GENDER MATTERS FROM
SCHOOL TO WORK

MODERN EDUCATIONAL THOUGHT
Series Editor: Professor Andy Hargreaves,
Ontario Institute for Studies in Education

This important new series contains some of the very best of modern educational thought that will stimulate interest and controversy among teachers and educationalists alike.

It brings together writers of distinction and originality within educational studies who have made significant contributions to policy and practice. The writers are all scholars of international standing who are recognized authorities in their own particular field and who are still actively researching and advancing knowledge in that field.

The series represents some of their best and most distinctive writing as a set of provocative, interrelated essays addressing a specific theme of contemporary importance. A unique feature of the series is that each collection includes a critical introduction to the author's work written by another influential figure in the field.

Current titles:

Roger Dale: *The State and Education Policy*
Jane Gaskell: *Gender Matters from School to Work*
Andy Hargreaves: *Curriculum and Assessment Reform*
Martyn Hammersley: *Classroom Ethnography*
Jean Rudduck: *Innovation and Change*

Gender Matters from School to Work

JANE GASKELL

OPEN UNIVERSITY PRESS
Milton Keynes · Philadelphia

For Jim, with much love

Open University Press
Celtic Court
22 Ballmoor
Buckingham
MK18 1XW

and

1900 Frost Road, Suite 101
Bristol, PA 19007, USA

First Published 1992

British Library Cataloguing-in-Publication Data

Gaskell, Jane
    Gender matters from school to work.
    – (Modern education thought series)
    I. Title II. Series
    305.30835

    ISBN 0–335–09692–1
    ISBN 0–335–09691–3 (pbk)

Library of Congress Cataloguing-in-Publication number is available

Typeset by Inforum Typesetting, Portsmouth
Printed in Great Britain by Biddles Limited, Guildford and Kings Lynn

Contents

Acknowledgements

It is a pleasure to bring together some of the writing I have done over the past ten years, to be able to rethink it, and to wonder about its significance. I would like to thank Andy Hargreaves for suggesting the project, and for being a discerning critic.

Chapters 2 to 6 of this book are edited versions of work published earlier. Chapter 2 was originally published as 'Course enrolment in the high school: the perspective of working class females', in *Sociology of Education*, volume 58 (1985; pp. 48–59). Chapter 3 was written with Marvin Lazerson, and was published as 'Between school and work: perspectives of working class youth', in *Interchange*, volume 11, number 3 (1981; pp. 80–96). Chapter 4 was published as 'The reproduction of family life: perspectives of male and female adolescents', in the *British Journal of Sociology of Education*, volume 4, number 1 (1983; pp. 19–39). Chapter 5 draws from an article originally published in *Curriculum Inquiry* as 'The changing organization of business education in the high school: teachers respond to school and work', volume 16, number 4 (1986; pp. 417–37). Chapter 6 is based on material published in *Atlantis*, volume 8, number 2 (1983; pp. 12–24) as 'Changing conceptions of skill and the work of women: some historical and political issues'.

I would like to acknowledge and thank the Social Sciences and Humanities Research Council of Canada, the University of British Columbia Small Grants Fund and the Killam Research Council for research funding that has made all the difference at strategic points over the past ten years. For the record, I think the SSHRC is a model research granting agency, and UBC has been a good place for me to work.

Thanks are due to many who have, in discussions over the years, taught me and encouraged me in this work. Marvin Lazerson helped me conceive the project and convinced me I could and should do it. Nancy Jackson worked through many of the ideas and some of the fieldwork with me. Jean Anyon, Madeleine Arnot, Dan Birch, Shauna Butterwick, Arlene McLaren, Roger Simon and Dorothy Smith have been particularly important in my learning. May the conversation continue.

For clerical assistance, I owe a large debt to Kaari Fraser and Betty Reid. For research assistance, to Barb Williamson, Bill Macjieko, Leslie Savage, Ted Rieken, Joyce Costin – and again, Nancy and Shauna. For editorial assistance, thanks to Robin Van Heck. And for reading the manuscript and making such useful suggestions, thanks to Allison Tom and J. Don Wilson.

The young women and men, and the teachers, who allowed me into their classrooms and their lives were wonderfully gracious and informative. Their willingness to tell me about their work made the research possible. I am very grateful and hope they might find the discussion interesting.

Unlike the model families I have read about in other acknowledgements, my family gave me a hard time when I wanted to withdraw and work on this book. I am glad they care more for me than for my text, and I like spending time with them, too. Thanks to Joanne for editing and cuddling, to David for caring and babysitting, and to Jim for understanding and picking up the pieces.

Critical Introduction:
Travel and Travail

SANDRA ACKER

This volume is a timely and welcome series of essays on young people's transition from school to work. I read it when I myself was in transit, moving from Britain to Canada, an experience which sensitized me to what I came to see as a key theme of the book: journeys and transitions. Clearly the young people who are of focal concern here have embarked on their own journeys, potentially treacherous travels through channels, choices and curricular options that may challenge or confirm their social positions and self perceptions. Simultaneously, as the cohort itself moves into adulthood, the social and economic structure of the society is being reproduced or renewed. The transition from school to work – or its macrosociological counterpart, the relationship of education to the economy – is a classic preoccupation of the sociology of education. How it is conceptualized and interpreted varies, however, across time and space: the idea itself undergoes journeys and transitions. Finally, the interpretation travels with the interpreter, as her positioning in a biographical and cultural nexus influences the discourses available to her and her choices among them. I shall elaborate on these 'journeys' in the remainder of this introduction.

From school to work: choices in context

Jane Gaskell's research derives from two linked studies. The first is a series of interviews with 35 male and 47 female students. In the spring of 1977 they were in grade 12 (age 17 or 18) in working-class Canadian secondary schools and were planning to take up employment, rather than further education, in the following year. Students were interviewed then and again a year later. Chapters 2 to 4 are based on data from this study. The second project took place from 1983 to 1987 and both narrowed and widened the focus of the original inquiry. Its specific target was the organization of clerical training, a form of job preparation favoured by young working-class women in high school. Its broader focus came from institutional and historical analysis, which enabled Jane Gaskell to place the vocational choices students make in a social context. The gendered notion of skill becomes a key component in this analysis. The final chapter explores some of the policy and research implications of her work. The essays and the data collection span a period in the 1980s when it might be expected that a number of simultaneous changes occurred: the typical views of youth might have changed to respond to altered opportunity structures in the labour market or ideological currents such as feminism; fashions in sociological interpretations of the transition might also have been in flux; and indeed so might the researcher's perspective.

It is tempting simply to see the young people's views as trapped in a time warp:

> What was striking . . . was what they took for granted: that men couldn't bring up children; that school was boring; that clerical jobs required a simple skill that could be picked up in a few courses in high school; that students who had rehearsed routine technical tasks would be more employable.
>
> (Chapter 7)

Yet there was some hint of change. Not all the young women harboured a romantic view of domestic life and there were examples of challenge and resistance to traditional patterns, plans to postpone marriage or childbirth for example. 'The young women are certainly not so committed to traditional patterns that new opportunities would make no difference' (Chapter 4). The key is that such opportunity structures, whether or not they 'really' exist, are perceived either not to exist, or to be unavailable to people like themselves. Non-traditional occupations that might be options for middle-class girls from educated families are not part of their world view. Clerical work is. It meets (they think) all the right criteria. They can train for it while still in school (true of few other fields) and get a head start on their relatively short time in the labour market before they leave to have children. Business courses offer a sensible (i.e. useful) option in the 'pointlessness and childishness of school' (Chapter 2). Clerical jobs are believed to be easily available and students can see many women around who hold them. They have relatively high status and security compared to some alternative blue collar jobs. Some of the alternative courses, like industrial arts, are too male-oriented.

What is interesting is that even girls who saw business courses as boring and unsatisfying *still* chose them. Just as for many years teaching was the inevitable destination for middle-class, relatively academic girls, for these girls clerical work was the quintessential safety net, the only realistic 'choice'. So we have the social reproduction scenario: the young women's 'conscious, rational, self-preserving calculations helped to reproduce gender segregation for themselves and others. They did not see this as a predetermined or imposed fact but as one they actively chose as best for themselves' (Chapter 2). In a study of two rural secondary schools in England, Sheila Riddell (1988) found a parallel phenomenon, reinforced by parents' perceptions. The girls didn't have to *like* typing – they might even loathe it – to opt for a course and a future as a typist.

To document the reproductive process *vis-à-vis* class and gender is itself an accomplishment, especially given the concentration on men's choices and chances that has been so central to the sociological literature on education and stratification for so many years (Acker, 1981). However, Jane Gaskell goes beyond such documenting to engage with another of sociology's preoccupations, perhaps the central one: the tensions between structure and agency in the social order. As she puts it in the concluding chapter, the research was 'shaped by a desire to emphasize human agency in the context of structural analysis, and to understand gender as integral to social structure'. This is no easy accomplishment. It requires balancing on a tightrope, trying to handle macro and micro perspectives simultaneously, allowing for freedom and determination, choice and constraint, reproduction and resistance. Like Willis (1977), Gaskell is unwilling to explain young people's avoidance of the better opportunities seemingly on offer as simply the overdetermined outcome of social and economic forces. As suggested above, their choices *are* realistic, given the messages and examples all around them. 'Concepts about how the world actually works are located in one's experience of the world' (Chapter 7).

Change, even for those who desire it, is perceived to carry 'unacceptable levels of self-sacrifice, risk-taking or unhappiness' (Chapter 7). Who is to say they are wrong? I found some perhaps unexpected parallels in my own recent study of primary school teachers in two schools in England (Acker, 1990c). They, too, came to terms with an unfair world, one in which men had massive advantages in the promotions stakes, while women shouldered heavy domestic responsibilities as well as demanding and stressful work ones. But, I concluded, an overtly feminist response would have been counterproductive in their circumstances. Teachers with outspoken feminist views ran the risk not only of being unpleasantly labelled in the staffroom, but also of sinking into discontent without an obvious means to alleviate it. There were ways in which the teachers could shape their own destinies and they preferred to stress these, creating and recreating definitions of careers and commitments that suited their circumstances (see also Biklen, 1985; Nias, 1989; Evetts, 1990). There were compensations for any difficulties and disadvantages: the teachers were doing a job worth doing, and they enjoyed the camaraderie and warmth of a small community of mostly women (also available in the business courses – see Chapter 5). Moreover, life was full of what I came to think of as 'accidents'. Career plans on the stereotypically male professional model would have been highly *un*realistic, as real life produced an unpredictable mix of health and illness, domestic stability and upheaval, childbirths and miscarriages.

Like Jane Gaskell, I felt it was too limiting to analyse 'choices' and 'views' only in terms of the individuals concerned. To go further, the researcher must bring in a repertoire of concepts and frameworks to make sense of what is happening to other people. So an analysis is imposed on the data. But which analysis? In sociology we have competing frameworks and perspectives and, further, we have travelled to the point where we no longer feel comfortable arguing that our particular pet theory is *correct*. In some recent accounts, all our frameworks are temporary constructions of a historical time, and none deserves pride of place. In fact, it has long been an open secret that data did not speak for themselves, that any given finding had alternative interpretations, that part of the pleasure of the sociological pastime was to find or construct an explanation sufficiently elegant and parsimonious that it evoked commitment and carried conviction. Such reproaches run the risk of inducing intellectual paralysis and a sensible compromise is to carry on using our conventional conceptual frameworks, while developing a more sensitive appreciation of where they come from, why we favour them, whether analysis from a different location (intellectually, culturally) might produce different priorities. Thus it is necessary to go beyond simply reporting the views of young people (or teachers) to try to locate the views in an explanatory framework. To do this Jane Gaskell moves from the individual to the institutional level, investigating the factors in the school environment that form the context and culture in which curricular and vocational choices are made. Beyond the school, as she shows in Chapter 6, there is the labour market itself and the definitions of skill contained therein, historically developed but continually struggled over and negotiated. These two chapters are important and original contributions to our understanding of the transition for young women from school to work. I particularly valued Chapter 5, perhaps because it resonates most closely with my own work on what I have come to think of as the 'work-place culture' of teachers. Chapter 5 demonstrates that career choices are produced and reinforced collectively, in a cultural context.

Here we encounter another enduring interest of sociology of education, that of the nature of school processes. This interest may or may not connect up with macrosociological issues; that is, what happens to children (or teachers) in schools might be seen as a consequence of the wider requisites of, say, capitalism or patriarchy; but equally they can be seen as part of the necessity for control and standardization of outcomes for large numbers in small places (Bidwell, 1965); or they might be understood as reflecting both sets of imperatives. Peter Woods titled one such study *The Divided School* (Woods, 1979) and that, in a nutshell, is what it is. Children are divided into groups based ostensibly on age, sex, ability, interest, destination; often these turn out to coincide suspiciously with sex, social class and race (see, for example, Ogbu, 1974; Rosenbaum, 1976; Ball, 1981; Pratt *et al.*, 1984; Oakes, 1985; Riddell, 1988). Recently there has been a particular interest in the gender dimension of such divisions. Madeleine Arnot developed the notion of 'gender codes' (MacDonald, 1980) and Kessler *et al.* (1985) that of 'gender regimes' to describe the processes whereby schools construct and reinforce boundaries between what is acceptable as masculinity and femininity. Processes of timetabling, allocating, option choice; routine encounters and use of language in classrooms and between peers; textbooks and examination materials all produce a gender regime, 'the pattern of practices that constructs various kinds of masculinity and femininity among staff and students, orders them in terms of prestige and power, and constructs a sexual division of labour within the institution' (Kessler *et al.*, 1985, p. 42).

Schools do not have identical gender codes. The school studied in Chapter 5 was, Gaskell points out, a conservative school, and one where the average income and educational level of the local area was below the city's average. Contrast, for example, the responses of middle-class girls in Weiler's (1988) study who, drawing on *their* home background, were 'natural allies' of feminist teachers. Moreover, a gender regime is a 'state of play rather than a permanent condition' (Kessler *et al.*, 1985). A school may change its ethos over time, for example with the advent of a new principal or headteacher (Nias *et al.*, 1989; McGrane, n.d.), a change in the social mix of the surroundings or alterations in the local labour market. Interviews with longer-serving primary school teachers in my research also confirm this phenomenon.

Chapter 5 of the present book considers one change to which the school is trying to adapt: alterations in the demand for clerical work in the labour market and in the level and type of technical competence expected. The school will never be able to afford the latest sophisticated office equipment and the teachers are faced with several options: attempt to upgrade technical skills, as best they can; alter the conception of business education to one which fills the largely remedial function of improving literacy and numeracy skills; or branch out into 'life skills', less tied to an office as future work-place and useful (they hope) to both girls and boys as they become adults. The tendency was to lean towards the last solution, which avoided the loss in status of the second option and had the advantage of appealing to students in its combination of usefulness and fun. The business courses were above all sold as vocational: although hard evidence was lacking, a shared belief that there would be a pay-off in the job market for those who took these courses was repeatedly reinforced. The classes made a conscious effort to mimic the work-place, with an emphasis on simple tasks, careful, correct procedures and knowing one's place as a good employee who would identify with the 'business point of view'. The job was presented as one where the worker simply carried out orders without questioning them, and any questions which arose that might have led to interruptions in the web of assumptions were simply deflected. The second strand that made up the appeal of the business courses rested on their claim to be 'easy', to promise the less-academic student a route through high school. In the marketplace of competing curricular options, business education teachers, helped by the lesser government scrutiny that accompanies an elective course, traded on the twin appeals of vocational – it will help you get a job – and educational – it is an easier way through school – rationales. The teachers felt frustrated at the endless succession of low-ability students, but at the same time gained a sense of purpose from the niche they carved out: they care, they can reach the students the other teachers neglect. One cost is a need to negotiate the curriculum, to trade down the requirements whenever students fail to meet them, and Jane Gaskell gives an evocative description of this process.

The school knits in nicely, if not isomorphically, with the labour market, as clerical work is historically and currently identified with women. Like child-care, it is disguised as 'easy' and remunerated accordingly. Jane Gaskell argues convincingly that 'skill' is in the eye of the beholder and forged in the political arena: 'When people overlook women's skills, devalue them, give them low ratings, it is not a technical glitch, but a reflection of the status and power women have not had in the world' (Chapter 7). It can be seen that the reproductive process is not simply located in the choices of individuals. The processes in schools have a hand in it; and these in turn are linked into socially constructed definitions of skill and its gender connotations, feeding back into the school the understandings that non-academic, unambitious, domestically oriented, conventional 'girls' are wanted, indeed go to the head of the queue, for these jobs. The actions of the school and the teachers become comprehensible, even praiseworthy; is it any better to hitch the entire system to an academic illusion that reinterprets class privilege as talent?

Must this journey be repeated in the nineties as in the eighties, and beyond? Jane Gaskell argues that there are policy options and ways in which social scientists can contribute to creating a 'conversation' with the subjects of their analysis. The emphasis should be on showing, rather than telling, girls (and teachers?) that change is possible. There is room for critical pedagogy, for making the effort to increase awareness of options, changes and contradictions. A recent study from the Canadian Teachers' Federation (1990) involved 97 discussion groups with girls aged from 11 to 19 across Canada. The girls saw their lives as complicated and stressful; many had part-time jobs and heavy extracurricular activities as well as commitments to family, friends and boyfriends. The researchers argue that the 'problem' is no longer one of encouraging girls to want careers; rather it is a hopelessness about how to get to their goals that needs tackling. One of the barriers is the advantages males enjoy, deeply resented by many of the respondents. Another is the focus of schools on simple tasks, facts and information; the girls wanted discussion groups like those of the project itself, where they could explore the contradictions in their lives. It is possible that the spectrum of their concerns is wider – including drugs, alcohol, AIDS, the environment, world poverty – than that of the young women studied by Jane Gaskell a few years earlier but, as in her study, there is an underlying vocational outlook and an awareness of gender inequities. Both Jane's study and the CTF one suggest a need for schools to rethink their approach to adolescent women. The simplification of 'tasks for the office' could be replaced by a conception of the adolescents as rounded people, with social and personal concerns deserving of serious treatment, to be tackled rather than downplayed by the school. Perhaps the life skills approach offers a chance if teachers can see its full potential.

This essay has so far considered the transition of the young women: whose purposes does it serve, how do the participants perceive it, is it inevitable? In the remainder, I wish to consider the intellectual and personal transitions of which this volume is a part. I take my lead here from Jane Gaskell's statement in her concluding chapter:

> The social location of social scientists informs and constrains their inter-
> pretations. The state of the academic field at any point in time, the

university's allocation of work and rewards and, most importantly, one's own biography and political commitments shape one's scholarship.

(Chapter 7)

Sociological journeys

Jane Gaskell's introductory chapter reminds us of the concerns of the 1960s and 1970s. Mainstream sociology in the United States and Canada was relatively conservative, concerned with order in society and influenced by a functionalist and human capital perspective that saw social arrangements as consequences of society's survival needs. Sociologists of the time regarded education as relatively unproblematic, a positive mediator between family and work. The dominant paradigm for linking education and the economy was the status attainment approach which sought to measure the relative inputs of family background socioeconomic status (SES), educational attainments, and sometimes other variables on occupational attainment. Favoured approaches were quantitative, statistical, 'scientific'. Status attainment research 'focuses solely on individual differences, assuming that these characteristics are what will differentiate those who are successful from those who are unsuccessful' (Chapter 1). This seems, in hindsight, odd coming from a discipline whose claim to uniqueness is its focus on the influence of the *social* context. What was even odder, as Jane points out, was the adherence to a framework that entirely failed to address the lack of congruence between *women's* educational and occupational achievements.

Jane and I were both studying sociology in graduate departments of education at elite institutions in the United States in the late 1960s. I was at the University of Chicago taking courses from 1966 to 1969; she was doing the same at Harvard from 1968 to 1971. Jane had the advantage of an undergraduate degree in sociology from Swarthmore, while I came almost new to the subject. Sociology of education, I naively expected, would be about changing the world, alleviating disadvantage, curing poverty, transmitting liberation and fighting racial prejudice (sexism had not yet been 'discovered'). It turned out to be an intellectual rather than a practical enterprise, where one debated concepts of power and authority, or theorized about youth cultures, or predicted occupational attainments. Positivism was the prevailing methodological paradigm, as the sociology of education journals of the time will show. Functionalism was the dominant theoretical approach. The 'Chicago School' of sociology, we understood, had long since abandoned Chicago for California, but several of our teachers kept the symbolic interactionist tradition alive as an alternative to functionalism – the loyal opposition, it was sometimes called. Jane writes: 'My thesis was developed within this paradigm [status attainment] and used path analysis, factor analysis and questionnaires to demonstrate how young women's attitudes towards sex roles affected their aspirations for school and work' (Chapter 1). Although I took a year-long course on participant observation, my own thesis was a survey. I studied women and men graduate students, trying to determine under what conditions women's career ambitions were as high as men's. I did some pilot interviews, Jane a few post-survey ones.

Both of us wondered why the interviews seemed so much more gripping than the survey results, reflecting complex realities rather than snapshot responses. We were ready for theoretical and methodological breaks with tradition.

Jane writes of her exposure to 'models of class conflict . . . so useful in shocking me as a graduate student into understanding the ideological under-pinnings of sociology theory and educational practice' (Chapter 1). My graduate courses were silent here. Perhaps Jane's slightly later years of study were enough to make the difference; perhaps it was the difference between institutions. At that time Chicago did not require a central theory course for its sociology or sociology of education graduate students, and Marxist models were barely mentioned in the courses I followed. Yet the political upheavals of the late sixties – the protests against the Vietnam War, the movements for the civil rights of minorities and women, student demands for a relevant curriculum and an end to oppressive grading practices – surrounded both of us. My real 'shock', however, came after I left Chicago and moved to England in 1971. Sociology, and with it sociology of education, were like new subjects. I learned a lasting lesson about the relativity of cultural perspectives, how the 'study of society' was often if not always the study of a particular society. In the UK, Marx was a key figure, Parsons a marginal one. Although there was a strong tradition of 'political arithmetic', empirical work on education and the economy, there was little need to learn complex quantitative methods; to be steeped in theory was more honourable. Moreover, when we had considered disadvantage in my undergraduate and graduate studies, it was racial or cultural disadvantage, usually focusing on black people but sometimes including other ethnic groups or displaced migrants from the Appalachian south of America to the northern cities. Differences related to possession of income and wealth were called socioeconomic status (SES), not social class. In Britain, SES was either an unknown term or regarded as a euphemism for the prime differentiator, social class.

Not only did I personally have to relearn some of my sociology, but a wave of innovative thinking was gathering momentum within British sociology of education, which came to be known as the 'new sociology of education'. It was exemplified in *Knowledge and Control*, a collection of essays edited by M.F.D. Young (1971). These writings sought to render the curriculum problematic, to argue that not only people but also knowledge was processed in schools. Like most such ideas, its origins could be found in writings of classic theorists, but the impact on the thinking of the time was great. We had to ask why some knowledge was considered of more worth than other knowledge and who set the agendas and shaped the curriculum. The 1970s and the first half or so of the 1980s were extremely productive and creative years for British sociology of education. A series of annual conferences at Westhill College in Birmingham brought together scholars in the field on a regular basis, and the *British Journal of Sociology of Education* provided a high quality outlet from 1980 for research and theory.

Competing 'strands' whose proponents pursued their own research agendas and argued with each other soon arose. To oversimplify, there were the neo-Marxists, the ethnographers and the feminists. In practice, some sociologists were all three, although the debates were real. Neo-Marxism was influenced by the 'new sociology' and by certain works from the United States, especially *Schooling in Capitalist America* (Bowles and Gintis, 1976). The ethnographers built a British version of Chicago-style symbolic interactionism and drew upon it to explore processes in schools and classrooms (see, for example, Woods, 1979; Burgess, 1983; Delamont, 1984; Ball and Goodson, 1985). Both these traditions changed over time: the neo-Marxists being influenced by Willis (1977) and Apple (1979) to move away from rigid reproduction models towards those which incorporated resistance and respected the perspectives of the people; the ethnographers raising thorny theoretical issues as well as producing descriptive monographs. Both traditions were challenged by feminism, for as with most sociology of education before 1980, there was little attention paid to gender. Reproduction and resistance theorists had to try to understand the sexual as well as the social division of labour (David, 1980); the ethnographers had to consider whether the experiences of girls might differ from those of boys (Davies, 1984).

Jane was exposed to these currents, not only in their published versions, but through her visits to England and a sabbatical in 1981 at the Centre for Contemporary Cultural Studies at the University of Birmingham. CCCS was concerned with education, among other topics, and it produced some dramatic research challenging prevailing concepts of cultural studies and of youth. Paul Willis, there at the time, must certainly be one of the most frequently cited British writers in sociology of education. So much good British work never crosses the Atlantic that this feat is all the more extraordinary.

One of Jane Gaskell's chapters was originally published in the *British Journal of Sociology of Education*, and she displays a greater familiarity with British work than many North American writers. To someone as transatlantic as I have become, the mutual ignorance of the different national sociologies is highly frustrating. There are other British studies of young women and their educational experiences that might complement Jane's work; similarly, their authors are unlikely to know about counterparts from Canada and the United States. In his Critical Introduction to Martyn Hammersley's *Classroom Ethnography*, Louis Smith (1990) marvels at the same phenomenon. The references in the American textbook Smith uses for courses on ethnographic method had little overlap with those in Martyn Hammersley's book. It may be that commissioning introductions like this one from persons outside the immediate frame of reference of the author will alert more scholars to the riches to be found in a series of countries, not just one's own. I hope my own recent move to Canada provides me with the opportunity to find the local treasures.

In North America, a series of works in the 1980s sought, like Paul Willis's study, to add resistance to reproduction and develop what has sometimes been called critical education theory. The studies represent a move away from the pessimism and determinism of correspondence theories such as the one outlined in *Schooling in Capitalist America* (Bowles and Gintis, 1976). Influenced by Paolo Freire, they try to retrieve the liberating potential of education and emphasize individual agency as well as (or instead of) structures. Kathleen Weiler (1988) explains how neo-Marxist insights are often retained but production rather than reproduction of cultures becomes central, thus establishing some links with phenomenological or other interpretive perspectives. Critical education theory, and its classroom counterpart, critical pedagogy, claim to be different from other approaches because they offer an explicit moral commitment to empowerment and emancipation. Weiler's own study of feminist teachers provides one such example; another is McLaren's (1989) *Life in Schools*, an account of the author's year teaching in a Canadian school and his subsequent efforts to theorize it. The claims of critical pedagogy have been rather sweeping and some criticisms of its pretensions and assumptions have been launched (Ellsworth, 1989). Although Paul Willis might be claimed as a cousin of this tradition, it remains a largely North American movement. British sociology of education, in contrast, appears to be moving away from theory and strongly into educational policy analysis and research. This is symbolized by the merging of the London Institute of Education's Department of Sociology of Education with the Department of Educational Policy Studies, upon the retirement of Professor Basil Bernstein (Atkinson, 1991). The field is suffering from a long period of Conservative political rule, which has been anti-sociology and has failed to provide institutional conditions under which critical scholarship could thrive. Teacher training curricula and in-service work have undergone great changes, one consequence of which is that sociological input has been squeezed down or out. Universities and polytechnics have been in constant crisis and contraction. The Education Reform Act of 1988 represented such a dramatic transformation (or attempted transformation) of the education system as previously constituted that studying anything else now seems rather perverse. Moreover, as it is clear that government policy has been entirely untouched by prevailing trends in sociological criticism, researchers hope to gain some credibility with decision-makers. So policy analysis is 'in', by virtue of an attempt to make a political difference, by virtue of lack of money available for any other purpose, and by virtue of a sense of crisis hanging over every endeavour.

Growing up in the time of status attainment and functionalism, maturing when Marxist models were coming into view, influenced by Willis and the critical education theorists who seek to add the person back in to the process, Jane Gaskell skilfully blends these sociological traditions into her own research. Perhaps the only important strand that she has not taken much from is the symbolic interactionist revival of 1980s Britain, although Chapter 5 fits well with that tradition. Symbolic interactionism emphasizes respect for individuals as well as for the socially constructed (but always negotiated and changing) nature of the context in which individuals come to shape their understandings. A series of concepts – including self, identity, perspectives, commitment, culture, career, strategies, negotiation – provides the toolkit of this approach (see, for example, Woods, 1983; Nias, 1989), which seems ideally suited to exploring the culture of teachers (Nias *et al.*, 1989; Acker, 1990b; Hargreaves, 1991). In Chapter 5, Jane begins the important task of seeing teachers with the same sympathy and empathy accorded to the young women and men students. Edith Black, in a study of secretarial studies teachers in an English college of further education, also finds teachers promoting an apparently reactionary view: 'In well over 300 hours of classroom observation I have not heard any teacher express criticism of the status quo while in the presence of students' (Black, 1989, p. 148). But she calls for a more sympathetic understanding of the occupational culture of these women teachers. The teachers were former secretaries who had worked their way up the office hierarchy, taking extra courses at night and eventually acquiring teaching qualifications by an arduous part-time route. They were proud of their secretarial skills and enjoyed teaching them to others. They were aware of injustice and sexism in the workplace but, like the students Jane studied and the primary school teachers in my research, adopted a 'rational strategy for survival . . . accommodation to perceived limits and constraints' (Black, 1989, p. 148).

Gender and scholarship

Perhaps I have saved the best journey for last. Jane's work falls not only into the traditions of sociology of education but also into the area variously known as sociology of women's education, or gender studies, or feminist research. I have already made several allusions to the importance of research that accords the experiences of women a central role. Without this, as, for example, Jane shows for status attainment approaches, findings are seriously defective.

For women in America, the late 1960s was an exciting time to be a graduate student not only because of the politically charged ambience generally, but also because the women's liberation movement gave us a new understanding of our own (and our mothers') lives. Consciousness-raising groups offered the chance to share these awakenings. We talked about how the desire to please others – especially men – had influenced our decisions and about how men intimidated us into silence in class and professors failed to take us seriously. In retrospect, of course, the analysis was unsophisticated and the divisions among women underplayed. But it is important to realize that this resurgent social movement challenged us personally, politically and professionally. Up to that point we had taken for granted the use of 'he' to include 'she'; the studies on all-male samples; the paucity of research on women; the scarcity of women on the faculty. Now all those 'social facts' could be challenged and perhaps changed. The intervening years have shown us that change is a good deal more difficult than we thought, but they have also seen a vast outpouring of feminist scholarship and debates over feminist pedagogy and research. In 1969, when I taught a course called 'The Sociology of Women', there were only two or three suitable books and a couple of articles on the topic.

Both Jane and I opted to do our PhD dissertations on 'women', then an innovative, even risky, choice. I had great difficulty finding a woman faculty member to be on my dissertation committee; there were very few in the university. Both of us, however, remained within the prevailing methodological paradigms and both of us drew upon what might be called the sex roles genre, characteristic of most American research on women in the early 1970s. The individualistic framework Jane criticizes for status attainment research was here, too. Our efforts were directed to finding out what attitudes or roles women held that led them to be different in their aspirations and ambitions from men. The tendency was to attribute women's lesser achievements to sex-stereotyped socialization and role conflict, for example, the competing demands of family responsibilities or a husband's career. It was only later that 'lesser' might be seen as 'different' or even 'better'.

Gradually, it became evident that this approach tended to take whatever men typically did or said as a norm against which women were being unfavourably compared. Feminist theory developed in various directions to provide alternative frameworks and empirical research began to fill in some of the gaps in knowledge (Acker, 1987, 1990a). Was there a distinct feminist method? A feminist pedagogy? The direction taken by such debates varied by discipline (DuBois *et al.*, 1985) and by country. Feminism itself takes different forms under different political systems (Gelb, 1989). An analysis I did of articles on education in three major British sociology journals from 1960 to 1979 (Acker, 1981) found few all-female samples and only one theoretical article with some consideration of gender. Certain topics, such as youth culture or the education of elites, inevitably considered males only. Even when 'sex differences' were reported, researchers had no idea how to explain them or investigate them further. Textbooks and collections of readings also treated the topic of 'women' superficially or not at all.

Issues of the *British Journal of Sociology of Education* since 1980 show how much has changed. Gender has found its way into the mainstream. The 'sex roles' approach, always more characteristic of North America than Britain, Australia or New Zealand, has declined. In Britain, liberal feminist views dominate official rhetoric but sociological scholarship is more likely to draw from socialist (or sometimes radical) feminism. Postmodern challenges to the categories used in feminist theory and research have set off vigorous debates in North America. Although there is British writing from this perspective, it tends to be associated with literary rather than sociological studies and British feminist sociology of education has not yet engaged with this debate to any great degree. (See Lovell (1990) for observations on the impact of different academic traditions on feminist criticism.)

Canadian feminist scholarship on women and education is probably better known in the United States and Britain than Canadian sociology of education *per se*. Dorothy Smith (1987) and Margrit Eichler (1988) are leading international figures. *Resources for Educational Research*, a journal produced at the Ontario Institute for Studies in Education, has wide circulation and there is a new edited volume from OISE's Centre for Women's Studies in Education (Forman *et al.*, 1990). Jane Gaskell's work is also well known. With Arlene MacLaren she edited a key collection, *Women and Education: A Canadian Perspective* (1987; updated in 1991), and together with Arlene McLaren and Myra Novogrodsky, wrote *Claiming an Education: Feminism and Canadian Schools* (1989).

There are different understandings of what the criteria are for research to be regarded as authentically feminist. Among these are usually the centrality of gender to the analysis, an appreciation of the 'personal as political', and a commitment to improving the situation of women in some way. While reading the first chapters of Jane's book at the hairdressers, in England, in mid-December 1990, I had an experience which underlined the practical reality of Jane's topic as well as its poignancy. I was startled to see a young girl working there who had started school on the same day as my daughter and who had been a good friend of hers in the early years. Now aged 14, they were no longer particular friends, but they did attend the same school. My daughter had just returned from a week's workshop (paid for by parents but sponsored by the school) with writers in Devon; she was excited and stimulated by the creativity and challenge. In contrast, here was Louise, shampooing my hair and sweeping the floors when she should have been in school. She rarely smiled; there was obviously not much creativity there for her. It was, I thought, no coincidence that she is a white, working-class, female, non-academic teenager. Jane's stated commitment is a feminist and humanitarian one: to give some real choices and a better future to Louise and all the others like her.

References

Acker, S. (1981). No woman's land: British sociology of education, 1960–1979. *Sociological Review*, **29**, 77–104.

Acker, S. (1987). Feminist theory and the study of gender and education. *International Review of Education*, **33**, 419–35.

Acker, S. (1990a). Gender issues in schooling. In H. Entwistle *et al.* (eds), *Handbook of Educational Ideas and Practices*, pp. 91–9. London: Routledge.

Acker, S. (1990b). Teachers' culture in an English primary school: continuity and change. *British Journal of Sociology of Education*, **11**, 257–73.

Acker, S. (1990c). Women teachers at work. Paper presented to the Canadian Teachers' Federation Women in Education conference, Vancouver, BC, November.

Apple, M. (1979). *Ideology and Curriculum*. London: Routledge and Kegan Paul.

Atkinson, P. (1991). Appreciating Bernstein. *Network*, **49**, 4.

Ball, S.J. (1981). *Beachside Comprehensive*. Cambridge: Cambridge University Press.

Ball, S.J. and Goodson, I. (eds) (1985). *Teachers' Lives and Careers*. Lewes: Falmer Press.

Bidwell, C. (1965). The school as a formal organization. In J. March (ed.), *Handbook of Organizations*. Chicago: Rand McNally.

Biklen, S. (1985). Can elementary school teaching be a career? *Issues in Education*, **3**, 215–31.

Black, E. (1989). Women's work in a man's world: secretarial training in a college of further education. In S. Acker (ed.), *Teachers, Gender and Careers*, pp. 139–50. Lewes: Falmer Press.

Bowles, S. and Gintis, H. (1976). *Schooling in Capitalist America*. New York: Basic Books.

Burgess, R. (1983). *Experiencing Comprehensive Education*. London: Methuen.

Canadian Teachers' Federation (1990). *A Cappella: a Report on the Realities, Concerns, Expectations and Barriers Experienced by Adolescent Women in Canada*. Ottawa: CTF.

David, M.E. (1980). *The State, the Family and Education*. London: Routledge and Kegan Paul.

Davies, L. (1984). *Pupil Power: Deviance and Gender in School*. Lewes: Falmer Press.

Delamont, S. (ed.) (1984). *Readings in Interaction in the Classroom*. London: Methuen.

DuBois, E., Kelly, G., Kennedy, E., Korsmeyer, C. and Robinson, L. (1985). *Feminist Scholarship*. Urbana: University of Illinois Press.

Eichler, M. (1988). *Nonsexist Research Methods: a Practical Guide*. Boston: Allen and Unwin.

Ellsworth, E. (1989). Why doesn't this feel empowering? Working through the repressive myths of critical pedagogy. *Harvard Educational Review*, **59**, 297–324.

Evetts, J. (1990). *Women in Primary Teaching*. London: Unwin Hyman.

Forman, F. *et al.* (1990). *Feminism and Education: a Canadian Perspective*. Toronto: Centre for Women's Studies in Education, Ontario Institute for Studies in Education.

Gaskell, J.S. and MacLaren, A.J. (eds) (1987). *Women and Education: a Canadian Perspective*. (Second edition, 1991.) Calgary, Alberta: Detselig.

Gaskell, J., McLaren, A. and Novogrodsky, M. (1989). *Claiming an Education: Feminism and Canadian Schools*. Toronto: Our Schools/Our Selves Educational Foundation.

Gelb, J. (1989). *Feminism and Politics*. Berkeley: University of California Press.

Hargreaves, A. (1991). Cultures of teaching. In A. Hargreaves and M. Fullan (eds), *Understanding Teacher Development*. London: Cassell; New York: Teachers College Press.

Kessler, S., Ashendon, D., Connell, R.W. and Dowsett, G.W. (1985). Gender relations in secondary schooling. *Sociology of Education*, **58**, 34–48.

Lovell, T. (ed.) (1990). *British Feminist Thought*. Oxford: Blackwell.

MacDonald, M. (1980). Socio-cultural reproduction and women's education. In R. Deem (ed.), *Schooling for Women's Work*, pp. 13–25. London: Routledge and Kegan Paul.

McGrane, G. (n.d.). *The Social Construction of Masculinity*. Unpublished PhD dissertation, Bristol, UK, University of Bristol School of Education.

McLaren, P. (1989). *Life in Schools: an Introduction to Critical Pedagogy in the Foundations of Education*. New York: Longman.

Nias, J. (1989). *Primary Teachers Talking*. London: Routledge.

Nias, J., Southworth, G.C. and Yeomans, R. (1989). *Staff Relationships in the Primary School*. London: Cassell.

Oakes, J. (1985). *Keeping Track: How Schools Structure Inequality*. New Haven, CT: Yale University Press.

Ogbu, J. (1974). *The Next Generation*. New York: Academic Press.

Pratt, J., Bloomfield, J. and Searle, C. (1984). *Option Choice: a Question of Equal Opportunity*. Windsor: NFER-Nelson.

Riddell, S. (1988). *Gender and Option Choice in Two Rural Comprehensive Schools*. Unpublished PhD dissertation, Bristol, UK, University of Bristol School of Education.

Rosenbaum, J. (1976). *Making Inequality*. New York: John Wiley & Sons.

Smith, D. (1987). *The Everyday World as Problematic: a Feminist Sociology*. Boston: Northeastern University.

Smith, L. (1990). Critical introduction: whither classroom ethnography? In M. Hammersley, *Classroom Ethnography*, pp. 1–12. Milton Keynes: Open University Press; Toronto: OISE Press.

Weiler, K. (1988). *Women Teaching for Change*. South Hadley, MA: Bergin & Garvey.

Willis, P. (1977). *Learning to Labour: How Working Class Kids Get Working Class Jobs.* Farnborough: Saxon House.

Woods, P. (1979). *The Divided School.* London: Routledge and Kegan Paul.

Woods, P. (1983). *Sociology and the School.* London: Routledge and Kegan Paul.

Young, M.F.D. (ed.) (1971). *Knowledge and Control: New Directions for the Sociology of Education.* London: Collier-Macmillan.

1 School, Work and Gender

The view that education can be a collective and individual pathway to prosperity makes education an important social priority. That schools should prepare young people for work is axiomatic for parents, for young people, for policy-makers, for employers and for unions. The belief accounts for most of the funding that has gone into education since the Second World War. But many people question how adequately school does prepare students for work, and proposals to improve the relationship are legion. As a result, the relations between school and work have been central to both analysis and policy in education over the past 30 years.

Much important sociology of education during the same period has explored the connection between education and work. This is partly because analysis of work is central to much sociological theory. The rise of 'industrial' society and its attendant institutions has been the focus of sociologists from Durkheim to Parsons to Foucault. Marxist traditions are anchored in the primacy of production for understanding any aspect of human activity. There are also some practical reasons for the attention sociologists of education have paid to the work-place. Political concern about economic issues makes research funding available for studies exploring relations between education and work. In Britain, in response to government initiatives with new vocational programmes and new ways of managing the transition from school to work, scholars have produced a large and mostly critical body of literature. In North America, the literature is more often in the service of government inquiries and technical reports, though not exclusively so.

There are, of course, those who think that the connection between education and the economy has been stressed too much. That schools are 'loosely coupled' institutions, relatively autonomous and able to create values and knowledge independently of the work-place. That they are strongly affected by families, the state and ideology. That educators' claims that schooling can increase our economic well-being are self-serving and cannot hope to be realized. That the demands of employers to have schooling serve the work-place distort educational priorities and reduce the quality of the schooling young people experience. That schooling should be justified by its relationship to loftier values like critical enquiry, the love of knowledge, or participation in democratic processes. .

Much of this makes sense. Economic influences are not the only influences on education. Economic goals for schooling often do conflict with other, more important, goals. But the fact remains that economic processes and purposes have shaped and will continue to shape schooling, for good reasons, based on the priorities of most of the participants. It is important to understand this, rather than to deny it. And it is important to see how this works, so that the processes become open and discussable. Doing social science entails involving oneself in an informed way in the debate about school and work, and becoming better equipped to suggest changes.

School and work: the academic literature

The analysis of school and work has an extensive and distinguished history in the academic literature. I will not provide a comprehensive review of it here, but I will illustrate through a few key works some of the ways scholars have approached this analysis. The changing modes of enquiry and understanding are linked to some of the most important academic and social developments since the Second World War. The linkages between academic analysis and social and political movements are undeniable.

In 1959, Talcott Parsons, who was probably the most influential sociologist throughout the 1950s and 1960s, analysed schooling in the following way:

First, from the functional point of view, the school class can be treated as an agency of socialization. That is to say, it is an agency through which individual personalities are trained to be motivationally and technically adequate to the performance of adult roles. . . . The socialization function may be summed up as the development in individuals of the commitments and capacities which are essential prerequisites of their future role-performance. Commitments may be broken down in turn into two components: commitment to the implementation of the broad values of society and commitment to the performance of a specific type of role within the structure of society. Capacities can also be broken down into two components, the first being competence of the skill to perform the tasks involved in the individual's roles, the second being the capacity to live up to other people's expectations of the interpersonal behavior appropriate to these roles. . . .

On the other hand, it is, from the point of view of the society, an agency of 'manpower' allocation. It is well known that in American society there is a very high, and probably increasing, correlation between one's status level in the society and one's level of educational attainment.

> Both social status and educational level are obviously related to the
> occupational status which is attained.
>
> (Parsons, 1959, pp. 297–8)

Functional theory, to which Parsons was a major contributor, holds that in any stable society institutions contribute to each others' functioning, producing a well-integrated whole. Parsons' work on schooling called attention to the links between the organization of schooling and the organization of the society at large, particularly of the economy. Schools serve two functions for the economy. They teach, or 'socialize' students, developing their skills and capacities to participate productively in the economy. And they allocate students to occupational roles, by evaluating their skills and capacities to do well, ensuring that those who perform most ably in school will get the best jobs. Values as well as skills affect what must be taught and what must be evaluated.

This view puts in sociological form many of the common-sense, meritocratic beliefs of democratic, industrialized societies. Schools teach what you need to know to do well in life. Stay in school and get ahead. Those who do well in school will get the good jobs, for the spheres of both school and work reward the same intellectual and social capacities. And as the economy becomes more complex, more highly technological and more productive, it requires increasingly highly educated workers. Thus education is, and will continue to be, critically important for one's opportunities in life.

The functional framework was used in Canada by John Porter to provide by far the most influential analysis of Canadian schooling available during the 1960s and 1970s (Porter, 1965). Porter stressed the role education played in preparing students for work.

> The content of education is affected by the emphasis in industrial societies
> on the marketability of skills. In terms of its social function, education
> should be thus affected, because an educational system fails when it does
> not train people in sufficient quality and quantity for occupational
> roles. . . . There has never been, in any society, knowledge for its own
> sake on a democratic scale.
>
> (Porter, 1965, p. 165)

Porter was also interested in social justice and equal educational opportunity, which he defined as allowing the more able to get ahead. 'The principle of equality and the principle of the rational use of economic resources thus have a mutually reinforcing function' (p. 167).

There has been a good deal of empirical research that uses a functional framework to look at the worlds of school and work. This research has found much that documents and specifies the functional relationships between the two spheres. In relation to 'allocation', correlational studies show that, on average, those persons who stay in school earn more. Studies of young people moving from school to work show how education mediates the transition. In terms of 'socialization', studies of curriculum show ways in which the skills and values learned at school are similar to those rewarded at work (Dreeben, 1968).

A particularly important research tradition that arose out of the assumptions of functional theory was 'status attainment research' (Horan, 1978). This research explores the allocation of school leavers to the labour force (e.g. Blau and Duncan, 1967; Sewell and Shah, 1968; Jencks *et al.*, 1972, 1979; Porter *et al.*, 1982; Kerckhoff, 1990). It appears to be a straightforward technique for determining what factors have an effect on attainment at school and in the labour market. The researcher takes various indices of individual characteristics – socioeconomic status, educational achievement, IQ, attitude measures, self-concept measures and the like – and sees how well they predict occupational attainment. Attributes are ranged numerically on scales, from high to low, and then entered into multiple regression equations that estimate the amount of variance explained by each.

What is striking about this research is that it focuses solely on individual differences, assuming that these characteristics are what will differentiate those who are successful from those who are unsuccessful. The labour market is assumed to be unitary, competitive and responsive to individual characteristics. Status attainment research tends to show that occupational status is better predicted by educational attainment than by anything else, including social class background. Thus it supports Parsons' contention that in modern industrialized societies educational achievement rather than ascriptive criteria increasingly allocates people to economic positions.

This kind of modelling has close links to an economic view called 'human capital theory'. If a single person can get ahead as a result of education, it follows that an entire economy also can. More educated workers have more skills and therefore are more productive workers. A society with more skilled and productive workers will be a more productive society. At the level of economic theory, the correlation between investment in education and economic growth was elaborated and demonstrated by Becker in 1964 in his book *Human Capital Theory*. Empirical support for the theory has been marshalled at the levels of the individual, the firm and entire countries. There is a correlation between 'human capital', in other words education, and wages. This theory forms an important part of introductory texts and lectures in labour economics. It shaped economic policy in Canada during the 1960s and 1970s, leading to huge increases in the funding of education, which it was hoped would increase economic prosperity (Economic Council of Canada, 1965).

All of this theorizing and research is based in an optimistic and meritocratic version of education and the work-place. The harmony of individual and collective interests, of employers' and employees' interests, of parents' and students' and employers' interests is taken for granted. Judgements of competence are assumed to be based on a universally agreed-upon scale that is competitive and known to all. The institutions of schooling take the form they do as a necessary consequence of these agreed-upon criteria. No one would benefit from anything else.

This relatively complacent vision of school and work stemmed from the prevailing liberal ideology of the 1950s and 1960s. Both championed individuals' responsibility for their own success or failure. Both viewed social progress as intimately linked to increasing levels of education. Both believed in the potential of education and work to bring social progress and economic prosperity. These views informed most government documents discussing education, and most educational policy in the United States, Canada and Britain.

By the 1970s, the persistence of social inequality in increasingly affluent societies was reaching the political agenda. The war on poverty and the civil rights movement in the United States had poked some holes in the myth of equal opportunity and called attention to the continued disadvantages of poor and minority students. In Britain, the Labour Party's social democratic policies, designed to increase access to education for everyone, had led to little change in the life chances of working-class students (Centre for Contemporary Cultural Studies, 1981). But the policy response, and much of the academic response, continued to be based in the assumptions of functional theory.

It was still assumed that the problems were located in the students. If the school system taught and rewarded those things that were necessary for the work-place, and if poor students were not performing well in school, one needed to give them extra help to catch up, to make up for the advantages wealthier youngsters enjoyed because of their home backgrounds. If the children of poor families were ending up in poverty themselves, they needed more education, for it was education that provided the passport to economic prosperity. The problems (and the solutions) were with the students and their families, not the structure and organization of schooling. And a great deal of research effort went into specifying exactly what these problems were, and how they might be corrected.

The political movements of the late 1960s and early 1970s did, however, spawn some further political movements and ideologies that ultimately challenged the assumption of a harmonious, 'post-industrial' society achieved through increased education for all. The politics of the civil rights movement and the new left, of Marxism and of social democracy, in at least some of their guises, had a major impact on academia, challenging the received wisdom of functionalist theory, and providing a new set of concerns about the relation between the worlds of school and work. Some important new theoretical approaches and a vibrant new scholarship arose as a result. The emphasis shifted from an assumption that schooling served everyone, to an assumption that schooling served some better than others. The question became who was served by the existing organization of schooling, and how those with less power could be better served. Marxist theory provides the clearest example of this, and its revival in academic circles challenged much previous work on the relationships between school and work.

Marxist models of society assume a fundamental conflict between capital and labour, a conflict which capital dominates. Schooling then becomes the agent of capital, producing workers who accept their alienation from their work and fit into an exploitative work-place. Schooling becomes the social agency that reproduces class divisions from one generation to the next, making the process appear fair and competitive. The institutions of schooling, in this view, reflect the dominance of some groups over others, not the needs of the whole, the collective good.

Perhaps the most influential statement of this position was Bowles and Gintis's *Schooling in Capitalist America*, published in 1976. Bowles and Gintis write (p. 11):

> Education in the United States plays a dual role in the social process whereby surplus value, that is, profit, is created and expropriated. On the one hand, by imparting technical and social skills and appropriate motivations, education increases the productive capacity of workers. On the other hand, education helps defuse and depoliticize the potentially explosive class relations of the production process, and thus serves to perpetuate the social, political, and economic conditions through which a portion of the product of labor is expropriated in the form of profits. . . .
>
> Schools foster legitimate inequality through the ostensibly meritocratic manner by which they reward and promote students, and allocate them to distinct positions in the occupational hierarchy. They create and reinforce patterns of social class, racial and sexual identification among students which allow them to relate 'properly' to their eventual standing in the hierarchy of authority and status in the production process.

The educational processes of socialization and allocation are as central to Bowles and Gintis's theory of schooling as they are to Parsons's. But here they are treated quite differently. Gone is the harmony of interest. Gone is the meritocratic judgement of skills and competence. In their place is a class-segregated institution, a class-based version of successful performance that is stacked against working-class youngsters, and a meritocratic ideology that conceals the class basis of the whole system. For Bowles and Gintis, the form that schooling takes does not reflect the needs of a productive economy, but the needs of the ruling class for control, for cheap labour, and for the selection of their own children into good jobs. The school system cries out for reform, but, as it is controlled by those who benefit from it, little can be done without major economic change.

Various kinds of empirical studies elaborated and provided support for this general thesis. There were studies that moved inside the school to explore educational processes more carefully and critically. 'Revisionist' studies of the historical roots of schooling provided new insights into the ways schooling was used for social control of the poor and of immigrants (Katz, 1968; Lazerson, 1971; Spring, 1972). Studies of schools showed that working-class children are segregated from wealthy children, and are taught different things (Anyon, 1981; Oakes, 1982). Studies of classrooms pointed out how teachers reward docility rather than creativity, and social conformity and intellectual compliance as much as independence and intellectual competence (Sharp and Green, 1975; Whitty, 1985). Studies of school credentials questioned whether they foretell competence in a job (Berg, 1970; Collins, 1979). Studies of social mobility showed that parents' social status is an excellent predictor of youngsters' success in school and of their first job, even if the effect of social status is mediated through education (Bowles and Gintis, 1976; Halsey *et al.*, 1980).

In Canada, a resurgence of interest in the political economy of schooling led to a more critical look at educational practice, and a more engaged educational scholarship. Periodicals like *This Magazine Is About Schools* and collections of articles like *The Politics of the Canadian Public School* (Martell, 1974), *Reading, Writing and Riches* (Nelson and Nock, 1978) and *The Political Economy of Canadian Schooling* (Wotherspoon, 1987) argued that schools did not serve students well, and located the problems in the class structure of Canadian society.

Some of these observations were well known and could be explained within the old functional paradigms. Parsons knew that parents' status affected their children's success, and he stressed that conformity to values mattered as much as intellectual ability. What was debated and changed was the interpretive framework, and therefore the focus of research studies and the sociological meaning that was made of their findings.

Critical theory and Marxist theory, despite their impact on scholarship, made few inroads with educational practitioners, who were frequently the targets of the critique, or with policy-makers, who were told there was not much to be done anyway within the framework of a capitalist economy. However, the new scholarship did have policy implications because it suggested new ways to understand and attack educational problems. Instead of treating social inequality as a problem caused by children and their families, and a problem that could be solved by more education, this work saw education itself as in need of change. The organization of schooling and its links with the work-place, both material and ideological, needed reform, even if this was unlikely to go very far within the confines of a capitalist economy.

Although Bowles and Gintis challenged many tenets of functional theory, the tight and necessary relations between school and work posited by functionalism remained in their work. Bowles and Gintis labelled the phenomenon 'correspondence' rather than functional necessity, for it was based in power relations rather than in social need. But the inevitability of the relations that existed, whatever educators, students, employers or the state thought and did, suffused their theory, and made educational practitioners feel helpless and threatened. For if education was part of the problem, not part of the solution, and this was built into its organization and curriculum, educators would simply be making a repressive system work.

This dilemma pointed to the necessity of looking more closely at the relationship between individual action and social structure. To see what people do as an unproblematic outcome of social structure is inadequate. It leaves no room for anyone to change and think and move and struggle. It misrepresents individual consciousness as merely an internalization of the dominant ideology, when, as Giddens (1979) points out, 'a good case can be made that only dominant class groups have ever been strongly committed to dominant ideologies. . . . All social actors, no matter how lowly, have some degree of penetration of the social forms which oppress them' (p. 72). People are located in more complex ways than any simple correspondence theory would have us believe, and their ways of determining how to act are full of contradictory pressures and understandings.

Moreover, power is never as clearly located in a single group as the work of Bowles and Gintis, and other work in this tradition, suggests. Power resides in interactions between groups, not in a person or a group of people. No capitalist employer has only simple decisions to make. Even the most oppressed, whether the teacher, the student or the state bureaucrat, has some leeway for action. To quote Giddens (1979, p. 6) again:

> Power relationships are always two-way; that is to say, however subordinate an actor may be in a relationship, the very fact of involvement in that relationship gives him or her a certain amount of power over the other. Those in subordinate positions in social systems are frequently adept at converting whatever resources they possess into some degree of control over the conditions of reproduction of those social systems.

In other words, things are negotiated all the time. Schools change, work changes. The reproduction of social inequality is continually contested, though not in a democratic fashion, among groups with unequal amounts of power. Schools are agents neither of the capitalist class nor of the impoverished. They are sites of struggle. To look closely at these struggles, how they are experienced and waged, with what resources, what is believed and fought for, what is taken for granted and conceded: this is what we need to do to understand how school and work are structured and connected. In this complexity lies the interest of sociological and educational research, and the resonance research can have for educators, students and parents, who are themselves struggling to understand and act in the face of the complexity.

Paul Willis's (1977) study of working-class 'lads' in Britain was the best-known attempt to look at social reproduction in schools as an ongoing, contested and contradictory process. Informed by critical Marxist theory, but concerned for how young men actually experienced and acted in schools, Willis produced a combination of ethnography and Marxist theory that set a model for critical educational sociology.

Willis (1977, p. 1) began with the following observation:

> The difficult thing to explain about how middle class kids get middle class jobs is why others let them. The difficult thing to explain about how working class kids get working class jobs is why they let themselves. . . .
> There is no obvious physical coercion and a degree of self direction. This is despite the inferior rewards for, undesirable social definition, and increasing intrinsic meaninglessness, of manual work: in a word its location at the bottom of a class society.

He allowed for no simple answer to the question of social reproduction (or as Parsons would have it, 'allocation') through schooling – neither that it was necessary for the economy, nor that it was dictated by the needs of capital. Instead, he treated the young men he interviewed as active agents who produce a culture, a set of decisions and some concrete behaviours, not out of nothing, but out of the existing social conditions in which they find themselves. They understand some things, they resist some things, they confront some contradictory and complex conditions which they have to make sense of. How they do it Willis found intriguing and revealing.

The mechanical models of class conflict that were suggested by early Marxist writings in education, and that were so useful in shocking me as a graduate student into understanding the ideological underpinnings of sociological theory and educational practice, have been displaced by more complex models of human action and social structure. The complex determinants of human action, as well as of social structure, are explored in as much of their fullness and contradiction as I can manage. Unequal power relations of many kinds, but particularly those among different social classes, between men and women, and between teachers and students, must be central to any analysis. And the wisdom of students and educational practitioners (as well as their folly) must be incorporated into the analysis, for their understandings of how schools work are not only insightful, but are part of what makes things happen.

Gendered politics

The disadvantage women experience in the work-place has been well documented in recent years. Women earn about 60 per cent of what men earn. They work in jobs that are by and large different from the jobs that men work in. They are secretaries, nurses, teachers, service workers. They are not managers, professors, technicians, carpenters. They work in garment factories, not in mines. They take responsibility for most of the domestic work, with no pay. They bear and bring up the children. And they experience little power and autonomy in their work.

But most women are educated alongside men. Surely this poses a central problem for any theory that posits a close relationship between schooling and work. How can women's work seem so different from men's when their schooling seems so similar? How is gender learned in school, and how is it used, in conjunction with schooling or in conflict with it, to allocate students to positions in the labour force? Despite the fact that the questions seem to me both obvious and central, scholarship and policy exploring education and work have been mostly silent on the issue of gender.

Parsons did note the seeming anomaly of coeducation in 1959. Discussing generally the education of a woman, he noted: 'her adult status is going to be very much concerned with marriage and a family. This basic expectation for the girl stands in a certain tension to the school's curricular coeducation with its relative lack of differentiation by sex' (p. 217). Parsons's resolution of the contradiction involved a couple of arguments. First, women increasingly have a role in the community and in paid employment, and school is important in preparing women for these roles. Second,

The educated woman has important functions *as wife and mother* [emphasis in the original], particularly as an influence on her children in backing the schools and impressing on them the importance of education. I think it is broadly true that the immediate responsibility of women for family management has been increasing, though I am very skeptical of the alleged 'abdication' of the American male. But precisely in the context of women's increased family responsibility, the influence of the mother both as agent of socialization and as role model is a crucial one. . . . It is very doubtful whether ... the motivational prerequisites of the general process [of increased schooling] could be sustained without sufficiently high education of the women who, as mothers, influence their children.

(Parsons, 1959, pp. 217–18)

For Parsons, women's schooling was justified by its relationship to their domestic work. Women's primary location in the family was assumed – observed, taken for granted and justified. The necessary (functional) relationship between their schooling and their domestic roles resolved the seeming paradox.

The question of how women fit into status attainment research and human capital theory needed a different resolution, for these research traditions clearly dealt with income, with paid employment. Patterns for women were patently different from patterns for men, and women could not be easily fitted into the research. As a result, they were simply ignored, left out. Blau and Duncan (1967), in their extremely influential book on occupational attainment in the United States, explained that they dealt only with men because

men's careers occupy a dominant place in their lives today. . . . [A] knowledge of the occupational structure and of the conditions that govern men's chances of achieving economic success by moving up in the occupational hierarchy is . . . essential for understanding modern society.

(p. vii)

In other words, women are less important to the economy, and careers are less important to women. Moreover, women just did not fit easily into the model. How was one to rank 'housewife' in a status or income hierarchy and how was one to treat childbearing in an economic model? Women's consistently lower wages meant that correlations had to be corrected for sex differences if the models were to produce the expected answers. Too many assumptions would have to be questioned even to begin to deal with women's experience on the same basis as men's. Instead, the question was treated as relatively unimportant and dropped.

Becker, in his discussion of human capital theory, is not quite so cavalier. While it is clear that his theory and his data apply better to men than to women, he, like Parsons, notices that women's experience is anomalous, and tries to explain it, taking for granted in the process that women's positions in domestic and paid labour are fundamentally different from men's. He notes that income differences between well-educated and less-well-educated women are smaller than these income differences are for men. To explain this, he suggests that women might be receiving a rate of return on their investment in education equal to men's because the cost of women's education is less if one counts income foregone while in school as a cost of schooling. He finds that even this circular reasoning fails to make the lower rate of return for women disappear. He then suggests that a woman's husband's income should be treated as an income return to her education since she was able to marry a wealthier man by continuing her education. This again helps, but 'even when the gain from a more lucrative marriage is included, the money rate of return from college seems less for women' (Becker, 1964, p. 102).

None of this treats women as persons with a desire for independence and income like men's. None of it assumes employers should treat women as they treat men. None of it calls attention to men's marriages and children. Sexist assumptions about women's roles are built into the scholarship, as they were built into the ideology of most people at the time.

Bowles and Gintis (1976) listed the women's movement among the other social movements that rocked the complacency of earlier times and inspired a new look at the role of schools in the social order. Their focus on how education served some groups at the expense of others, and how curriculum, selection and socialization were structured by the perspectives of dominant groups easily suggested some problems in relation to women. But they discuss only class inequalities. Gender, sexism and women do not appear in their index. The data they use to argue about the impact of schooling on economic status are drawn only from 'non-Negro males, aged 24–65 years, from non-farm background, and who are experienced in the labor force' (p. 315), as was the tradition in status attainment research. Gender equity was simply not an issue that was part of the analysis.

Willis's (1977) study of working-class British lads occasioned a great deal of feminist discussion, for here was a study that was explicitly anti-racist, Marxist and feminist, but that continued the tradition that studies of youth culture, at least interesting and important ones, are studies of males. Although his opening question was about working-class 'kids', his research had to do only with boys. Moreover, the lads were in many ways sympathetically portrayed in the book, even though they were outrageously misogynist and racist. The author often seemed to enjoy their company (although he wrote little about his own role) and saw these young men as potential resisters to bourgeois society, even while he deplored their racism and sexism.

Probably most importantly, it is hard for a woman to read the text without getting angry at the comments the lads make, and without wanting to make these comments the focus of the analysis. Sexual imagery is used constantly by the lads, in a way that insults and degrades women. As Angela McRobbie (1978, p. 41) writes:

> One striking feature of Willis' study is how unambiguously degrading to women is the language of aggressive masculinity through which the lads kick against the oppressive structures they inhabit – the text is littered with references of the utmost brutality. One teacher's authority is undermined by her being labelled a 'cunt'. Boredom in the classroom is

alleviated by the mimed masturbating of a giant penis and by replacing the teacher's official language with a litany of sexual obscenities. The lads demonstrate their disgust for and fear of menstruation by substituting 'jam rag' for towel at every opportunity. What Willis fails to confront, I think, is the violence underpinning such imagery and evident in one lad's description of sexual intercourse as having 'a good maul on her'. He does not comment on the extreme cruelty of the lads' sexual double standard or tease out in sufficient detail how images of sexual power and domination are used as a kind of last defensive resort. It is on these terms that the book's closing lines can best be understood. When Paul Willis gently probes Joey about his future, he replies, 'I don't know, the only thing I'm interested in is fucking as many women as I can if you really want to know'.

As a woman, to read the book is to be confronted with comments that are hurtful and upsetting. What is central to the female reader is only tangential to the text, to be incorporated into the analysis of class reproduction, but not to be explored, traced to its roots and critically examined for its own sake. In the context of such unrelenting sexism, this is hard to accept.

This is not to argue that Willis ignores sexism. He analyses the role of patriarchy in the reproduction of capitalist production. The lads equate mental labour with school and femininity, and feel superior to and contemptuous of both. They see themselves as masculine, therefore fitted for manual labour. In a three-page section, he demonstrates the ways the lads define their superiority to young women, putting them in one of two categories: the 'easy lay' or the 'girlfriend'. The easy lay is a social outcast with no power to discriminate: 'once they've had it, they want it all the time, no matter who it's with' (p. 44). And the character of the girlfriend is illustrated by this quote:

> She wouldn't look at another chap. She loves doing fucking housework. Trousers I brought up yesterday, I took 'em up last night and her turned 'em up for me. She's as good as gold and I wanna get married as soon as I can.
>
> (Willis, 1977, p. 45)

The Willis study does open up the question of where such misogynist views came from, and how they can be explained and perhaps combated. Gender inequality is an issue that is made visible, and the framework Willis developed can be used to explore how ideologies and material practices are both changed and continued. But still issues of gender are secondary, used to help explain social class reproduction, but not themselves the subject of analysis.

Feminist scholarship that did make gender issues central to understanding all aspects of social life arose in the 1970s, in conjunction with a renewed feminist political movement. Analysing the socialization of young women and their allocation to positions at work was what feminist scholarship and feminist politics were all about. Why did women cluster in so few jobs, and why were they paid so little? What were the social conditions that reproduced gender inequality, and what were the social conditions that might change it? To answer these questions, feminists drew from the same ideological currents and sociological theories as other analyses of education and work (see Arnot, 1981). But they added to and rethought previous scholarship in the light of women's experience.

The functionalist paradigm suggests that if members of a group do not do well at work, it is because they do not do well at school. Some feminist scholarship amounted to an attempt, in this tradition, to show how women did not perform appropriately at school, and therefore did not get good jobs. The solution, given this analysis, was more and better schooling for women, in order to ensure that they could compete equally with men.

Two kinds of arguments could be adduced. The first was that women did not stay in school long enough to get the *amount* of education they needed. Until recently, women have been less likely than men to obtain university degrees, and this was the focus of reports in several countries. However, focusing only on university education, where men were ahead, hid the fact that, at least in industrialized countries, women in the labour force were on average better educated than men in the labour force, because they were more likely to complete secondary schooling. This point is too often overlooked, and it poses a basic challenge to the notion that school-based skills are rewarded at work. Women have lots of school-based skills, more than men. But they do very much worse than men at work. Schooling makes women's disadvantage in the labour market harder, not easier, to explain.

The second argument contended that women did not get the *kind* of schooling they needed to compete at work and to be attractive to employers. It was pointed out that even though they are in coeducational classes, young women are rewarded for different things from young men. Females learn femininity, instead of masculinity; they learn, in other words, to be docile and subservient instead of independent and thoughtful. As Levy (1972, p. 27) summarized the impact of sexual stereotyping in schools,

> the 'masculine' characteristics are related to intellectual development and self-actualization, whereas the strong, consistent pressures on girls to be 'feminine' and 'good pupils' promote characteristics that inhibit achievement and suppress females' full development.

This line of argument makes visible some of the discrimination that young women face in school. It points to differential socialization in coeducational classrooms, a phenomenon that is easy to document as soon as someone looks (Sharpe, 1976; Stanworth, 1983; Lees, 1986), and one that teachers must learn to notice and change. But the argument about stereotyping in schools also overlooks a great deal. Traits that are linked to femininity are treated as the cause of low achievement, while male traits are used to 'explain' male success. Such research does not pay much attention to the positive value of feminine characteristics like sociability and cooperation, characteristics that are usually valued in the school environment and that need to be valued in society and at work. It also suggests a bifurcation of personality characteristics that is not supported by the evidence on sex differences. Socialization to gender norms is not very successful (Anyon, 1983). There is a big overlap between males and females in their sociability, their aggression, their independence (Maccoby and Jacklin, 1974). The overlap in personality characteristics is much greater than the overlap in status and income at work; personality characteristics can therefore provide only a very partial explanation for the differences between men's and women's success in the work-place.

Researchers also pointed out that, especially as students reach the end of their schooling, many classrooms are not coeducational. Young women and men get very different kinds of preparation for work. At the secondary level and even more dramatically at the level of job training and post-secondary education, young women and men 'choose' to take courses and programmes that are predominantly filled with one sex or the other. Thus they enter the labour market with different skills and interests that lead to differential treatment by employers.

This observation calls attention to an important structural feature of the school system, its specifically vocational curriculum. The organization of this curriculum along gendered lines is central to linking school preparation to economic position. The question is how to interpret the significance of such organization and how to understand its existence.

Functional theory and human capital theory understand its existence as a necessary reflection of the differential strengths of students, and their differential productivity and therefore wages at work. If both schools and employers evaluate on universalistic, achievement-related criteria, differences in skills and performance will account for curriculum placement and ultimately for economic placement. Marxist theory, on the other hand, stresses the ascriptive characteristics involved in curriculum 'choice' and employers' desire to get work performed at the lowest possible wage. Instead of assuming a competitive school system and labour market, Marxist theory suggests we enquire about the way each is organized to segregate and disadvantage the powerless, in other words the working class or, perhaps, women.

Different strands of feminist theory understand the organization of curriculum in different ways. Feminist theory is often divided into liberal, radical and socialist tendencies, even while these categories are not mutually exclusive and any particular piece of work may borrow from more than one. To overgeneralize a bit, liberal feminist theory tends to adopt the view of functionalism, to assume that the world works well, and that the problem is to fit women in on an equal basis. Structural inequalities in school would be overcome by having more women enrolled in the higher-status streams. Radical feminism assumes that the dominance of men has shaped the world in favour of men, and argues that women's point of view must be articulated, valued and given power to transform the organization of the society. When it comes to streaming, this suggests that the curriculum where women predominate needs to be revalued. Socialist feminism rejects the unitary notion of a 'women's' point of view and argues that class as well as gender shapes the world, and that power must be redistributed more equally to all. More recently, attention to racial and ethnic differences has added more emphasis to the observation that women have very diverse lives. 'Woman' is not a unitary category, and if it is used as a unitary category it serves to conceal the experience of minority women (hooks, 1984; Lorde, 1984; Minh-ha, 1989). For the study of schooling, this entails the study of power and cultural differences as they have affected the organization.

What is reproduced in school is a gendered as well as a class society. What we want young people to learn in school is shaped by gender relations and by notions of what young men and women will do differently at work. Thus, gender is involved in socialization and in the curriculum at school. Gender is also involved in the allocation of young people to work. But gender relations are not the only power relations that matter. Social class matters. The meaning of gender in the experience of students and teachers is shaped by race and ethnicity, by country and city, by family structure and popular movements. The experience of gender itself is constructed by school and by work.

The politics of research

Research should be an attempt to find answers we don't already know to questions we care about. Sometimes, of course, research programmes are carefully crafted merely to prove an already-identified contention, to score political points, to settle old scores. But most research, and certainly the research I do, is done out of curiosity to find out how something works.

To be clear about this is not to argue for a moment that research is free of political agendas and attempts to show the limitations of someone else's work. Research questions arise in dialogue with existing scholarship and practice, a dialogue that reflects the researcher's politics, values and experiences. Research strategies must be carefully adapted to the questions the researcher wants to answer, for there is no one correct way to find out what goes on in the world.

I began to do research on young women, their schooling and their job expectations, as a graduate student in the 1970s, when the feminist movement was resurgent and campuses were highly politicized by the Vietnam War. The prevailing sociological paradigm for understanding young people and their career plans was status attainment research. This appeared to be a straightforward technique for determining what factors had an effect on aspirations and ultimately on attainment at school and in the labour market. My thesis was developed within this paradigm and used path analysis, factor analysis and questionnaires to demonstrate how young women's attitudes towards sex roles affected their aspirations for school and work. A few interviews were appended to the data-gathering exercise to give me some sense of the community I was working within. My conclusion: 'The research suggests that even after social class and academic achievement variables are controlled, measures of sex-role ideology continue to be significant predictors of women's aspirations' (Gaskell, 1973).

In the process of carrying out this research, I learned two things. First, that interviewing was more interesting, and gave me more new information, than administering well-developed questionnaires with reliable scales. The sentence after the conclusion noted above stated: 'The conclusion that beliefs about women's place in the world influence the way women plan their futures may seem unexciting.' After a couple of years' work, I seemed to be restating the obvious. What was exciting was learning about how young women experienced being female in high school. Comments like the following were amazing and intriguing to me:

Career? I never want to make a career. I want to get married and have kids. If you get all involved in a career, I think something happens to the kids. They need their mother, not their father. Women just work on week-ends. With their husband around, they can go out and waitress and get the extra money they need.

A guy has to go to college to get a good job and support a family to find out about life. A girl has to have something in common with a guy to talk to him.

To a highly educated, career-oriented graduate student like me, these insights into the world in which these young women moved were fascinating. I wanted to learn more, to understand where these views came from and what their impact was.

The second thing I discovered was that the critical Marxist models of schooling that were beginning to be discussed in my graduate seminars were much more intellectually appealing and politically relevant than the assumptions underlying my status attainment models. To find causation in individual characteristics, whether academic abilities or sex-role attitudes, was just not adequate. Again, this change of heart is reflected in the comments I made in the conclusion to an article based on my thesis:

Job opportunities for women are limited, as are day-care centres and other alternative methods of looking after children. Sex-role ideology and its impact on aspirations can be expected to change only when there is a general change in the social and economic supports for sexism in the society.

(Gaskell, 1977)

The work I have done since, the work that is collected in this book, tries to incorporate the fascination that interviews and observation of schools still hold for me within a theoretical framework that questions the way power relations shape schooling, particularly the relations between schooling and work. I would describe this work as feminist, as political, as engaged. No research can take a photograph of the social process. All research involves the researcher, in that she or he chooses a particular point of view from which to ask questions and a particular lens through which to see the answers. The researcher must take a stand as a political actor, not hide behind the supposed neutrality of 'science'.

Donmeyer (1985) usefully summarizes three levels at which research can be criticized, pointing to three ways in which a researcher must make choices about framing research. He discusses three levels at which research can be analysed, three levels at which the researchers' conclusions can be questioned. Referring to these three levels as potential 'mistakes', he writes:

> First order mistakes occur when the evidence cannot support propositions that have been framed by using a particular language. . . . Second order mistakes occur when the language used to frame propositions is not adequate for particular purposes. . . . Third order mistakes relate to the inadequacy of the purposes themselves.
>
> (Donmeyer, 1985, p. 19)

First-order mistakes involve careful gathering and weighing of evidence. Here are the technical questions of reliability, and of validity, sampling error and interviewer bias. Good research must sift and weigh evidence carefully. As Lather (1986) has argued, we must develop and refine techniques that ensure the credibility of our data, and minimize the distorting effects of personal bias on the logic of evidence.

Second-order mistakes involve the usefulness of a conceptual framework for the purposes it is being asked to advance. Here researchers must ask methodological and theoretical questions in light of the overall purposes of the research. For example, will interviews or questionnaires answer the questions better? How should questions be asked? Should the unit of analysis be individuals or institutions? Should students or teachers be questioned? The researcher must clarify how questions of individual agency and structure are being handled, and what the methodology will illuminate and conceal. These decisions require knowledge of competing frameworks and conceptual languages, and an appreciation of their different implications. The questions of what the research is trying to understand and what the political purposes are should underlie these kinds of decisions. My earlier discussion of competing paradigms – functionalist, Marxist, liberal, radical and so on – enters at this level of analysis.

Third-order mistakes involve an analysis of the political purposes themselves. The relativist view that one person's purpose is as good as another's, and that differences among research frameworks are simply a matter of personal political preference, trivializes the most important questions about our commitments as researchers and educators. To justify one's research choices is to engage in discourse about political questions, about the nature of good education in a good society. This dialogue is a critical one. It brings political discussion to the heart of the academic process.

Political self-consciousness means not personal confessionals at the beginning of research reports, but rather a serious conceptual analysis of the frameworks that are being used, and an argument for their usefulness. Politically situating the research in this way can help the research have an impact, while at the same time improving the conceptual logic and academic value of the study.

This research, then, is placed within a feminist agenda to explore who is served by the structures of the relations between school and work, and how these structures are recreated and resisted, particularly by young people and teachers in schools. There is relatively little analysis of work, for my concerns are with education. There is particular focus on women, for their experience has been ignored in the previous theories and models in the literature. My political commitment is towards providing young women with more control of their lives.

Introduction to the book

This book starts from the assumption that one must not take the existing structure of schooling and its relationship to the work-place for granted as the requisite for preparing young people for jobs, but that one must instead enquire into who is served and who is not. The nature of schooling and the way it is linked to work are actually intriguing and peculiar. They have been historically contested, and should continue to be the focus of policy and educational debate today. They have been shaped by political contests, contests stacked by unequal relations of class and of gender.

The chapters in this book follow in more or less chronological order, and thus reflect my developing sense of my own intellectual agenda. The first three chapters are based on interviews carried out in 1977 with 82 students in three Canadian secondary schools. All three schools were located in working-class neighbourhoods, because I wanted to find students who were moving from school directly into the labour force, not into a community college or a university.

The school counsellors asked any grade 12 (age 17 or 18 years) students who were planning to get a job next year to sign up for interviews. In some cases, guidance counsellors asked specific students if they would be willing to be interviewed, in order to help me find a diverse and fairly representative group of students. More young women than young men were interviewed, because the experiences of the young women were of particular interest. Eventually, 35 male and 47 female students were interviewed.

With a research assistant I conducted two open-ended interviews of approximately one hour each with each student. The first series of interviews took place in the spring of 1977 in the school. Students were asked about their school experiences and about their plans and expectations for the coming year. The second series of interviews took place between February and April 1978, when 80 of the original 82 students were tracked down and asked about their work, the transition from school to work, and their retrospective views of high school.

These interviews were transcribed, then read and re-read. On each transcript, comments relevant to the themes being explored in one or other of the papers were highlighted and retyped. As interpretations were developed, I would go back to the original interviews to check on the meaning in context, and to add material that was relevant. A research assistant would often be employed to re-read interviews to check my interpretations, or to find counter-examples and alternative meanings. This method is necessarily impressionistic and interpretive. It was used before computers offered researchers a more streamlined set of procedures and software for keeping track of interview data. But it allowed the researcher – in this case, me – to stay closely in touch with the words of the young people involved.

Chapter 2 grows from an interest in the way schools stream students and prepare them differentially for work. It grows from the recognition that gender issues were ignored in most of the research on streaming. The chapter focuses on how these young people choose their high school courses. It looks at these 'choices' as a product of the structure of the high school curriculum and of young people who are actively trying to find a satisfying and useful education.

Chapter 3 explores the views of these young people as they move from school to work. It was written with Marvin Lazerson, and inspired by a conversation we had about whether school or work was worse for young people. The focus is on the ways young people understand the transition from school to work; why they choose to leave school, why they value the low-paying, low-status jobs they are able to get. The influence of Willis's work is unmistakable. Why do working-class kids choose working-class jobs?

Chapter 4 explores a question that Paul Willis posed to me while I was on sabbatical at the Centre for Contemporary Cultural Studies in Birmingham. Why do young women choose domestic jobs? If the unequal assumption of domestic labour is the source of gender inequality, why do women buy in? The answer to this question is explored in relation to constructions of work, of schooling and of gender in the lives of these young women.

This exploration of the experiences of young people turned my interest towards understanding more fully the world that they experienced. It was not constructed by them; it was constructed elsewhere. They were responding within structures of school and work that had been put in place long ago and that continued to be shaped by teachers and employers. How did this work?

To answer this question, a second major data-gathering project took place with the aid of the Social Sciences and Humanities Research Council of Canada from 1983 to 1987. This time, there was more money for research assistants, more computer-assisted data analysis and a much more ambitious agenda. The organization of clerical training, in its historical and contemporary forms, was to be explored, because the organization of this training was so important for understanding the experience of women in school and at work.

The research included work in the archives, observation of classrooms, the collection of documents and, again, extensive interviews. The analysis was as time-consuming and painstaking as before, despite and sometimes because of the advent of computer technology. Interpretations of the data this time were checked not only by members of the research team, but also by the teachers and students in the field who provided the data.

Chapter 5 uses the observational and interview data to explore the construction of skill in a contemporary high school business education classroom. What is being taught and why? The answer is sought both in the structural properties of schools and the changing labour market, and in teachers' constructions of and responses to them.

Chapter 6 uses some of the historical work to explore the construction of clerical training and, more particularly, the construction of the notion of skill that underpins contemporary ideas about what vocational training involves. The argument is that clerical skills have been devalued because they have been women's skills, and that the present organization of clerical training reflects the lack of power women have had in the labour process.

The final chapter explores the implications of this enquiry for public policy and research. It argues that policy must start from the concerns of young people, instead of criticizing them for having the wrong values and attitudes. It explores the debates about vocational education and argues that education for the hand and for practice must be reintegrated with education for the mind and for theory. It examines policies that demand wages for education and shows how such policies can both help and hurt the cause of women's – and human – equality.

2 Course Streaming in the School

The school creates differences among students by offering them different kinds of knowledge. Some students take French and some take German. More significantly, some take physics and some take business fundamentals. Some get high-status knowledge that prepares them for high-status jobs; some get low-status knowledge that prepares them for low-paying jobs. Here we have, quite concretely, in the organization of schooling, a process of social reproduction and production of social inequality. Here the functional relationship or correspondence between the school and the work-place can be seen in its most straightforward form.

Differential course enrolment sets students on different paths towards the labour market. Academic courses prepare them for college or university and for professional and managerial jobs. Industrial arts courses orient students towards blue collar work. Maths and science courses allow them to enter technological fields. Business courses teach them what is involved in secretarial or sales jobs. Home economics courses prepare them for domestic tasks. In a very concrete organizational form, one can see in high school course enrolments the genesis of divisions that shape adult life.

Much of the discussion of course enrolments, 'streaming', as it has been called in Canada, or 'tracking', as it has been labelled in the United States, has taken place in relation to class and racial inequalities (Oakes, 1985; Page and Valli, 1990). Working-class students and minority students are more likely to be enrolled in the lower tracks, in the courses that lead to lower paying jobs. There is a strong relationship between track placement and previous academic performance, especially on standardized tests which have been developed for the very purpose of sorting out students and placing them in different courses in the high school. This can be accounted for partly by the bias of tests against children who are not white and middle class. But social class has an effect on track placement over and above its effect on academic performance (Heyns, 1974; Rosenbaum, 1976; Vanfossen et al., 1987). Class and race themselves make a difference, through factors like the teachers' perceptions of a child's potential, the parents' preferences and knowledge of the school, and the students' goals and attitudes. Moreover, there are differences among schools in how the relationship works (Garet and Delaney, 1988). Some schools create more differentiation by class and race than others.

Tracking by gender has been analysed much less. But any statistical profile of women's enrolment in educational programmes shows dramatic differences between the kinds of courses taken by men and by women. Academic performance is a poor predictor of gender differences in course enrolments. Gender itself matters, and this chapter will explore how it does.

At the university level, the small number of women enrolled in engineering and science has frequently been noted. Women are much more likely than men to be enrolled in nursing, education, the fine arts and most humanities disciplines. At the college level, women are under-represented in trades training and in technologies, but are over-represented in community services and in secretarial and accounting courses. In high schools, the differences occur not so much *between* academic and non-academic courses, where racial and class differences are found, but *within* each. Young women are more often in senior French and history courses than in senior physics and computer science courses. They are more often in domestic science and business education than in industrial education.

Why? The patterns are identifiable, but the social processes that produce such consistent relationships need to be understood if teachers, guidance counsellors, parents and students are to sort out what might bring about change. Documenting and deploring the process is not enough.

The processes involved in course enrolment are not well understood. In the academic literature, terms such as 'placed in', 'elected', 'decided on', 'chose', 'channelled into', 'assigned to' and the non-committal 'end up in' can all be found describing the process whereby students are enrolled in different courses. The confusion in terms reflects the confusion about exactly what happens. Do students choose or do teachers place? Ability grouping, which is done by the teacher, has been equated with curriculum differentiation, which is more freely chosen (Persell, 1977; Garet and Delaney, 1988). Little attention has been paid to how the process is conceived of by the school, or by the students.

In general, sociologists attend to the ways that course enrolment patterns are produced by the organization of the school. They explore the criteria the school uses to sort students (Heyns, 1974; Davis and Haller, 1981) and the role school records and counsellors play in placing students in different tracks (Clark 1960; Cicourel and Kitsuse, 1963; Rosenbaum, 1976). Cicourel and Kitsuse's (1963) study of the way guidance counsellors classify and place students using knowledge of their social class backgrounds has become a classic in the literature. The assumption on which the study is based is that counsellors are gatekeepers who control the careers of students, and that their constructions of social processes are the mechanisms of social reproduction. Literature on school classrooms has pointed out the ways teachers' constructions of gender influence what goes on in class (Levy, 1972; Stanworth, 1983). All these are ways of seeing how the school has an impact on students' 'choices'.

There is, however, an extensive literature that emphasizes students' characteristics as the determining factor, and stresses the importance of students'
attitudes, aptitudes, self-concepts and psychological traits (Meece *et al.*, 1982).
Like status attainment models, this literature looks for individual characteristics
that set apart those students who enrol in high-status or, in the case of women,
non-traditional courses. Differences in aptitude and achievement are too small
to explain much of the gender gap, although there has been a good deal of
attention to differences in spatial perception and maths ability (Benbow and
Stanley, 1980, 1982, 1983). Women's 'fear of success' (Horner, 1970), their
confidence, anxiety and aspirations have all been used to account for why they
enrol in traditional courses. The implicit assumption is that they can choose,
or, alternatively, that the criteria of the school are (of course) meritocratic.

The issue is partly empirical and should be studied more carefully. There are
important variations between schools and over time in the relative importance
of student choice and school assignment in determining course enrolment.
Historically, North American high schools have moved from a relatively similar
course of study for all students, through a rigid hierarchy of curriculum tracks,
to a more open system of curriculum options (Porter *et al.*, 1982; Boyer, 1983).
The causes and consequences of these variations are worth exploring. The
'smorgasbord' of courses that students take for granted today is neither universal
nor necessary. Many would argue that it should be replaced by a common core
curriculum, or at least by more common requirements for high school
graduation. This would quickly change the relationships among class, gender,
race and curriculum content. Any regression equation that specifies relationships between course enrolment and student characteristics must specify the
context in which the study was done, and therefore how far it can be
generalized.

There are also variations within schools between different kinds of courses,
so it is important to specify what kind of course is being discussed. Bernstein's
(1975) notions of framing and classification are useful in analysing these
differences. Enrolment in a highly framed and classified subject like English is
strongly influenced by the school's assessment of ability. Enrolment in art or
music classes is more open to student choice. The two may be linked, as in the
school Rosenbaum (1976) studied, where ability grouping in core subjects in
the junior high school was translated into a wide variety of curriculum options
in the senior high.

The question of choice versus placement involves more than empirically
sorting out which model applies in any particular case. It involves theoretical
issues concerning the relationship between individual agency and social structure. In every case, both the student's orientation and the school's organization
are involved. Even in a relatively open system, where students feel able to
choose among options, school staff limit the available choices, shape the way
students see themselves and their options, and offer advice, veiled threats,
encouragement and strongly worded suggestions. In a relatively closed system,
where the school assigns students to courses, students must still comply. The
system will work best if students are encouraged to see that the courses they

are taking are in their best interests. The problem, then, is to reconceptualize the issue of 'choice' in a way that incorporates both the orientation of the student, that is, individual consciousness, and the organization of the school, that is, social structure.

This takes us to the heart of a major problem in social theory. Structural theories and correspondence theories have for too long regarded individual action as an unproblematic reflection of social structure. As I discussed in Chapter 1, such theories construct students as if they internalize the beliefs of the teachers and the school. Clearly students do not. They think for themselves, they question authority, they try to make sense of their own worlds. They do all this by borrowing the language and the ideology in which they have grown up, and within social locations that they did not opt for, but this does not make them passive ciphers.

Moreover, teachers are aware that students have to be convinced. They know their power to dictate depends on cooperation from the great majority of those they work with. Students must be actively persuaded of the logic of the educational enterprise, and some are never persuaded. The process of 'structuration' in Giddens's (1979) terms is the active construction of social structures all the time through the actions of teachers and students. This captures the process better than any notion of structures that act on people.

I will look, then, at students as active participants in the process that produces differential course enrolments. But in emphasizing students' choices, I want to avoid a model that reifies and decontextualizes their attitudes and traits. As Laws (1976) points out in her discussion of women's work aspirations, motivation is dynamic and responsive to the social context, rather than static and individually 'owned'. An individual may be hard-working in one setting but lazy in another if one setting provides more incentives and a more congenial atmosphere than the other. To label an individual hard-working or lazy is to miss the structuring of what look like individual characteristics by social structure.

Willis's work (1977, 1981) is an attempt to deal with these complexities. He explains how a group of working-class British lads 'chose' working-class jobs, and he carefully analyses the structure of the school and the society in which the choices emerged. He emphasizes their 'sense of activity and practice and what feel like (and are to the participants) circumstances creatively met' (Willis, 1977, p. 3).

In this chapter, I will explore how course enrolment differences arise, adopting this theoretical orientation and emphasizing students' belief that they choose, while embedding their orientations in a specific institutional context. This approach avoids some of the problems in earlier research on course tracking and points to the need for more case studies of specific tracking practices in specific courses and schools.

The context

The data for this study are drawn from a series of interviews with 47 young women in Vancouver, Canada, as described in Chapter 1. Vancouver schools have little ability-grouping before grade 10 (age 15 or 16), and curriculum options open up, subject to a complex set of distribution requirements, in grade 11 (age 16 or 17). The options are defined not as ability tracks but as a series of choices in different departments – music, history, business education, French, home economics, and so on. Relatively speaking, the process seems fairly open to student and parent input. The official school-board policy is that enrolment decisions are ultimately the responsibility of the family, although the school has some input. The student handbook states that course decisions are 'a joint responsibility shared by students, parents, and staff, to ensure a suitable program is undertaken, but final responsibility rests with the parents.' This is different from the school policies described by Cicourel and Kitsuse (1963) and Rosenbaum (1976).

Instead of focusing on all course choices, this chapter focuses on the choice of business courses. The taking of business courses marks both a class and a gender divide. Choosing business courses means opting out of the academic, that is, high-status, stream. This is an important step towards reproducing one's class position. Academic courses prepare students for post-secondary schooling. Professional and managerial jobs are likely to require post-secondary schooling, working-class jobs are not. Much concern about curriculum differentiation has arisen from its functions in segregating and channelling working-class children (Lazerson and Grubb, 1974; Bowles and Gintis, 1976).

Enrolment in business courses is overwhelmingly by female students. This gender division in course enrolment corresponds to the sexual segregation of the labour force. Secretarial and sales jobs have all the characteristics of quintessentially female work – little responsibility and power, low pay and little room for advancement. Thus, the young women in this study chose courses that were likely to reproduce not only their class position but also their subservient gender position.

The issue of choice

There is a good deal of evidence that students believe they choose their curriculum track, whatever the coercive practices of the school actually are. Jencks *et al.* (1972) note that 84 per cent of all students surveyed in the 1968 US Congressional Survey of Equality of Opportunity said they were in the track they chose. Rosenbaum (1976) reports that 87 per cent of his non-college students stated that they chose the track they were in. Davis and Haller (1981) also found a strong relationship between what students chose and where they ended up. They note that two-thirds of those whose choices are discrepant with their placement are in a higher track than the one they chose, which reinforces the importance of understanding what makes non-academic curricula attractive to students.

The young women interviewed in this study were no different. It was striking that they saw themselves as completely responsible for their curriculum choices: 'I did what I wanted. It made sense to me'. They provided a variety of reasons for taking the courses they did and rarely mentioned pressure from their parents or the school. Only a couple of young women directly attributed their course enrolment to the guidance counsellor or to the school:

> The counsellors look at your grades. So I took commercial . . . basically because my counsellor told me. She seemed to think I would be better fitted to those courses.

> I wanted to take academics, but they wouldn't let me.

These comments suggest a number of things that have been pointed out in the literature. Grades are important, and curriculum tracks have many features similar to ability tracks. Moreover, counsellors can take an active role that goes beyond formal school policy. But the Vancouver counsellors appeared not to have the authority, resources, or respect to play a critical role in course selection.

> The counsellors we've got here are just completely terrible. They don't know what they're doing. . . . To tell you the truth, I think [names the school] counsellors just don't get enough training or whatever it takes to become a counsellor.

> There is not enough counsellors. They're having to take care of a whole grade of people. They're spending most of their time running through the papers and there's not much time for them to sit around and rap.

> Counsellors are no good. [They are] just phys. ed. teachers who have been moved to guidance.

Many of the students felt that counsellors could be ignored, and they exercised their power to disregard them.

> The counsellors suggested day-care, but that means one or two more years at Langara [a community college]. I don't want more school.

> The counsellors kept saying, 'You'll never get a job unless you can type'. But I just picked what I'd enjoy.

Like guidance counsellors, parents infrequently had a direct influence on course selection. Although they were given the official and legal responsibility for course choices, they were not part of the everyday processes of the school and thus were least likely to be well informed. Few students reported a direct intervention by their parents. Most of the students said that their parents let them do whatever they wanted: 'They let me make up my own mind'. If advice *was* offered, it was to include academic courses and to keep open the options for post-secondary education.

> My parents encouraged me to take arts and sciences, to go to university and be a teacher.

> My dad advised science. I didn't like science, but I figured he knew better.

But now I wish I had taken more business courses. They were what I really liked. I thought they were fun.

These students saw themselves making choices, often creative ones, designed to resolve the dilemmas that arose out of the structure of schooling, femininity and work. Understanding why they took certain courses thus involves understanding their reasoning, rather than simply understanding the power and interests of parents, teachers and guidance counsellors. Their assumption of responsibility for course choice was important because it led them to accept the consequences of their choices and to blame themselves for the restricted options they faced later. It affected the organization and morale of the school, because students tended not to blame or feel beholden to the teachers or counsellors on issues of course enrolment. In these ways, the students' consciousness both drew on the existing structures and served as part of the process of recreating those structures.

Why choose non-academic courses? The reproduction of class

One of the major divisions among courses is between academic courses, which fulfil the prerequisite for university entrance, and other courses, which do not. Most of the literature on tracking has conceived of a single vertical axis of differentiation with academic courses at the top. The use of this axis arises from and clearly displays the class hierarchy involved in course selection.

The school's student handbook highlights the importance of the post-secondary/no post-secondary divide by printing the entrance requirements for universities and community colleges. Course descriptions clearly indicate those courses that are designed for potential post-secondary students:

This is a valuable course for students in preparation for further English courses at the university.

This course is required for most universities and technical institutions.

Feedback from BCIT [a technological college], Langara [a community college] and university students indicate this course is of tremendous advantage to biology-related courses in their area.

The handbook also indicates the academic ability required for entrance:

A better than average achievement in English is necessary for success in this course.

An average or better mark in mathematics correlates well with success.

In emphasizing the relationship between a student's achievement and her choice of academic courses, schools construe class differences as achievement and ability differences. Those who are less bright take vocational courses and get working-class jobs. Such is the IQ ideology (Bowles and Gintis, 1974) or the masking of cultural privilege through an ideology of unequal giftedness (Bourdieu and Passeron, 1979).

Was this the perspective of these young women? A few of them did describe their choice of courses in the light of some fairly stable notions of their abilities and their personalities, which suggest a hierarchical world in which brains and hard work are rewarded:

I'm not university material. I don't have that much brains.

I'm lazy. I wouldn't work unless I have to.

But most of these young women believed that their choices arose not out of their unequal giftedness but out of a quite sensible inability to tolerate the pointlessness and childishness of school. They did not like school, especially the academic courses, and they did not think that what they could learn there was useful. They suggested that in such an environment, any reasonable person would opt out:

It was ridiculous. . . . Maybe ten minutes of it you can learn.

School is boring. You can't change it.

I don't like the rigid system – hour after hour – or demanding notes if you are sick or late. I miss classes because I won't be missing anything.

I stared out of the window and at my hands, like everyone else.

These young women questioned the justificatory ideology of the school rather than being socialized into it. They located difficulties in the educational environment that confronted them and in the lack of decent opportunities that existed there, instead of in their own abilities and attitudes. But this unmasking of the school's ideological rationale did not lead them to challenge the organization of the school. It led them to find ways around it, to try to pick the best set of courses they could out of a bad lot. They tried to come up with personal solutions that would minimize the discomfort schools caused them. They took courses that were easy (i.e. courses that did not intrude too much into other, more important aspects of life), fun (i.e. courses that involved less time sitting at a desk, more work experience and more interaction) and useful (i.e. courses that transmitted skills that had some direct utility in the labour market or in leisure activities). These criteria led them far away from an academic programme.

Bowles and Gintis (1976) suggest different motives for the selection of vocational courses – motives deduced from structural differences in the schooling and work experiences of working-class and middle-class families. Working-class jobs and vocational courses are more likely to be characterized by alienation, a clear hierarchy of control and punitiveness (see also Oakes, 1982). Therefore, working-class families prefer stricter, more routinized educational practices. Similarly, 'that professional and self-employed parents prefer a more open atmosphere and a greater emphasis on motivational control is a reflection of their position in the division of labor' (Bowles and Gintis, 1976, p. 133). Track assignment, they conclude, springs from working-class students' self-concepts and preferences, which are appropriate to their future position at work.

Such a straightforward correspondence does not characterize the consciousness of the young women in this study. They saw course differences in more substantive terms. They rejected academic schooling not because it was too open but because they believed it was irrelevant. Vocational courses were perceived as less regimented and less confining than academic courses. Other studies suggest that this explains a good deal of the appeal of work/study and career awareness courses (Farrar *et al.*, 1980; Watts, 1980).

Willis (1977) explains that his lads chose working-class jobs because they valued manual labour over mental labour, they resisted authority, and they wanted diversion and enjoyment. Although these young women were more diverse in their cultural traditions and expressions of disenchantment with mental labour than Willis's lads, there were some common themes in their responses. They were quite able to question the educational paradigm that asserts the fair exchange of cooperation and work for knowledge and moral superiority. They wanted a break from regular schooling and saw practical job skills as more worthwhile than irrelevant academic information.

The young women's accounts construe course divisions as horizontal rather than vertical: some people like some things, others like different things. However, they live in a world where higher marks and academic pursuits are associated with higher status, more economic opportunities and more money. In schools, marks are the official currency, and as the course descriptions make clear, high marks go with academic courses. It is hard for an aware participant in the school or the society to ignore completely the vertical nature of the divisions.

These young women produced accounts of course differences that indicate an awareness of the hierarchical nature of school programmes. According to them, students in academic courses 'think they're better', and 'university is necessary to get ahead these days'. These comments were not offered as easily or as often as other accounts, but the contradictions and diversity they indicate must not be ignored. To some extent, different students produced different emphases in their accounts. A few were more likely to say, in effect, 'I am dumb and the bright kids go to university'. Other students were more likely to indicate that school is boring and that anyone sensible would have as little to do with it as possible. But sometimes one individual gave contradictory accounts. These contradictions suggest, as Sennett and Cobb (1972) have indicated, that there are hidden injuries associated with non-participation in academic success, even when cultural forms and an understanding of oppressive relations make alternative meanings available. These injuries are hidden in that they are not easily elicited in interviews with higher-status persons. They may be produced more often in the kind of in-depth and personal discussions used by Sennett and Cobb.

Does this mean the young women really believed that they were inferior or that the system was unjust? The question is unanswerable in these terms. Different methodologies will reveal more of one account than the other. What are at issue in this study are public, everyday, easily and frequently elicited responses. These have both political and practical significance in the school and in the labour market. The young women discussed the choice of vocational courses as a choice to avoid the worst stresses and irrelevancies of school. The structure and organization of school was critical for them. They suggested that if school work had been more involving or more useful, they might have chosen otherwise. Their acquiescence in the process of selecting themselves out rested on their understanding of the school experience. Their critique of school did not go very far. It focused on individual teachers, counsellors, and specific course content rather than on the organization of the entire venture. It did not lead these young women to suggest much in the way of alternatives except better teachers and more work experience. They overwhelmingly rejected the value of school and the school's equation of academic performance with merit and deserved power, but they accepted the school's power to create links between academic performance and success in the labour market.

Why take business courses? The reproduction of gender divisions

In the high schools I studied, not a single young woman took industrial education at the grade 12 level (age 17 or 18), but almost all the young women who were not planning to continue their schooling took at least one business course. The gender segregation of courses is pervasive, but its existence has been ignored in the literature on tracking because a single vertical axis has been used to describe the differences among courses: 'The use of the terms high, average, and low track classes seemed to cut through the terminology differences at the different schools and levels, and identify classes according to their essential characteristics in terms of student classification' (Oakes, 1982, p. 201). Although a unidimensional vertical ranking of courses displays class divisions, it makes gender divisions disappear. Young women are just as likely to be on the high-track, academic courses. Gender divisions appear as horizontal divisions within each track – for example, as language versus science options in the academic track, or as business versus industrial options in the vocational track.

Gender divisions in the school curriculum correspond to divisions in the labour force, just as class divisions do. The correspondence between school tracks and gender divisions must be taken as seriously as the correspondence between school tracks and class divisions. Occupational segregation by gender has influenced the way curriculum options are defined at school, and the organization of this school training has affected the shape of occupational segregation by providing a generous supply of skilled female workers trained at the public's expense for a narrow range of jobs.

Why did the young women choose the business courses and not the industrial courses? There were four factors that were mentioned in their accounts: the advantages of clerical work, the availability of specific skill training in business courses, the lack of opportunities in industrial work, and the impact of domestic labour.

The young women overwhelmingly chose business courses in order to prepare themselves for clerical jobs. The course descriptions make clear that this is the purpose of the courses. In the school calendar, the business course descriptions stress usefulness in the labour market, specifically in secretarial work: 'as many types of written language projects as are relevant to office work will be included'; 'should be capable of handling books in a small business firm'; 'qualifies a student for a high standard secretarial position'. These are the courses that were most attractive to the young women. Other, more general courses attracted a greater mixture of males and females. These include: courses in general business ('investing your money, conditions of employment, home-ownership and mortgages, etc.'); accounting, marketing and distributive education ('to develop in the student personality and skills which will enable him to become an intelligent consumer and achieve success in the field of marketing'); career exploration ('to overcome the tendency of students to drift into careers with the result that they find their jobs largely unfulfilling'); and personal finance ('to enable students to make the best possible use of their income through sound money management').

Why is clerical work attractive? Most importantly, the jobs that are available to women in a competitive labour market are clerical jobs.

> I don't like typing, but it is the easiest way to get a job. It's boring and tedious just sitting there. But if you can get a job, you might as well take it.

> The only jobs are for secretaries these days. You might as well get trained.

> [I took commercial courses] because I wanted to be someone's secretary. You know, there is a big demand for secretaries.

This perception, many would argue, is a misguided one. Clerical jobs are disappearing with the introduction of new technology. There are more opportunities for women in other areas of work (Menzies, 1981). But one-third of all employed Canadian women and over half of all employed female high school graduates work in clerical jobs (Statistics Canada, 1980). The young women accurately perceived that there are a large number of clerical jobs of many different types in many different locations. The women they knew who had jobs had clerical jobs. It is difficult for a counsellor or a new economic survey to discount the students' overwhelming experience of where the jobs are.

Moreover, the literature on youth employment shows that youths are twice as likely to be unemployed as adults are and that they tend to take the first job that comes along (Blackburn and Mann, 1979; Osterman, 1980). In a period of economic crisis, this is even more pronounced. Instead of young people choosing jobs, the jobs choose them. As the young woman above said, 'If you can get a job, you might as well take it'.

Clerical work had other attractions besides its relative availability. It has higher status than blue collar work and provides more security and better working conditions. When asked why she took commercial courses, one student responded

> To fall back on commerce. My mother forced me to. She is a janitoress and said I could do better than her. She sees all these women working in an office and she said, 'You're going to do better than that'.

It provides a setting that is comfortable to work in, where there are likely to be other young working-class women to socialize with. It is attractive because it is a woman's occupation: 'Girls together can be funny and dirty. I can be more open with women around'.

The organization of training for clerical work also provides an incentive to take commercial courses. The young women pointed out that these courses were directly relevant in finding a job, unlike other courses in the high school. The courses in industrial education prepare students not to enter a trade but to embark on trades training after graduation ('recommended for students going on in engineering or architecture'; 'designed to fulfill the requirements for admission to vocational school') or to develop avocational skills ('the skills necessary to repair and maintain his own vehicle'; 'constructing a stereo') and sometimes intellectual skills ('to illustrate the fundamental principles of science'). They do not provide the edge in the labour market that commercial skills do. If anything, they have such low status that employers and community colleges prefer academic students. Carpentry courses do not make one a carpenter. One still has to go through an apprenticeship. The same is true for other industrial arts courses and for the home economics courses.

Only commercial courses provide skills that give an immediate advantage in the labour market. If they did not learn to type and understand office work, the young women were running the risk of getting no job at all. In a competitive labour market, taking clerical courses was the best way these young women could prepare themselves for the jobs that they saw as available to them.

This view that business courses are the only sensible option for non-academic young women was shared even by young women who could provide extremely negative accounts of clerical work and business courses. They regarded these as boring or, at best, 'not so bad': 'It's always inside and just sitting down at the desk and doing nothing'. These young women felt pressed to take the business courses 'to fall back on' in case they couldn't find another job. The courses were a safety net, the wisest choice because they were directly relevant to finding a job.

If the advantages of office work and training were not enough to attract a young woman, the disadvantages of the male alternative, industrial work, were likely to repel her. Many of the young women felt that the industrial courses and industrial work were difficult, dirty and uninteresting. The most common response to the question 'Why didn't you take industrial education?' was 'I'm not interested'.

> It's OK for girls to do whatever they want – be carpenters or whatever. But it's not for me. I just don't like it.

They described how socialization had shaped their responses:

> Maybe it's the way I've been brought up.

> We've always been taught to be the soft touch, like the cute sex, just sitting there.

> I was pushed away from it as a little girl – dolls, not hockey and trucks.

They even had plans to change it:

> I think [young women] should be encouraged into other jobs, but not just from our age. I think from elementary school, because you get dolls and the little guys get trucks. So you're always influenced on that kind of a path.

> You've got to be trained from the beginning to make things equal. I'd like to start a camp. I wouldn't tell the kids who were boys and who were girls. No girls' and boys' bathroom. Everyone would be exposed to everything – trucks and dolls.

There *were* young women who found blue collar jobs attractive. The status, activity, money and even unfamiliarity of male work gave it a certain appeal.

> I like to do the jobs men do. I think they are more interesting.

> I wish I had taken woodwork. I like working with wood.

> It would be exciting to be a truck driver. But I wouldn't know how to go about it.

> Men's jobs pay more.

However, their perception of barriers inside and outside the school came into play. Peer and teacher pressure, which often amounted to sexual harassment, made industrial courses a very difficult choice.

> When I was going into grade 10 [age 15 or 16], I tried it [auto mechanics] but it was a mistake. There were all guys in the class and I felt too stupid.

> The second year I was the only girl in the class, and I felt really stupid, so I didn't want to go back.

> This year I got into Auto Mechanics 12. It was all guys and when I walked in they thought I was really stupid. You know, 'Oh, we got a girl', and they were irate, so I transferred out.

> Because I am a girl, and there are only boys taking the courses, I'd get a name in the school. Girls are rowdy who take it.

> The teacher is a male and he doesn't encourage females. He gives us mostly written work. We used to complain, and he would say, 'Well, the boys can do it for you'. He probably thought it [auto class] was dangerous for us.

Barriers in the labour market also seemed to make industrial courses a waste of time:

> They wouldn't hire a female. It distracts everyone.

> I was thinking of going for an electrician, and then someone said something: 'What? You're a girl!'

Furthermore, they felt that the working conditions would be difficult:

> Truck drivers are weird people and they would harass her.

> You couldn't talk about the same things if men were around – what you did last night, and all that.

Thus, socialization and the perception of opportunities combined to make industrial education a much less favoured option. Socialization did not 'take' with all the young women, but the perception of opportunities ensured that even those who were not traditional in their interests still chose the traditional options.

A final factor in course selection was the issue of domestic labour. Most of the young women assumed that they would have primary responsibility for the domestic labour in their families. This by no means arose from a wholesale endorsement of the domestic ideology. Although about a quarter of the young women said domestic work was what they wanted to do, most said they would feel trapped at home, wanting the independence provided by a paying job, and said housework was a chore that should be shared. But they wanted husbands and they wanted children, so they felt they would have to do the domestic work for a variety of reasons based on their perception of the world and the opportunities available to them. Men, they said, would not or could not do it.

> Sharing the housework would be wonderful. But it is not going to happen. He'd [boyfriend] never help with the floors or the dishes. I know him too well.

Alternative forms of child-care, which could free them for a paying job, were perceived to be inadequate. No man could or would stay home with the kids, and

> Day-cares and babysitters are not good enough for children.

> You'll be a better mother if you stay home with the kids and not throw them out with the babysitter . . . because they learn bad habits.

Moreover, as women they were likely to be contributing less to the family income than their husbands, so they felt they should be the ones to pick up the extra domestic work and, when necessary, give up their paying jobs.

> The most practical approach would be the one with the most money would work.

As a result of all these calculations, even those young women who had no particular desire to do domestic labour expected to drop out of the labour force or work part-time when they had small children. Even though many assumed that they would return to work after their children had grown up, their views of this later period were very hazy. What they planned for was largely the next five to ten years. They wanted to get their training over with quickly so that they could get a job and have some independence for a few years. They were less likely than boys to feel that they had years to explore the labour market. This added to the attractiveness of business courses and clerical jobs. They could do their training quickly in high school, and the training would develop a skill that would always be useful and flexible. Furthermore, clerical jobs were relatively available and could be pursued part-time.

What these young women knew about their world produced the obvious choice of business courses. They saw a world in which business courses had many advantages and industrial courses had few. Their knowledge was based in some very tangible structural conditions – the opportunities in the labour market, the vocational role of business courses, the existence of sexual harassment in male occupations and the assumption of family responsibilities by women. The young women sometimes objected to this structure. They did not like sexual harassment in class. They felt that employers should hire women in non-traditional jobs. They did not want to do all the domestic chores in the home. But for all these perceptions of different conditions for men and women and their professed commitment to equality of opportunity, their conscious, rational, self-preserving calculations helped to reproduce gender segregation for themselves and others. They did not see this as a predetermined or imposed fact but as one they actively chose as best for themselves.

There were different routes to the same decisions. Some young women incorporated domestic ideology more fully than others. Some resisted secretarial work more strongly than others. Some found the option of work in male areas more tempting than others. While their choices may not have been made with the sense of elation and confidence that Willis's lads expressed, they were regarded as reasonable, even good solutions to the problems the social structure confronted them with. What is striking is not that some young women resisted, but that despite their resistance, so many of them continued to choose very traditional paths through school, paths that reproduced both class and gender categories.

Discussion

Why is it important to examine the young women's perceptions of the world? It scarcely needs to be pointed out that these young women did not produce adequate analytical accounts of the process of course selection in high schools. Their representations are interpretations, as all accounts are, involving selecting, highlighting, cutting and editing. In their stories, they underplayed some of the things they knew in order to maintain their own dignity. They used the same factors that others used to justify different choices. Their information on labour markets, men, teachers and so on was based on specific experiences and particular ideological assumptions.

These accounts highlight some aspects of school and work and gender relations that are concealed by other investigations. As Smith (1977, p. 16) points out in a brief history of the development of the women's movement:

> Shifts in the women's movement came about in part as women from other spaces than those originating the movement began to be heard and listened to − housewives, for example, who refused to be despised, women who had children or wanted children and could not accept the derogation of motherhood that was important in the early stages. . . . Issues and analyses had to shift and deepen accordingly.

A political process is different from an academic one, but the conception of how new knowledge is developed is useful. Working-class women's knowledge of the world and the questions they ask have not been part of academic discourse. Awareness of their views challenges the silence of social science on some issues and points out the biases inherent in the formulation of others.

These young, white, working-class women stressed their self-direction in selecting courses, challenging academic work that construes them as simply assigned to places by the school. They highlighted the importance of job opportunities and sexual harassment in course choice, issues that have often been overlooked in school-based research. They pointed out the unique role high school business courses play in providing saleable skills, which raises structural and historical questions about why business education was incorporated into the school curriculum in a form that so closely reproduces work relations and skills, while industrial and home economics courses take a form that is much less closely linked to work.

These young women stressed the role of domestic labour in career planning and course choice. They challenged the view that the important differences between courses can be represented by one vertical axis of academic respectability and that vocational courses are more attractive because they are more closely supervised. All these perspectives need to be added to the literature on curriculum differentiation in the high school.

An understanding of the perspectives of these young women gives us a more adequate understanding of how class and gender categories are reproduced in the school. Research on education has tended to assume that reproduction occurs when the relatively powerless internalize the views of the powerful. Studies of schooling have emphasized a process of socialization to the hidden curriculum, which ensures acquiescence and explains students' consciousness. Analyses of what the school's message is − the IQ ideology, the traditional gender code − have substituted for analyses of the students' understanding of these messages. This approach produces theories of reproduction in which subordinate groups appear as 'cultural dopes', so oversocialized into dominant ideologies that they cheerfully behave in ways that counter their own experience of the world, as well as their own interests. Its factual claims are wrong: people do not so completely believe dominant ideologies. Its political and policy implications are also profoundly undemocratic. Such an approach treats subordinate groups as misguided, backward and conservative rather than as aware and self-directed actors in a world that is stacked against them. It thus suggests that they will have little that is useful to say about what changes should take place.

The limits of socialization and the more problematic nature of consent have been increasingly recognized in studies of the labour process, and some of the parallels to schooling are worth noting. From Braverman's (1974) assumption of management's power to control the conditions of production, we have moved to studies of 'contested terrain' (Edwards, 1979), 'manufacturing consent' (Burawoy, 1979) and working-class culture (Palmer, 1979). There is also a tradition in feminist scholarship that has emphasized that women's consciousness is not simply an internalization of male forms but contains its own alternative interpretations, commitments, and connections (Rowbotham, 1973; Rubin, 1976; Olsen, 1978; Janeway, 1980; Bernard, 1981; Finn and Miles, 1982; Gilligan, 1982). The relation between women's consciousness and man's world (Rowbotham, 1973) is complex and involves accommodation, resistance, and self-imposed and externally imposed silences. Correspondence does not account for their relationship.

This brings the issue of structural change back into an intimate, but dialectical rather than mechanical, relation with consciousness. For these young women, change would have involved a far-reaching shift in their perception of reality. It would have meant new notions of where job opportunities lie, what men are like and what skills are valued by employers. Their beliefs about these things were forged in their daily experiences, and new accounts that contradicted their experience were likely to be found wanting, to be reinterpreted, or to lead to distrust of the source of the new account. They knew, for their own good reasons, what the world was like, and their experience acted as a filter through which any new message was tested, confirmed, rejected, challenged and reinterpreted. Changing their minds would have meant changing the world they experienced, not simply convincing them of the desirability of a new set of ideals about equality of opportunity and of a different world.

3 Making the Transition from School to Work

The transition from high school to full-time work has been seen as the transition from a sheltered and benign world of adolescence to a competitive and harsh world that must be negotiated alone. The transition, which is difficult at any time, is exacerbated when economic conditions deteriorate and the number of young people seeking to enter the labour force increases, as happened in Canada during the late 1970s and early 1980s. The result was an extraordinary outpouring of concern about youth employment and the transition to work (Canadian Council on Social Development, 1977; OECD, 1977; Mangum and Walsh, 1978), and a variety of policy initiatives designed to make the transition easier.

Most of the concern arose because of employers' perceptions and rising unemployment rates. But how do young people experience and understand the transition? A distinctive pattern has emerged in the literature on youth employment. Young people work for low wages in low-skill jobs; whatever skill they need is usually learned on the job in a very short time. Young men operate in very different labour markets from young women. The youth unemployment rate is at least twice as high as the national average, very sensitive to changing economic conditions and especially bad for high school drop-outs and racial minorities. Most young people change jobs frequently, a process variously described as a 'moratorium', 'shopping around', 'floundering' or 'drifting'. They get jobs through personal contact, and they are less satisfied with their jobs than adults. While high school graduation makes a considerable difference to the chances of getting a job, employers pay little attention to school grades (Burstein, 1975; Collins, 1977; Hall and Carlton, 1977; OECD, 1977; Freeman and Wise, 1979; Osterman, 1980; Furnham, 1985).

Much, then, is known, yet a great deal remains uncertain, especially about how youths understand the transition to work and their place in the occupational structure. Why do some leave the seemingly protective school environment for poor jobs with low pay and poor working conditions? How do they sustain their faith in themselves and their society in the face of such a transition?

Do they develop severely disaffected attitudes, becoming bitter about their school experience and about their work? A few studies have explored these kinds of questions from the perspective of working-class youth. A summary done by the OECD found that throughout western Europe, Japan and North America, students complain that classes are irrelevant to the work they will do after graduation, even though they recognize the necessity of finishing second-ary school in order to get a good job (Centre for Educational Research and Innovation, 1983). Willis (1977) looked at the culture of a group of working-class 'lads' in Britain, concentrating on their opposition to school and the way their attitudes towards work develop. A Canadian study (Hall and Carlton, 1977) examined the relationship between skills learned at school and the jobs high school graduates get. Sennett and Cobb (1972) assessed working-class attitudes towards school and work, but dealt with adults (again, only males) who had had years to figure out their adjustment to work. Griffin (1985) finds that young working-class women move from wanting to work in male jobs to an acceptance of 'more acceptable' choices. Wallace (1987) shows how young people adapt to unemployment by reducing their expectations. This chapter builds upon and reassesses these studies by following a group of working-class youth from school to their first job.

The students

The young people interviewed for this chapter participated in the longitudinal study of high school students in Vancouver, Canada, described in Chapter 1. While the students were not randomly selected and thus are not statistically representative of Vancouver's working-class youth (much less those of Canada, North America or the industrialized west), the jobs they got suggest that they were typical of young people who go to work immediately after high school (Collins, 1977; Osterman, 1980).

Table 1 shows the distribution of their jobs by sex. Although some students were unemployed at the time of the second interview, their last job is reported, even if it was part-time. The office jobs included a wide range of low-level functions – typing, operating the switchboard, photocopying, filing, delivering mail and running errands. The sales jobs were in department stores and in small bakeries, hardware stores, clothing stores and so on. Youths who got jobs classified as 'distribution' were working in warehouses or delivering goods. The factory jobs were primarily in saw mills and plywood mills, reflecting the importance of the forestry industry in British Columbia. The other jobs were in service areas – caretaker, dental assistant, armed forces personnel.

The average hourly wage for the young men was $6.88; for the young women it was $5.62. The young men's hourly wages varied from $3.50 to $10.60, the higher figure reflecting wages in the saw mills. The young women's hourly wages were all between $4.50 and $6.50. Few jobs offered chances for promotion. Stability of employment was also low. One-third of the young

Table 1 Distribution of jobs by sex

	Office	Sales	Waitress	Factory	Distribution	Misc.	Total
Female	24	8	8		2	3	45
Male	1	9		9	6	10	35
TOTAL	25	17	8	9	8	13	80
% of Total	31	21	10	11	10	17	100

men had changed jobs within the year. Many had experienced some unemployment and were only able to find part-time work.

Most of the youths found their jobs repetitious and low in status. 'I don't think it's my bag, just stacking groceries. If people ask you what you do, you just say, work at Safeway'. 'It's very boring in a way, very routine'. Working conditions were often bad. 'The heat, the smell, I get really bad headaches'. 'The foreman is always watching you and writing down what you do'. Low status, low wages, tedium, lack of promotion opportunities, insecurity of employment – these seemed to be the defining characteristics of the working-class youth labour market in Vancouver, conditions that prompted such strong assertions as 'This must be the worst job anyone can have', or the more plaintive 'I don't have much ambition, but more than that job'.

These jobs conform to those typically available to working-class youth just out of high school. How have these young people coped with their transition from school to work? Were they content or angry with their move? Resigned or rebellious? How did they explain why they were working when many of their classmates went on to post-secondary education? What benefits and losses did they see in the transition to work?

Modes of coping

Each student, of course, had a different story to tell. Each individual had to create meaning out of her or his experience as well as out of existing ideologies. But as the interviews were read and re-read, patterns emerged, 'strategies' of coping with the transition from school to work. Most youths used more than one of these 'strategies'. Any one person's articulation of a strategy was incomplete, groping, tentative. The presentation of their responses tries to make more coherent the assumptions and ambivalences they expressed, while keeping the data in a form they would recognize.

Several assumptions are widespread. The young people stressed the opportunities available to them as individuals; then, by and large, they accepted responsibility for where they were and how they got there. They thought about their jobs with reference to and in comparison to schooling. They assumed that the young women would have a short time at paid work and would soon become involved in child-rearing as a full-time occupation. These assumptions were pervasive, and they reveal a great deal about the power of schooling, the ideology of individualism in a capitalist society and the strength of sexism. But despite these common assumptions, not all the youths evaluated their move to work in the same way. In order to understand how working-class youths move into and evaluate the transition to work, it is necessary to understand the distinctions they draw. Five patterns of response usefully summarize the differences among the young people's accounts.

'It's too much school for me'

Bowles and Gintis (1974) argue that 'the IQ ideology operates to reconcile workers to their eventual economic positions primarily via the schooling experience'. Having accepted the school's definition of them as unintelligent, workers believe that the distribution of rewards in school and at work is fair and that they therefore deserve their low-status jobs. The youths interviewed here manifest some but not all of these characteristics. While a few have internalized notions of 'dumbness', most discuss their position in terms of choice. Where they place blame, they pin it on themselves or on individual school teachers or guidance counsellors. Sometimes they blame both themselves and individuals in the schools.

A few of the people in this study believed that their economic options were limited by their cognitive inability. They put it quite simply: 'I'm not university material. I don't have that much brains'. Or 'I took English 12. I thought I needed it for vocational school. But it was more than I could handle'. Lack of brains was not, however, the central assumption among those who believed that low school achievement had hindered their chances for economic success and high-status jobs. Much more prominent was the view that school was a drag and that they 'chose' not to achieve in school and were 'guided' away from academic courses. The distinction between lack of ability and lack of interest was often blurred.

> I would like to be a lab technician, only I don't have the brains for it. I didn't like the science courses. There is no way because I didn't want to take those kinds of courses – sciences and all that. I did take one science course, but I didn't do that well in it.

After all, who wants to keep hitting her head against a brick wall, sitting in a class where she does not understand what is happening, and continually being confronted with this by the teacher.

> I stared out of the window and at my hands and at everyone else. I picked what I'd enjoy.

> I picked easy courses.

Most often the youths did not emphasize that they were 'dumb', but that they did poorly in school because school itself was inadequate. They left school to go to work in order to leave a place that was boring, useless and intrusive.

> I've had enough with school. No more.

I'm not interested in academics.

I think school is a waste of time. . . . There is so much else I'd rather be doing.

Flight from school was seen as best for them, even though they recognized that not continuing beyond high school meant giving up on preferred and more high-status job options.

I'd like to get into interior decorating, if I could do it without years of study.

I'd like to be a teacher, but it's too much school for me.

The youths accepted the importance and legitimacy of schooling for high occupational attainment and acknowledged responsibility for their choices. The experience of unrewarding work, however, made them ambivalent and often regretful about their school experience, and they blamed both themselves and school personnel for limiting their job opportunities. Repeatedly, a number of the young people expressed regret over their decisions.

I didn't enjoy those courses at the time. I wouldn't goof off if I went back now.

If someone had only told me, you need more academics to get into another institution.

I wish I'd taken university entrance courses. I never thought I'd go on in school. It's too much work. Now I see that that's what you have to do to get where you want to go.

I wish I'd done better. I never went to class or did any work. I'd like to work with kids, but I don't have Math 10. I wasn't good at math.

I think I missed by not taking the sciences in grade 11 and 12. I never took it. I think I maybe should have taken at least one or two of them, because there is lots of things I found out that need, say, grade 11 or at least one science.

Because course choices were often seen as the cause of limited opportunities, school guidance counsellors who advised the youths were especially singled out for criticism.

I wanted to take academics, but they wouldn't let me.

Advice from guidance counsellors is not too swift. They're up in the clouds. They don't tell you nothing. All he did was screw me up – made me take French and auto mechanics.

One mode of coping, then, recognized that past decisions about schooling – the product of limited abilities and uninterest, of poor choices and poor advice – have forced these young people into low-status jobs. They believed that their life chances could have been better if they had worked harder in school and had received better advice. If they had regrets, these rarely took the form of hostility directed to the school system itself. On the whole, they did not judge themselves as stupid; they have not internalized the IQ ideology, as Bowles and Gintis (1974) suggest. Rather, they believed that they had made a choice about their courses and about leaving school, and that their choice had landed them in their current situation.

Sennett and Cobb (1972) suggest that a sense of regret about opportunities lost in school is common among American adult workers who, in turn, project their frustrations onto their children, urging them not to be like their parents. Over time these youths may well follow that pattern. But it is also possible that they will become critical of the fact that job access and economic success are dependent on school attainment. Because credentials for job entry get inflated so that they bear little relationship to what happens at work, and because these youths have to compete for jobs against community college graduates with credentials but no job experience, the legitimacy of credentialling may be challenged. These projections are not mutually exclusive. They suggest, however, that the initial view – that schooling has legitimately limited people's options – may change over time. For now, accepting responsibility for choices made in school is for young people an important way of handling the frustrations they feel towards work.

'It's OK for a short time'

A second way of dealing with a tedious and unrewarding job is to see it as a stop-gap measure that merely fills in time until you can go on to better things. This kind of adaptation involves a low commitment to the job, planned instability and not having to accommodate your sense of self to your job. Work may now be full-time, no longer interrupted by long periods of schooling, but it is still treated pretty much as summer or part-time jobs were. The job is transient, an interregnum before a move on to something more rewarding. Much of the literature on youth employment points out how pervasive this attitude is (Davison and Anderson, 1937; Burstein, 1975; Osterman, 1980). This sense of transiency – of 'moving on' – was the most frequently articulated 'mode of coping'.

It's boring. It's very routine. But I don't mind it for a short time.

A good job, but nothing I'd want to do for the rest of my life. One of the hardest jobs around.

I like working there, but I wouldn't want to do it for a very long time. It's monotonous. You get like a robot.

All right for a summer job, but not forever. It's boring.

It's a good job. But just a job, not a career.

Young men expressed these views more frequently than young women: 75 per cent of the young men and 60 per cent of the young women expected to leave their jobs in the near future. Even more striking, however, were the contrasting expectations between the sexes about what 'moving on' meant. In spite of the fact that many of them had experienced considerable frustration getting a job at all, almost half of the young men who planned to leave their jobs expected to change to a better job. The prevailing view was 'I'll stay till I find another job I like better'. They believed that with luck, with contacts, with age, with 'shopping around' they would be able to come up with something better. Sometimes the goals were concrete. A number wanted to join a police force, but had to wait until age 21 to apply. Others hoped to get specific jobs as soon as openings became available. The young men believed a range of opportunities existed in the world of work, but rarely did they expect to advance through on-the-job mobility; they had little sense of career ladders in the jobs they presently had. Advancement required looking around, learning about the job market, and trying out a number of different jobs.

I might try electronics, or selling stereo sets. I wouldn't mind that. Or work in a grocery store.

The other half of the young men planning to 'move on' expected to go back to school, usually into post-secondary trade training programmes. As a result of wrong high school course choices, course requirements were a constant worry to them, as were long waiting lists at local trade and technical schools, having to find money and fears about their ability to succeed. Although a few of the young men had well-organized plans about returning to school, usually their ideas were quite vague – 'I'm going to work for one or two years, then go back to school, because the job market isn't very good'. Many of them expressed confusion and self-doubt about returning to school. When pressed, the promise of schooling seemed a thin reed to hang on to, an aspiration more than an expectation.

The young women had fewer alternative job and school plans. In part, this reflected their greater job satisfaction. But much more important was their overriding sense that work was itself temporary. Unlike the young men, who assumed they would work for a living all their lives, and indeed would have to work harder once they were married, virtually all of the young women planned to marry soon, have children quickly and be full-time child-rearers. The promise of motherhood was the promise of change and of a more rewarding work-life in the home. It allowed young women to treat their jobs as temporary, without having to consider alternative wage-labour. Many hoped they would not have to return to work when their children were older. To some, a part-time job to 'keep busy' was acceptable, but even for these young women motherhood appeared to be the true source of their adult identity, a future that allowed them to treat their jobs as temporary. Another illustration of the temporary status of work was the number of young women – 11 per cent – who expected to stop work and travel. Not one young man expressed a similar expectation.

The young women were also more concrete in their plans, looking to special programmes for dental assistance and legal secretarial work, to community

colleges for studies in child-care, journalism or interior design, and to universities for degrees in social work or teaching. Few of the young women planned
to shop around the job market in ways similar to the young men. This reflects
in part the structure of 'female' jobs, where credentialling is clearer and training
is done before entry rather than on the job at the employer's expense. It also
reflects the young women's greater satisfaction with their schooling.

The differences in attitude towards work and school between young men
and young women were striking. None the less, both sexes were optimistic
about the future. They believed that opportunities were out there. The
prospect of movement, of not being stuck in unpleasant work, diminished
frustrations with their present work. The young people professed faith in
themselves and in the economic system. They believed in the individual's
ability to shape her or his destiny by making choices in an open and potentially
rewarding marketplace. Even though they did poorly at school and decided to
leave because they did not like it, and even though many had been unemployed
and were aware of tight job markets, they did not take these barriers seriously.
Far from being resigned and cynical, they had a continued faith in their ability
to find a 'good' job, advance through schooling, or enjoy being a housewife
and mother.

These are not irrational attitudes. All the statistics suggest that levels of
unemployment and job instability will diminish over time. Formal and informal
age restrictions on hiring will matter less as the youths get older. Those who
go back to school can expect improved job conditions. Many of the young
women are likely to withdraw from the paid labour force when they have
children. Eventually, the youths may 'settle down' to more rewarding jobs in
firms that have internal labour markets and offer promotion opportunities
(Freeman and Wise, 1979).

Things will not improve as much as the youths think, however. The young
men's hope that they can overcome the irrelevance of their high school
experience through practical vocational courses is counterbalanced by their
deep hostility toward schooling itself. Much of the movement from job to job
will be horizontal rather than vertical, a change with little real improvement.
The frustrations for the young women are also likely to continue – most
obviously because a large proportion will continue to work even after childbirth, the proportion increasing as their children get older (Labour Canada,
1977; Gerson, 1985). To the extent that they expressed job satisfaction, low
levels of aspiration and willingness to do 'women's work' stem from their belief
that their jobs are temporary, so the reality of continued work to support their
families may come as a rude shock. Likewise, their return to schooling may fall
short of their expectations, although the young women were much more
positive about schooling than the young men and were more concrete in what
they expected to gain from post-secondary programmes. At what point the
youths will realize the barriers to their aspirations, or whether the aspirations
for moving on continue in altered form – as small business fantasies or living
for the vacations, for example – is uncertain.

In any case, both young men and young women will have to reconcile their expectations about moving on to better things with the realities of continuing to work in working-class, moderately paid jobs. For the moment, however, the transition from school to work is made easier by a continued faith in the ability to move to something better.

'I do it for the money'

In a study of school and work in a community in Ontario, Hall and Carlton (1977) argue that students and young workers do not treat their work as very important; they go through the motions only because it provides them with a pay-cheque or, with schooling, a credential for a pay-cheque. 'Over the past two decades', they write, 'consumption and the good life have taken precedence over hard work and thrift. . . . Continuing high expectations of income and leisure now appear to accompany work commitments which are declining' (p. 270). The problem is cultural, the creation of a consumer society where challenging work is no longer valued, and 'poor work, low productivity, insubordination, instability and absenteeism' are acceptable (p. 204). This thesis echoes the better-known work of Goldthorpe *et al.* (1969), who argue that workers have become interested solely in the amount of money they can earn and not in the intrinsic satisfaction of their work.

Such an analysis seems misleading for these young workers. Most of the youths interviewed stressed a strong desire for interesting and involving work.

I'm not particular about money that much. I want to like my job.

A good job is challenging. You look forward to it every morning. There are different things to do.

I'd like something where you'd have to think because you don't really think in typing. It's not hard to do. . . . Bookkeeping is quite challenging. You use your brain.

If you don't accomplish anything, you feel kind of run down.

I'd like something, being constructive.

I like to be busy, not crowded with work. I figure you're here to work, not to fool around.

I like doing something useful, a feeling of accomplishment, working with my hands.

Work with variety, interest, challenge and pleasant work-mates was overwhelmingly preferred. Writing off the work-place as a drag was not a common strategy for these young workers, fresh out of school, starting on a new life (see also Burstein, 1975; OECD, 1977).

Alongside the desire for stimulating work, however, lay another reality: the jobs these youths actually had. Since their work was rarely challenging, they justified it in terms of money.

I hate it but it's good money – boring, but for $7.70 an hour, I can put up with it.

Sometimes I miss school because I'm not learning anything, but I get paid and I can do more things. I have more free time.

I do it for the money.

It's a boring job, but good money.

For those who had just left school, where their 'work' was unpaid, money had a special attraction.

I'd rather be working than be in school. Making the money. I wouldn't work if I didn't have to make money.

I want to get out of school. Make some money. Get a car, boat, a better stereo.

I prefer this year because I make my own money.

When I don't have money, I get down.

Money meant consumption, having what you could not have before: new clothes, a car, gifts for friends. Most important of all, it meant independence from parents, the emergence of adult status and the right to be taken seriously. This is strikingly similar to the views women express when moving from unpaid work in the home to the paid labour force; see, for example, Rubin, 1976; Gerson, 1985.

This year I am my own person. I have my own life and I'll run it myself. I have my own apartment. I feel like a totally new person. Last year I was dependent on my parents. I figured that if they said no, that's no. And I had to listen to what they said. I feel really independent now; it's a crazy feeling.

When money is the primary reward for working, attitudes towards the work itself can be expected to deteriorate. Instead of enthusiasm for keeping busy and learning something new, these youths come to do as little as possible in the job so as to have energy left to enjoy themselves. They want their jobs to claim as little of them as possible.

These attitudes paralleled attitudes towards school. As Sennett and Cobb (1972) suggest, 'Adults who move into the institution of work react to its demands for performance the same way the children did to the demands of school: they think about the meaningful time they spend outside the institution' (p. 93). Like their jobs, school, which should have been challenging, was boring and alienating. The youths claimed they did as little as possible in order to get by.

I didn't take school seriously. I sort of slacked off after grade 10 [age 15 or 16].

I took the easiest courses because I was failing.

School's major benefit was the credential, which, like money, came to justify staying in school. In the case of both school and work, the youths wished the institution to intrude as little as possible on their lives.

Yet differences between work and school outweighed the similarities for these young people. At school, they could effectively opt out of participating, show up infrequently, slide by without much pressure and, indeed, without much concern. They could do all this and still receive their credential. Their experience led both to nostalgia for the easy days of school and to bitterness at the little regard their teachers and administrators had for them. Getting paid, however, justified the more insistent regulations of the work-place. 'It doesn't matter if the job is hard, if it pays like it'. Because it was paid, it could demand more, and the demands themselves were taken as a sign that the youths were held in higher esteem than they were in school. The calculations were thus complex. The job provided money, something schools could only promise. The demands of work were legitimate because they were paid for, even though the youths were disappointed in the quality of their jobs.

The emphasis on money produced its own constraints: while money liberated it also controlled. Full-time work increased the youths' income, but it also increased the costs of living. For those young people who moved out of their family homes, their wages barely covered rent, food and living expenses. Even those who lived at home were usually required to start paying rent and sometimes board.

I have to spend my own money this year.

I've got to budget. Now I've got certain commitments.

There are more things to pay for this year.

I didn't go to vocational school because I wanted to work again so I would have enough money. And it looks like I still won't; I mean, after rent and that.

The struggle to make ends meet undermined the enthusiasm that came with the pay-cheque. Their wages became necessary, a trap forcing them to stay on at unrewarding work when they would have preferred not to stay.

I thought of quitting. There is so much pushing. But I'll probably stay for a while. The money makes you stay.

It is no wonder that, as Hall and Carlton (1977) found, money was so prominently mentioned by young workers fresh from school. By contrast to lack of income in school or the small wages of part-time and summer work, the pay-cheque that came with employment after graduation looked munificent indeed. The fact that these young people were getting paid for their work was itself a sign that they were valued, something they had very little recollection of in school. The resort to money was thus not a simple cultural trend towards consumerism, as Hall and Carlton suggest; it was much more job-specific. They turned to money because they found, much to their disappointment, that it was one of the few rewards of working, and certainly the clearest.

Whether this will remain the case over time is hard to predict. As adults, they may give up any expectation that work ought to be challenging and become resigned to their job for the money it provides. Low wages that now seem so satisfying will come to seem increasingly inadequate as school recedes and as pressure to provide for families grows, even though their wages will undoubtedly improve. The result will be still greater pressure for more money to compensate for the inadequacies of work itself. Alternatively, they may retain their initial belief that work ought to be satisfying, which would result in greater expectations about job tasks and working conditions and an unwillingness to let wages 'buy off' those expectations.

'I'm expected to be more responsible'

Sociologists tend to see the organization of schooling as similar to the organization of work, reproducing the social relations of work in order to socialize the young to adulthood. The Parsonian perspective stresses the essentially benign functionalism of the schools (Dreeben, 1968). A more radical position sees schools replicating or corresponding to the hierarchical and alienating nature of work institutions (Behn *et al.*, 1976; Bowles and Gintis, 1976). While this latter perspective correctly emphasizes the class basis of both institutions, the youths frequently dismissed this similarity and pointed instead to the differences between school and work. Despite the complaints about their jobs, they claimed they felt freer, more independent, and more grown up at work. These perceptions made moving into work attractive, and counteracted feelings of failure, of being trapped and exploited.

> At school you're treated like kids, but they act like kids. This year I'm expected to be more responsible, to work.

> High school treats you like a little kid. This year I'm doing my own thing. Don't you bother me. I'm not mommy's little young man going off to school.

> You're not babies this year. People respect you.

> I like it a lot better this year. I get on better with my parents. They used to say don't get in late and don't get drunk. I felt really babied last year. Sometimes I felt like telling my teachers where to put it. They were talking to me like I was five years old.

Being at work means being seen as and treated as an adult. School, on the other hand, defines students as children. It is a 'people-processing' or custodial institution, preparing youths for adulthood, defining them as not yet fully responsible. Its similarities to other total institutions were pointed out in the comment, repeated several times, that 'school is a jail'. In part, the contrast between school and work was based on the pay-cheque; getting paid was itself a statement of responsibility and value. But the change also reflected the move from an institution where supervisors were more concerned with how one behaved and with 'moral development' than with the accomplishment of tasks, be it writing an essay, learning to speak French or solving mathematical problems. In school, getting the task done was only a stepping-stone to learning something else or becoming a better person.

The developmental nature of school tasks made it difficult for these young people to gain a sense of mastery and control. At work, job tasks were repetitive and easy to learn. This led the youths to say that they had more control over their tasks at work, a strange observation when they were so clearly at the bottom of the job hierarchy, with tasks defined by others.

> I can manage my own time. There is not someone over my shoulder all the time.

> I feel so free this year. In school you have to listen and write down what they say. Now I can move at my own speed and get paid for it.

While they acknowledged and sometimes resented the existence of supervision at work, they contrasted it with the supervision exercised by teachers. At school, they could not go for long without being told by a teacher what to do or how to do it. It was being told that was irksome – in effect, having their noses rubbed in their inferior positions. Being at the low end of the hierarchy was bearable if it was not impressed on you by the daily social relations of your work, if you could forget it for a while or push it to the back of your mind. The dilemma was summed up by one young woman: 'No one tells you what to do [at work] unless you don't know what to do. If you're supposed to be doing something and you're not, they'll tell you'. Other young people reiterated this in different forms.

> You can learn what you're expected to do during the day. No one has to tell me what to do.

> At first, they had to tell me what to do. Now I can see it myself. I can make a decision about whether to take it back to the kitchen if someone complains.

> I can make up my own schedule, I can do it in any order.

> In the beginning I was told. Now I see a pile of typing and I do it. And I order supplies as I see fit.

> I like to catch on quick so I can do things myself and no one has to tell you.

The sense that one is regulated but still independent is tricky to maintain in most low-status jobs, and impossible in some contexts, like assembly lines with close supervision. But in many jobs, some variety of tasks, some physical movement and some flexibility of schedule provide a feeling of independence, responsibility and decision making not found in school work.

The same kind of contrast between school and work appeared when the youths talked about being evaluated. At school, evaluation and the sense of falling short were constant, but sanctions were minimal and easily avoided. While it was always possible to do better, it was hard to fail. Although there was a range of grading from A to D, D was still passing. At work, sanctions were more immediate, but the feeling of a job well done was easier to achieve.

> If you don't live up to it at work, they fire you. At school you just get a little talking to.

> You have to get up and go every morning. In school you're supposed to but you don't have to. You can't get docked pay.

> I have confidence now. I can do the job. I was nervous at school.

The differences produced ambivalent feelings. The youths 'chose' the easy way out in school, but they often regretted it and castigated teachers for not being tougher. Without sanctions for poor performance, they never knew whether they were performing well. Without sanctions, they did not believe they were taken seriously.

A formal consequence of moving out of an institution where you are being 'processed' and into an institution where you are doing the processing is that the work becomes clearly for someone else's benefit; that is, after all, why it is paid for. There is little pretence at work that typing a letter or moving a box makes you a 'better' person, the way that at school writing a better essay or understanding calculus is supposed to make you a better citizen, consumer or worker. At school, what is experienced as 'work', producing what the teacher wants, is not paid but is 'for your own good'. Producing something for someone else, something that is really valued, made these young people feel responsible and grown up. Instead of producing essays or bookends that no one cared about, they were producing work that mattered to someone besides themselves.

> I was away for a couple of days and when I came back my desk was piled high. When I'm here it is clear I'm needed. They'd be in trouble if I was no good. If they didn't have me – chaos.

In almost all ways, then, having a job means being an adult. In only one area did the young people consistently raise doubts about being out on their own: the loss of peer-group social life built into the organization of schools.

> I haven't met that many people since I've been out of school.

> I don't see my friends except for two. I don't even bump into them on the bus.

> You don't see your friends every day anymore.

The adulthood that the youths proudly assert is clouded by the isolation and loneliness of their first year at work. For a few, a fondness for school emerged: 'School is a good time because of the people.' Although some youths talked about meeting new friends at work, the age disparity and the family ties of older workers made social contact difficult. Whatever the limitations of age homogeneity in schools, it obviously fostered social relationships.

Loneliness was a price the youths initially paid when they were on their own. But it was insufficient to persuade many of them that it was better to be at school than at work. The move from being a child in a children's institution to being an adult in an adult institution was a powerful experience that allowed the youths to counteract the negative aspects of their jobs. Work was tough, exhausting, demanding, even lonely, but that was what being a grown-up was about, and they believed they had been denied that right too long.

The perceptions of these young people echo James Coleman's claim that 'education and work institutions are almost wholly distinct' (Panel On Youth, 1974). The stress by Coleman on the ability of jobs to offer opportunities for interdependent and collective tasks and to reward self-management, self-responsibility and sustained involvement in tasks conforms to the youths' perceptions of the transition from school to work. It similarly conforms to the feelings expressed by women who have moved from unpaid work at home into the workforce (Rubin, 1976). Accomplishing an externally defined if routine task, and getting rewarded for it, is a public definition of competence. It provides a public identity that compares favourably to the identity of the non-worker, whether student, housewife or welfare recipient. Not recognizing this and insisting that school and work are so much the same that Coleman's concerns are diversionary (Behn *et al.*, 1976) is not helpful. However, ignoring, as Coleman does, issues of class and contradictions of independence and responsibility in work settings that are hierarchical and controlling leads to a romanticizing of work that is also misleading.

The notion of adulthood was used by these young people to convert many of the negative aspects of their jobs into something positive. Herein lies a central paradox of the transition from school to work: the fact that they had to work harder at their jobs and that the regulations were more rigid was taken as an affirmation that the task was important and that they were responsible people; the fact that sanctions were real, that they could be fired, made keeping a job a statement of worth. Whether the youths will retain this attitude over time is questionable, however, for the references to responsibility at work were invariably phrased in contrast to being denied responsibility at school. As the distance from school increases and the youths find themselves contrasting their own jobs with other jobs, the satisfaction of the first year out of school will lessen, and the demands of work are likely to become less acceptable.

'I love my job'

The jobs of these young people were low in status, pay and challenge, something many of them recognized. Much of the literature on youth employment supports these findings on the nature of the jobs and on the amount of dissatisfaction associated with them (O'Toole, 1973; Burstein, 1975; OECD, 1977). However, some analysts have cautioned that jobs which look unrewarding to outsiders are not necessarily perceived that way by the people who hold them. Polls show that substantial portions of all occupational groups claim to be satisfied with their jobs (Burstein, 1975; Rinehart, 1978).

Real job satisfaction did emerge among a few of these young workers, primarily among young women.

> I love my job. It's really interesting. I'm still learning about it. Sometimes I work in the darkroom.

> I like the variety. I see customers, check orders, type correspondence, open accounts, type loan cards and loan applications, mail letters.

> I really like it. I look forward to getting up in the morning. I'm learning about auto parts.

> It's exactly what I wanted to do. I'm lucky.

> I admit, I really enjoy typing. I've always wanted to type. It just appeals to me most. I'm fascinated with pushing buttons. I love to type.

Separating this enthusiasm from the contrast to school or the sheer novelty of the tasks is impossible, but the enthusiasm of some should not be dismissed. The tasks at work offered a wider variety of chances for moving around, being outside and using physical skills than school did. The young men especially stressed how much they liked the transition from mental to manual labour.

For the young women in offices, work was the culmination of their school experience. While they were in high school, commercial courses were filled with the promise of a job, as Chapter 2 has shown. Now that they were out, that promise had been fulfilled. They could try out the skills they had learned at school in the 'real' world.

> I wanted to be a secretary. There is a big demand for secretaries. It's the best thing for a young woman.

Office work is white collar work. It offers relatively secure employment, often in large firms. It demands a level of skill that other jobs available to high school graduates do not. More than any other group, the office workers genuinely valued their work.

These findings provide another insight into debates on job satisfaction for youths. Female clerical workers do not fit many of the patterns of youth labour markets. Clerical workers are not as unstable as workers in other jobs. They often have skills which they feel pride in exercising. They are often employed by large firms with internal labour markets. While the size of the clerical labour force overall is beginning to decrease, the clerical workers in this study obtained stable employment, and they were much more likely than the other young people in the study to enjoy their jobs and use their skills in them.

Again, the dilemma of job satisfaction over time remains. While genuine enthusiasm for jobs exists even when these jobs are routine and low in authority, it is impossible to separate the satisfaction from novelty and release from school. When the novelty wears off, the tedium may become more burdensome. What is new and challenging after three months will be less so after three years. The problem may go deeper, however. Many jobs, particularly office jobs, are rapidly being fragmented so that a sense of craft, of concern with the quality of one's work, becomes impossible to sustain (Braverman, 1974; Hall and Carlton, 1977). The deterioration in responsible tasks may dim enthusiasm. For now, however, freedom of movement, variety and a sense of involvement in their tasks do sustain a few enthusiastic workers.

Conclusion

This chapter has tried to capture what young people feel about their move from school to work in the few months before and after high school graduation. They are glad to be out of school and are optimistic about their future work lives. It is a brief moment in their lives, but one that is critical. By making the choice not to continue their schooling, almost all of these youths have effectively chosen many of the same working-class occupations as their parents.

For youths of this age, there are two key educational decisions: the decision to drop out of high school or to stay on and graduate, and the decision to enter the labour force or to go on to post-secondary schooling after graduation (Spady, 1970; Boudon, 1973; Jencks *et al.*, 1979). These youths did not drop out of high school, it is important to remember. Unlike some of their peers, they hung on, almost exclusively because they believed that a high school diploma would help them on the job market.

This period also lays the basis for reproducing a sex-segregated labour force and a traditional family structure. The stage has been well set earlier, in course choices in high school and in cultural participation throughout adolescence, but when the youths leave school, they make individual choices to take sex-segregated jobs, the outcome of which is a reinforced ideological commitment to a sexist society.

The young women are less critical of school and are happier with their jobs than the young men. They are surrounded by an ideology that their primary place is as wives and mothers, and this belief becomes stronger as they seek an alternative to the frustrations that begin to appear at work. Their sense of family is not of release, but of additional responsibilities. Neither young women nor young men find anything in the transition to work which offsets these stereotypes.

While we see class and sex divisions being reproduced in the ways these youths move from school to work, they see individual choices, individual frustrations and individual compensations. It is true, of course, that interviews which ask individuals about their circumstances are biased towards 'individualistic' answers. But these young people's insistence on choice and voluntarism seems stronger than the methodological bias. For the moment, these youths are optimistic about the satisfactions work can provide, even while they criticize and complain about their jobs. They are also critical of their schooling, but they accept as fair the advantage that schooling provides in the labour market, and a good number want to return to school. Their frustrations and criticisms do not lead them to reject, in any fundamental way, the way education and work are organized. The future is bright, even with society as it is. The difficulties of the present are an aberration that can be overcome by continuing to make good choices. Their future, they believe, will bring, if not total fulfilment, at least a good life and a 'good job'.

The young people see through schools and the official claim of offering equal opportunity and meaningful experiences in preparing for adulthood. They see through their jobs to the unchallenging and low-status labour that the jobs actually are. But their quest for adulthood, their liberal and individualistic notions of the society, and their belief that woman's place is in the home are used to interpret these perceptions in a way that deflects any real demand for social change to alter school or work. This is not to say that the youths are passive, resigned or apathetic. They struggle to find meaning for themselves and to cope in ways that will preserve their dignity and their sense of efficacy. But at this juncture of their lives, they have few traditions available to enable them to interpret things differently.

This is particularly clear when it comes to their analysis of schooling, an institution they know well. As the various models of coping reveal, the youths choose to get out of school because they find it boring and meaningless, and they have a much more favourable view of work. To young people it is the differences between school and work that count, and in order to make school attractive, they want to make it more like work. Career and vocational programmes, work experience, tighter discipline and less 'babying' – all appeal to them.

The similarities between the two institutions may become more apparent as work ceases to be such a novelty. Both school and work are controlled from the top, demand conformity to similar codes of behaviour, and produce a great deal of alienation among the students or workers. However, some of the differences the youths point to are based on the different organizational structures of work and school. The educational changes they want – adopting the organizational structure of the jobs they hold – would result in a major restructuring of the educational system and would undermine many of the most basic hopes for education. When the youths favour work, they emphasize responsible decision-making, the money, being treated as an adult. In short, the youths want to change the school's role as *in loco parentis*, a rather drastic alteration of the notion of school as a socializing institution. Paying youths for school tasks, even if there were any chance that the costs would be borne by tax-payers, might be worth considering, but only under more obviously voluntary conditions, including the economic freedom that middle-class youths have. But much more fundamental is whether learning and the current structure of jobs even *ought* to be made more compatible. Learning is an ongoing process; at its best, each step should open up new questions and provide the tools to answer them. What is potentially most valuable in school is precisely what is missing from jobs. Literacy, critical awareness and exposure to new ideas on a continuing basis, which are what education ought to be about, are not what these young people's jobs are about.

4 Reproducing Family Patterns

The literature on the transition from school to work concentrates on the experience of males rather than females, as does a good deal of work in the sociology of education (Acker, 1981). Thomas and Wetherall (1974), Ornstein (1976), Willis (1977), Bazalgetti (1978), Ryrie and Wier (1978), Corrigan (1979) and Osterman (1980) constitute just some examples of research that has been carried out only on males. Even when both male and female young people are interviewed, the focus of the discussion remains the reproduction of class and ethnicity, not the reproduction of gender (Jenkins, 1983; Brown, 1987). This neglect of females' experiences has meant that findings on males are misleadingly generalized to 'youths'. In fact, we know very little about youths, though a fair amount about young men. The analysis remains incomplete, failing to question the basic assumptions on which men's lives are based, assumptions which assume the subordinate, helpful but invisible presence of a woman.

At least until the mid–1980s, most young men and the researchers who studied them assumed that growing up male meant getting older, marrying and 'settling down' to an uninterrupted work life, provided a job and a wife were available. The existing research on young men makes issues about the relationship between public and private life neither important nor problematic. But when young women are studied, this becomes impossible. As the two preceding chapters have shown, when researchers turn their attention from men's to women's experience of the labour force, one of the first variables that is added to the analysis is family plans (Sokoloff, 1980). Regression equations designed to predict how long and for what wages women will work are much more accurate when expected and actual family responsibilities are taken into account. A husband's 'support' and the necessity of interrupting women's work-lives for bearing and rearing children differentiate the labour-force behaviour of some women from that of others (Almquist and Angrist, 1975; Bielby, 1978). Qualitative research on women's accounts of their work-lives always includes extensive discussion of domestic issues (Rubin, 1976, 1979;

Gerson, 1985). Young women do not assume someone else will look after their children while they go to work, so they worry about domestic labour as well as about issues of paid employment as they approach working life. Their planning about where, when and how they will work is intensely connected to their ideas about domestic responsibility.

The continuing location of women in the family is central to understanding women's subordination in both capitalist and socialist societies (Kuhn, 1978; Barrett, 1980). Women continue to have primary responsibility for domestic labour, even as their participation in the labour force increases (Venek, 1974, 1980; Meisner, 1975, 1981). Employers and state agencies assume women are primarily located in the family (Coser and Rokoff, 1971; Wolpe, 1974; Thurow, 1975; David, 1980) and by basing policy on this assumption, serve to ensure its continuation. But it is not just women who are located in families. Fully theorizing the organization of families and the role they play in locating people is critical to an adequate notion of how paid work is treated by everyone, not simply to an understanding of the oppression of women.

This chapter explores the way these 17- and 18-year-olds in Vancouver, who are just leaving school and entering work, construct their family lives in relation to their work. It will address the reproduction of family life alongside the reproduction of wage labour. The problem is how these young people, male and female, come to expect and plan family lives where the woman takes primary responsibility for domestic work and where the man 'helps out'.

Of course, expectations and decisions at this age are not binding. The ways these young people anticipate and plan for domestic life may not last, and certainly will not take into account all the contingencies that will shape their behaviour over the years. However, the way they anticipate the future affects what the future will bring them. Their assumptions at this age are only a first step in determining how the allocation of domestic duties occurs, but they are an important step in reproducing families in which domestic work depends largely on women.

As Willis (1981) notes, the term 'reproduction' has come to subsume many different approaches. This chapter continues an analysis that tries to avoid two pitfalls.

The first potential pitfall is a structural analysis that accounts for the reproduction of family life through its functional necessity for capital accumulation or, in a feminist version, for patriarchy. Arguments that women's subordination in the family is 'necessary' consider the consequences of particular family forms, but do not show how they are produced, how capitalists or men manage to bring about conditions that ensure people will do what is not in their interest. Functional approaches over-emphasize the power and clarity of purpose of the dominant group. Capitalism and male domination have managed to survive many different forms of marital and child-rearing relationships. The forms these relationships take are affected not simply by what the powerful want, important as this may be, but also by the ways ordinary people have collectively and individually won space for their own ways of doing things. While structures of domination define some of the conditions that a new generation confronts, the solutions people work out for themselves are not predetermined. To understand them, we must move from the level of abstraction of structural theory to the level where individuals can be seen making decisions.

The second potential pitfall is an analysis based in 'socialization' theory, which locates reproduction in childhood learning of 'sex roles'. Many have attempted to explain the continuation of traditional family forms through the internalization of the dominant ideology by young men and women. Educational research on gender has emphasized the way images of women's domesticity are transmitted to the young in teachers' and parents' attitudes, and in school practices and textbooks. This research has made visible an important set of sexist practices. But as Anyon (1981) has pointed out, the assumption is that this socialization is, unfortunately, successful and that little girls emerge content to recreate traditional forms of behaviour. Recent research has begun to take seriously the resistance young people put up and the ways the dominant ideology is mediated through a prism of class- and gender-specific life conditions and experiences and only selectively incorporated. The result is a blend of oppositional tendencies and acquiescence, self-interest and acceptance of domination (Hall and Jefferson, 1977; McRobbie, 1978). This allows a more dialectic approach to ideology and structure, and makes change possible, open to human agency.

In this chapter, I will point to the ways structures of capitalism and patriarchy, and dominant ideologies of gender, impinge on the experience of these working-class youths, and on the ways they think about organizing domestic work in their own lives. I will present these young people not as passive recipients of cultural and economic imperatives, but as creative, active participants in the social process, making 'sense' and making choices for themselves. They do overwhelmingly choose, or at least plan for, patterns of domestic labour that continue women's subordination in the family and in the workplace. But neither the young women nor the young men are powerless in the process. They resist some aspects of it, they see through some of the inequity and they find advantages for themselves in traditional patterns. Looking at how they decide to organize domestic labour, and why, exposes the structural and ideological factors that become critical in reproducing old patterns, and the factors that might change and lead to different kinds of decisions, with different consequences for the young people themselves and for others. It exposes the struggle, the weighing of forces, the problems confronting them, rather than granting total power to the system.

The young women

These young women plan to work outside the home. It is this that has been emphasized as a change when analysts compare young women today with young women 30 years ago. However, when their words are compared with the words we would expect a young man to use, they are strikingly different.

Working for pay is still seen as an option, not an economic necessity. And the right to work outside the home needs to be justified, rather than being taken for granted. It is striking how many of them say women 'should be able' to work 'too':

It's OK for women to earn money. She is helping out.

I think if she wants to work, she can.

They all assume they will have primary responsibility for domestic work – for child-care and for housekeeping. They assume that paid work outside the house will be possible only when domestic duties have been taken care of. If they want to make space for other activities, they feel they are responsible for making alternative domestic arrangements – by working harder themselves, 'bullying' their husbands, finding someone else to care for the children or buying other necessary services.

This belief that work outside the home will be secondary to work inside the home is critical to an understanding of how these young women plan their lives and 'voluntarily' choose paths that will tend to reproduce their secondary status at work and, paradoxically, in the home. It limits their aspirations, or at least reconciles them to less-attractive jobs, as Chapter 3 showed. As the young women put it:

If I had a job that was really important, I probably wouldn't be able to raise my own children the way I want to.

I considered engineering pretty seriously [but] . . . if I'm going to get married that's the most important thing I'm looking forward to.

It also means that whatever jobs they do aspire to are treated as less important than their husbands'. They feel they must allow men to devote time and family resources to performing their jobs well, while they take time and resources from their jobs to help them do so. A woman's lack of resources, especially monetary, then limits her power in the home, even though she expends her energy there.

These young women are not part of a new generation of 'liberated' women who explicitly reject old expectations. Some young women undoubtedly do, and the processes involved in this need to be understood. But in this case, it is the continuation of the assumption that women shoulder the domestic responsibilities that needs to be explained. These young women fit the abstracted models of 'reproducing patriarchal structures' and being 'successfully' socialized. However, the young women arrive at what they expect to do not through a straightforward response to structural imperatives or through a complete internalization of a domestic ideology. To understand the processes involved, it is necessary to explore both ideological and structural factors, showing how individual beliefs and choices are dialectically related to social forces that are beyond their choice or control.

The domestic ideology and the role of experience

The 'domestic ideology' tells these young women that putting family responsibilities first is the preferred pattern for a woman. Domestic work will be as
satisfying, fulfilling and challenging as putting a career first. The woman's
assumption of the domestic work is based on a woman's special interests and
abilities, making her different from, but not unequal to, a man. This ideology
obscures power differences and uses gender, rather than choice or achievement,
as the criterion for determining who does what.

To the extent that these young women have been successfully socialized
into femininity, they should accept this pattern, prefer to do domestic work,
and see themselves as more suited to it than any man. About a quarter of the
young women did this, turning domestic work into a romantic idyll.

> Her main job is doing things that, you know, he likes. And making the
> house their own. Making it a nice and comfortable place to come home
> to. Supporting him and his problems, sort of thing.

Others saw it as a good alternative to the stresses of a paid job:

> I'd rather be at home. I don't want to work the rest of my life. I'd rather
> do the housework.

A rewarding way to spend time:

> The advantage of being a girl is that you have kids and bring up a family.

Or just the way it is:

> I feel that the woman's place is in the home and I feel that she should
> work at making their marriage work.

They have become interested in domestic work, they value it and they like it.
As a result, they prefer traditional patterns and use the domestic ideology to
defend their choice.

Although we can see them as 'too traditional', theirs is an active and
considered voice. They find advantages in traditional patterns. They discount
experiences that might bring their beliefs into question. A job is nice, they
admit, but only for a while. Housework can be a chore, but a tidy house is
satisfying.

The other three-quarters of the young women do not describe their
experiences as so nicely congruent with the domestic ideology. They have seen
that paid work provides status, money and independence. They are enthusiastic
about moving into jobs after high school, despite the low wages and the low-
level and boring jobs most had. They find that work provides a period of relative
independence in their lives, when parental control is eased, and the school's *in
loco parentis* role disappears. They are treated as responsible adults and paid a
wage, signalling that they are competent to perform a task that is of real value
to someone else. Furthermore, work provides more free time and the money
to enjoy it with.

These positive feelings about paid work are projected into the future, and buttressed by their observations of their mothers' lives. Sixty per cent of their mothers work, but the daughters of both working and non-working mothers share the view that life at home is isolating, boring and cuts you off from the 'real world'.

You get bored staying at home. Women should get into things more. My mum is at home. She doesn't know what is going on in the world.

I think women should be able to work. My mum did. She didn't do it because we were starving or anything. She did it because she was really bored. She needed to come out of her shell.

Rubin (1976) finds the same attitudes among married working-class women. Despite the fact that they are often forced to work because of financial pressures, 'most find the world of work a satisfying place – at least when compared to the world of the housewife' (Rubin, 1976, p. 169). Work provides independence and more ability to control one's own life, even when the jobs appear routine, low-paying and dead-end. The socialization into femininity which these young women have received has not been enough to convince them that paid work does not matter for a woman and that they should define their achievement simply in terms of a domestic role.

Most of the young women are well acquainted with housework. Eighty-five per cent of them were regularly expected to do household chores and half of them took a major responsibility for housework for the whole family. In their descriptions of how housework gets done in the family, it is clear that mothers take primary responsibility, whether they are working outside the home or not. Female children are the primary helpers and males rarely do much.

When I was younger my parents were working and me and my sister were young but we swept the floor and vacuumed and washed the dishes and then when mom came home she'd do the heavy stuff, like washing clothes, and that.

I don't have to do chores around the house. Like I help my mom with the dishes. Sometimes I'll wash and dry for a week if I feel like it. Sometimes I won't even touch them. But usually, I must admit, I either wash or dry for her, you know. . . . On Saturdays and Sundays, like, I clean the basement, mop it up and that. Saturday my mom does the upstairs. But I like to cook too, like a lot of times I'll come home and cook dinner.

Even young women who by their assessment 'didn't do much' were able to list household tasks that they performed fairly regularly. Females' responsibility for this work is so deeply ingrained that it is barely noticed.

Housework is seen, by and large, as unglamorous and boring work, not something that provides great rewards. At their most positive, the young women might say, 'Housework is tolerable. I will do it if it has to be done'. This view of housework feeds the desire for work outside the home, which is less boring, more socially rewarding and more challenging.

Child-care is the most critical and demanding part of domestic work and, although these young women were committed to having families, they were very ambivalent about the joys of mothering. They have experiences of babysitting and they have watched their own mothers. Some of the strongest negative expressions were:

> I don't ever want to have kids. I can't stand being around little kids. They drive me totally out of my mind.

> I think 95 per cent of mothers don't want their kids. You always have to do things you don't want to do. You don't have any respect for yourself. The kids are dirty and crabby and you get treated like dirt by your husband.

In milder language, many described women at home with small children as 'depressed and hypochondriac', 'tired out' and 'really bored'. This ambivalence about motherhood – I want children, but staying home for long periods with children is a nuisance – is also described by Prendergast and Prent (1980). Using a somewhat different methodology, they discovered that most young women's accounts of motherhood are dominated by fears of isolation, boredom and depression, rather than the stereotypical joy in children.

Three-quarters of the young women, then, valued paid work over domestic work. In this, they reflect and find support from the dominant achievement values of the society, if not from feminine values. But they overwhelmingly agreed that they would not be the ones who would take primary responsibility for earning money. How did they agree to this, agree to collude in their own subordination, to take on the less desirable tasks, if their socialization had not succeeded in making it a preferred choice for most of them?

Ideology and structures: the dialectic of reproduction

Even though these young women did not accept the whole ideology of domesticity, elements of this ideology exerted an important effect on how they interpreted what they saw around them, what they took for granted. These elements existed alongside a demand for equality, and an understanding of the way existing social structures prevented change from occurring. The particular mixture of critical awareness, social analysis and dominant ideology that they produce illustrates both the active part the young women themselves play in reproduction, and the role of ideological hegemony and social structure in reproducing forms of domestic organization that privilege men's paid labour.

Masculinity
Many young women said the barriers to change lay in the nature of men. Men, they said over and over again, cannot or will not share domestic work. They are not like that. So if you want a tidy house and you want to live in relative harmony with the opposite sex, you have to do it yourself.

I just couldn't picture my husband doing it – cleaning, making beds, making supper. I guess it's picturing my brother and dad.

Men don't know the first thing about a laundry machine.

Similarly, men are seen as incapable of, or at least not very competent at, bringing up children.

I can't give a distinct reason why a mother [rather than a father] should bring up her children, but I think it should be the wife that brings them up. It's because kids really relate better to mothers.

The woman has more affection for a baby when it is small. Men aren't used to it and don't want to do it.

Men are rough, their tone of voice. Babies like softness.

I don't think men are very good at raising children. From what I have seen of fathers, I don't think they could hack it. I guess that is just the way they were brought up when they were young. Women have a better knack for it than men do.

In all these ways, men are seen as incapable of being and/or unwilling to be full-time fathers. Their masculinity is threatened by involvement with small children. As one young woman put it, 'I always look at them as fags. I really do. I can't help it.'

This view of men, masculinity and the limits of acceptable or 'natural' male behaviour has been noted before (Oakley, 1974, pp. 153–60; Gaskell, 1977; Tolson, 1977). These beliefs show few signs of change, despite the women's movement and more media attention to the issue. The young women express an enormous amount of incredulity when presented with the notion that men might be domestic.

Their construction of masculinity is rooted in an ideology which suggests that what men *are* like is what men *must be* like. Biological explanations of the differences between men and women and the domestic ideology's construction of the special nature of men and women shape their perceptions. A culture based on gender differences makes it easy to incorporate this element into the way they construct their lives.

Their views are also validated by their experience of patriarchal family structures. They have not seen men in domestic roles. Their fathers, brothers and boyfriends do housework only as a special favour, for a woman. The knowledge that some men do housework – that it is not inherent in the nature of man not to do housework – seems hard to come by, but can be powerful when it does. One of the two young women who said they would fight for equal sharing of the housework said:

He [boyfriend] is neat and I'm not. The regular way is the way it's mostly done. You don't see people going against it. Why not? I want to be equal. Men and women should share the housework. I know guys who vacuum and sew and do the laundry.

When they were presented with the possibility of having a man stay at home while the woman worked, the young women also alluded to the role their experience played.

> It could be OK, I guess. It's strange because I'm not used to it. I still feel that a child needs his mother.

This view of men is important in shaping the dilemma the young women confront. It limits what they see as their options to having no children and a messy house, or making the adjustments themselves. Men remain outside the whole process of decision-making.

The labour market
A further constraint that these young women saw impinging directly on their ability to plan their futures was a realistic assessment of the probable earnings of themselves and the men they would live with. Men earn more money than women. In Canada, women can expect to earn, on average, about 60 per cent of what men earn. These young women were in and were expecting to continue in jobs that were firmly located within the female part of a sexually segregated labour market. Fifty-four per cent were in clerical jobs, 18 per cent were in sales jobs and 16 per cent were working as waitresses.

With occupational prospects like these, the young women realized that if they worked and their husbands stayed home to look after the children, the family would not be financially well off. Assuming a parent must stay at home with young children, it makes more financial sense for the women to be the ones who give up their jobs, if only for a while. This economic reason for the belief that it should be women who stay home was often cited by young women who wanted to keep working.

> It would be quite all right for him to stay home if the wife went to work as long as she made enough money to support them.

Young women with more traditional views were also able to point to economic constraints to bolster their opinions.

> One parent should be able to stay home until the kids are old enough for school. The most practical approach is that the one with most money would work. But really I'd probably stay home anyway. I'd have more patience.

Financial pressure also has the effect of pushing women into the labour market. These young women are aware of how tenuous the financial position of single-income households has become.

> I think that now most women are going to have to work. In our age it is impossible to buy a house or anything, and I think we are going to have to work and support him and work equally.

> I think if only one works, they don't have hardly any money. They don't eat good.

This push, however, is adding the responsibility of earning money to women's existing domestic responsibilities, not making the responsibility for domestic labour equal. Women will not earn an equal share of the family income, and Lein *et al.* (1977) have pointed out that this tends to make women feel they have to work even harder around the house to 'make up for' their lack of earning power. The fact that women can expect to earn lower wages than men becomes a critical structural element in reproducing a traditional division of labour in the home. It becomes a financially rational decision, incorporating an element of dominant ideology – the view that how much you earn determines the importance of your work. Financial criteria become the primary criteria for valuing work: work that brings in a lot of money deserves more respect than work that doesn't. This in turn serves to devalue domestic labour even further, as well as to devalue the work women do outside the home. Again, ideology, and the structural reality of a sexually segregated labour market, become the elements that combine to lead to 'reproduction'.

Child-care

Finally, the availability of acceptable child-care outside the family limits these young women's notion of how they will handle domestic labour and a paid job. This constraint need not differentially affect men and women. If domestic responsibilities were shared, the problems of finding substitute child-care would also be. But because, as we have seen above, the young women assume responsibility for it, child-care constrains *their* job planning and not the young men's.

Their view that child-care is a 'drag' and that paid work is rewarding coexists with the belief that to grow up healthy, happy and well-adjusted, young children need to be cared for by their mothers. This belief is widespread. Public polls reveal that Canadians overwhelmingly endorse equal opportunities for women, but just as strongly believe that 'when children are young a mother's place is in the home' (Gibbins *et al.*, 1978; see also Yankelovitch, 1974). It is this conflict that the young women must come to terms with.

Women with small children shouldn't work. It's hard on the kids.

One thing I learned in Child Care and feel strongly about, is if a woman is working she doesn't get to know the kids. Mothers shouldn't stick the kids with a babysitter until grade 1 [age five or six].

One thing I'm really against is leaving kids when they are really small. Kids come first. Wait till they're a few years into school.

This ideology exerts a powerful influence on these young women. It may be learned in a child-care course, as one of the young women above indicated, or picked up from family, friends, television, newspapers, magazines and child-care manuals. The view that one must stay at home with young children is also fed by the inadequacy of any perceived alternatives to child-care by full-time mothers until the school takes over at the age of five or six. Although school is an approved alternative to mother, other publicly available alternatives like babysitting and day-care at an earlier age are seen as 'dumping grounds', lacking in 'love' and alienating parents from children (see Lein *et al.*, 1977).

> I don't believe in leaving little kids at home with the babysitter and their mother not knowing them very well. I'd wait to go back to work until they were in about grade 1 or 2 [ages five to seven].

> Like when you have kids, you'd have to shove them off into a day-care [if you went to back to work]. But if you don't see them, it isn't so good.

> There's a day-care across the street and I feel those children won't grow up as part of those parents. Day-care workers have more influence. If both parents want to work, they should realize they can't give a child what he deserves. They shouldn't have children.

These views reflect the fact that the availability, quality and funding of day-care is less than desirable because of the very low priority given to it within the social service sector and the very low salaries that are paid to anybody embarking on a career in child-care. Decent child-care is hard to find, but then, one could argue, so is a decent grade 1 classroom. The notion that the age of five or six is the desirable age to have children in 'school' is clearly a reflection of the way child-care has been publicly organized in Canada – at five or six the state pays for and indeed demands attendance. Before that, the parent pays and the state only provides subsidies to parents with low incomes, making day-care a suspect institution, appropriate only for 'inadequate' parents. In this area the ideology of mothering, instead of being contradicted by experience, is supported by it. The organization of society – the structure – produces the experience that validates the ideology and produces constraints that any parent must contend with in order to change traditional patterns of behaviour. Ideology and structure come together to reproduce mother-centred patterns of child-rearing for another generation.

The potential for change
Elements of the dominant ideology, the constraints of child-care and the labour market, and their experience of men combined to produce in all of these young women the view that domestic work is primarily their responsibility. However, there are differences in the ways they plan to deal with the domestic responsibilities they assume. Some are more likely to challenge the usual behaviour patterns than others.

A couple of young women, seeing the dilemma, concluded that marriage and a family were not for them. The only way to stay independent was not to get married and not to have children. Although only two contemplated this as a long-term solution, many commented that they would put off marriage, and certainly having children, for a while (at least until they were 25, which seemed like a long time to them) in order to enjoy their independence while it was possible.

It was the potential availability of acceptable alternatives for child-care that was critical in setting apart that quarter of the young women who planned to return to work while their children were pre-schoolers.

I would work if my mum would take care of the kids.

I guess I'd have to stay at home for a while, at least until they're one-and-a-half or two years old. Unless my husband worked graveyard.

I'd go back to work when they were old enough for day-care – one-and-a-half or two.

The most acceptable alternative forms of child-care are family arrangements, with the husband or with the grandmother. But if day-care is seen as acceptable, it makes possible a much earlier return to work.

There were also a few young women who, while accepting that they should stay home for the sake of the children, were prepared to put their own needs above their responsibilities.

It would be better to stay at home, but personally, I don't think I could.

I hate staying at home. I'd really be going crazy without a job. But with children, part-time is best.

Similarly, a couple of young women were committed enough to sharing housework to be willing to do battle over it.

You should share everything when you're married. Even now my boyfriend does the dishes. He complains and bitches sometimes. Sometimes I do it. He is trying hard to change his habits. It creates tension between us.

Her expressed willingness to create tension and take on her boyfriend distinguishes her from the great majority of other young women, who if they do it, do it more quietly, less on principle.

The young women anticipate that experience in the labour market will also make a difference to how much paid work they do, and perhaps to the division of domestic work.

If I really love my job, and the boss needs me, maybe.

It should be the husband [who works], unless he's unemployed and I could get outside work.

This suggests that change can occur when a young woman takes her own needs seriously and when the social structure provides her with alternatives. Structural factors – the availability of child-care, male unemployment, women getting higher pay – may produce shifts in who does what, even if not immediately. The young women are certainly not so committed to traditional patterns that new opportunities would make no difference. These changes in behaviour would then become part of their, and other young women's, experience, and provide potential challenges to the received ideology. Understanding this dialectical relation between ideology and structure allows us to see how reproduction occurs systematically, but is not a necessary and inevitable outcome of the situation in which these young women find themselves.

The young men

The young men also make decisions about how they plan to manage domestic work. Although paid work is their primary focus in planning the future, they also want to get married and have children, just as the young women do. However, they do not plan to take a lot of responsibility for domestic tasks, which allows them to treat paid work as their main focus of concern.

It is perhaps easier to understand the young men's decision – who wouldn't want to have the more powerful and independent position and to let someone else take responsibility for getting the domestic work done? Who wouldn't like a wife? The dominant ideology supports their immediate self-interest, so reconstituting this ideology to make it congruent with their experience and desires is not as pressing for them. In this section I will outline the young men's notions of the division of labour in the home and I will examine how accurate the young women's constructions of the young men's views are.

The domestic ideology and self-interest

Most of the young men accept the traditional view of the division of labour in the home. They are significantly more conservative than the young women, significantly more likely to swallow the 'domestic ideology' whole.

I wouldn't let her work if I could support the family.

If I work and get a lot of money, I wouldn't want her to work. She could look after the kitchen or something. There's a lot to do.

I'm traditional. Women's lib. can never make a husband pregnant. Mother's place is at home until the kids can take care of themselves.

I don't think it should be equal. I think the wife should stay home and clean the house and cook, while the male goes out and works.

They accept some variations – the woman can 'help' the man by getting a paid job and the man can 'help' the woman around the house. But a differentiation of roles is assumed.

A wife helps out. It's not as important [for her to work] as long as you can get along on his wages. It's not right if she has a kid.

When the kids get to be about 16 and they're in school all day and she's got five hours to kill, she should go out and get a job not far from home so she can get home and make supper.

Well, if the husband happens to be at home and his wife is working (like if he's sick or something), there's no reason why he can't do the cooking.

And a reversal of roles is outrageous.

> I'd never let her do that. It's just a person's morals, It's how you're brought up . . . the man is supposed to go and collect the bread and the woman stays home.

> No, if you have a lot of kids, she's got to stay home all the time and he brings in the money. It's the husband's duty to keep the household going. I don't know why. That's the way it's always been.

It became apparent in the interviews that the young men had not spent a lot of time worrying about the division of family labour – it's 'just the way it is', they said. Their own households ran along these lines, and they took these patterns for granted.

> The males and females don't share the work in our house. The females got nothing else to do. When mother was working, she did all the housework too, but that's because my sister wouldn't do it.

> I sleep and eat. Sometimes I wash the dishes. Pick up the mail and paper if I step on it. I don't really care if the housework is done. Mother does it. She works part-time.

> The odd time I cut the grass, or work in the garage. Help dad fix things around the house. No housework, not even making my own bed. Mother does it. She doesn't work. My sister should help.

And they were quite aware of their own self-interest. They did not like domestic work. They did not want to change what was obviously an advantageous status quo. Although they said the same things as the young women – housework is a drag and child-care drives me nuts – they were much more willing to take their own self-interest seriously than the young women were.

> I just couldn't stand staying in the house, really. It would drive me bananas.

> I can't picture myself staying at home and looking after kids for five years, while she works. I'd just feel sheer lazy.

> For one thing, I don't like kids and housework, kids and housework. . . . I wouldn't want to do it all the time.

When they were prodded, they recognized that their assumptions were not quite fair – that they 'should' share. This was clearest in the area of housework.

> I don't do a hell of a lot. I'm too lazy. . . . I'm bagged after work. I want the weekends for myself. Biking, skiing, my girlfriend. I should help more – there should be two of me – one to stay around. My mum and sister do the work.

> If I marry, I should share; but I wouldn't want to.

If I marry my girlfriend, I'd help her out. I don't like doing it. If someone doesn't ask me, I won't do it.

If she's going to be a stickler about it, well, I guess I could volunteer sometimes. It depends upon the person.

In the area of child-care, it was not so much fairness as a desire to retain their primacy in family affairs that motivated them to take part in domestic work. They set out how important their role in child-care was, retaining the father's prerogatives and his ultimate authority, while leaving women to do the primary care-giving.

There's a difference between raising kids and looking after them. The woman might spend more time with the kids, but the father has the authority.

From age one to seven you are mom's boy; and then from seven to fourteen you are daddy's boy. The kids need the female, but they need the male image too. They act differently with males and females. They can get away with more with the female, like with their mother. But the father comes home and he's ready to hit the kid over the head.

In the interview, then, the young men overwhelmingly presented very conservative views. When asked the reasons for their views, what came most easily to mind was what their parents did, what the dominant ideology told them, a justification for their own present behaviour. This makes the young women's descriptions of men fairly accurate. The young men are, as the young women described, unused to and unwilling to do much about domestic duties. They incorporate the dominant ideology gladly, actively to serve their own interests.

Equality and structural barriers

The young men were not universally as reactionary as the above discussion suggests. Some young men did take seriously the notion of women's equal rights, especially to a job.

Sure I think [career women] are a really good idea. But I think it's going to be a long time before women are really into top positions . . . because so many men still feel that women should be at home and doing the routine jobs.

Women should be able to work outside the home. We shouldn't expect them to get married, have babies, and stay home. They do have their own freedom, their own life. They can enjoy it.

She should believe in something, you know, and she should go for it. What usually happens is that she just goes for the husband to complement him. Because I think women think that if they can please the husband that's what they're looking for.

The general values of achievement and fairness present a challenge to the traditional views of these young men. They admire women with more independence; they feel everyone should be treated equally. Achieving these goals, however, will involve some concessions by men in the area of domestic labour. Are they willing to follow through? To a certain extent they are, although it often becomes 'helping' rather than sharing equally.

Housework?

Yeh, they [men] should do that, you know; they shouldn't just say 'Oh I worked eight hours and I'm tired and I'm gonna go to sleep or something'. They both occupy the same house, and . . . we have to look [after] our own things, and if we can't split the duties. . . .

They should share. It's something that has to be done. I help my fiancée with her housework. She has a two-year-old son.

Child-care?

I think it's sort of an equal responsibility, too. If a man's home, why not be involved. He sort of groans changing those diapers. I'd probably end up doing it. Changing the kid at 2 o'clock in the morning...yuck. It's important, like...they have to do it.

The way it is in most families is what I don't want. I want to have some part in what the kids are doing. I want to be at home; I still want to have something that I would do as a career. But I really think that it should be equally done.

As with the young women, structural barriers become important in the young men's thinking. For them, these come down on the side of not taking equal responsibility at home, which is what they prefer anyway. The labour market makes it more reasonable for women to stay home because they earn less.

I wouldn't mind doing child-care if she had a large income; I would stay at home. But I would prefer to be working and have my wife at home.

I could stay home with the kids if her job was more [money] than mine. . . . Times change. I haven't heard of any men staying home, but it could be all right.

Staying home is a little weird; the guys have to be a little strange, or, unless the guy's a cripple and can't help it. . . . If she'd earn more money than him it would probably work out that she'd go to work and he'd stay home.

And the person who stays home should do the housework, so they can assume women will do it for them.

I figure if I'm gone all day and my wife is home she can clean up.

Whoever has the job shouldn't have to do the housework. It could be either person. But, I'd have the job.

I think the person who spends the most time at home should do the majority of the work.

If [my] wife wasn't working, I'd expect her to keep the house clean. Whoever has time should do it.

A woman might handle child-care in some other way besides staying home, but day-care is unacceptable, and alternative child-care is hard to come by.

If there was somebody to take care of the kids I wouldn't mind if she worked or when she is very well trained for or involved in her work.

She could have a small part-time job if she wants to. But not with the kids in day-care.

So it becomes 'reasonable' to assume the women will stay home, even for those more liberal young men who do not assume it is their prerogative to tell their wives what to do, and who do not find the notion of equality absurd even before it is circumscribed by factors in the real world. The application of universal principles – whoever earns most money, whoever is at home – becomes the reason for women to do the work.

For the more liberal young men, resolving the issue of domestic labour becomes a struggle to integrate principles of fairness and achievement with relegating women to the home. For the more conservative young men, this is a less difficult issue because the ideology of domesticity provides a rationale that reconciles their self-interest with fairness. For neither group of young men does their concrete experience play a large role in refracting and forcing them to reinterpret the ideologies they hear. The division of domestic labour is a much more abstract issue for them than for the young women.

Conclusions

I have argued that the reproduction of family life has been ignored in the mostly male research literature on the transition to adulthood. The issue of family organization is important in itself, and it makes visible a set of assumptions in which the vocational planning of young men and young women is embedded. Despite the initial similarity in their enthusiasm for leaving school and finding work, males and females make different long-term assumptions about what a paid job will mean, because of its relation to domestic labour.

In exploring the reasons for this, I have stressed the importance of domestic ideology, its interaction with social institutions – notably the labour market and the provision of child-care – and the way these combine to make young people's immediate experiences of family and friends confirm the impossibility of change. Income differences between men and women, the inadequate provision of public child-care facilities and the predominance of families with a traditional division of labour are all part of the world these young people know, and they interpret it through selected elements of the dominant ideology. Their experience then takes on meanings that lead to an expectation that traditional patterns will be continued. Whether these expectations will come to pass cannot be determined here, but I have suggested that changes in opportunities – a good job for a woman, an excellent child-care facility, a liberal husband – could make a difference. The trouble is that these changes are unlikely to occur on a wide scale in the immediate future.

Both the young men and the young women in this study expect that the young women will add work outside the home to their domestic work. Paid labour for women gets incorporated into the old directives that women be primarily mothers and housekeepers, helpmates to their husbands rather than equal participants in the labour force or the home. It means that while these young women are pleased by their transition from school to work and find their jobs important and rewarding, they still assume they will give them up in a few years and, for the most part, will not allow the demands of their paid work to interfere with their family life.

There is perhaps nothing surprising about this. Much of the literature tells us that although paid labour can increase women's power in the household, it does not equalize it. Women's jobs provide them with less income than men's do, and are seen as less important. Even working women continue to do most of the domestic labour, both reflecting and producing their 'secondary' status as workers.

These interviews provide some insight into the way this pattern begins in the expectations of young people about to embark on adult life and into the factors that begin to produce change in their expectations. A few young women accept happily, indeed glorify, the traditional role of women. They want to be primarily lovers of their husbands, mothers to their children. They see advantages in the traditional pattern; they appropriate the traditional ideology. They often recognize that their attitudes reflect the way they have been brought up, the way they have learned to deal with the world, the skills and abilities that they have developed over time. But they accept these prescriptions.

Most young women do not embrace these traditional tasks so cheerfully. The majority do not particularly like housework, and they see being at home with children as confining. Work brings them independence, responsibility and money, all of which they enjoy. Marriage and children bring a return to dependence on a male wage, little personalized control and authority in the family, and hardly any time that is not open to the demands of others. However, incorporating domestic duties into their lives seems necessary, given the way they see the men around them behaving, the state of child-care and the incomes they can expect. Elements of the domestic ideology still shape the way they see acceptable options. The social organization of child-care, the 'nature' of men and the segregation in the labour market make change unlikely. They therefore determine to cope with their lack of alternatives with good grace, not asking the impossible, not complaining about the inevitable.

I don't know if I'm looking forward to that, but I accept it.

I feel strongly that people should be equal, but how can you, unless you start from scratch?

In the young people in this study, we can see both the passivity that reproduces traditional roles and the beginning of discontent that provides the possibility of change. There are many youths, most notably a large number of the young women, who would challenge the idea that the traditional division of labour by sex is equally fulfilling for males and females, and is the only proper way to organize families and work. But it is clear that this discontent is not enough to bring about equality for men and women. The waning of domestic ideology among the young women is not enough to stop them planning their lives around it. Life choices come not merely from some abstract principle of what should happen, but from an assessment of the way the world works, what opportunities are open, what paths are possible. In this construction of how the world works, ideological elements incorporated from outside are critical. Young people with more liberal attitudes think that little change is realistically possible. Instead of expressing much anger about this, or trying to combat it, which might begin a process of change, they resign themselves to it and resolve to get on with life as it presents itself. Hoggart (1960, p. 322) writes:

> When people feel they cannot do much about the main elements of their situation, feel it not necessarily with despair or disappointment or resentment but simply as a fact of life, they adopt attitudes towards that situation which allow them to have a liveable life under its shadow, a life without a constant and pressing sense of the larger situation. The attitudes remove the main elements in the situation to the realm of natural laws, the given and the raw, the almost implacable material from which a living has to be carved.

This analysis implies that any attempt to give young people a sense of their own agency in the world, to show them that the world is constructed through a series of political and personal actions that might be changed, involves not just talking to them, but also showing them that conditions can indeed be altered. In other words, it involves not just ideological work, but also political movements for institutional change that demonstrate the possibility of change. This might occur in many ways – in a movement for satisfactory child-care that demonstrates its potential value, or in a struggle for equal pay that shows women's jobs are valuable and can be rewarded. The limits of reform will be set not just by how well an alternative account of the world can be conveyed, but also by how much the lived world of young people can actually be demonstrated to be changeable.

5 Inside the Business Education Classroom

Business education is a very important school subject for the young women discussed in this book. It has a major impact on how they plan their lives, at school and at work. It has a major impact on their experience of school. They take for granted its existence in the secondary school curriculum, its close relation to the labour market and its character as a school subject. But it is the job of the social scientist to look behind that which is taken for granted, to make the character of everyday life problematic, to ask why and how it came to have the character it has.

This chapter enquires about the nature of the business education curriculum, just as the earlier chapters have enquired about the aspirations and views of young people. Why is business education so closely connected to preparation for work for young women? What does this connection mean for the quality of instruction in the classroom? What does it mean for the reproduction of class and gender categories through schooling? What are the possibilities and directions of change?

It has often been observed that the vocational curriculum reproduces the social and technical relations of the work-place (Grignon, 1971; Bowles and Gintis, 1976; Tanguy, 1985). Vocational classrooms teach students how to be good workers, and this means learning one's place in a class society, carrying out procedures that allow business to proceed efficiently and putting the employer's needs above one's own, or seeing them as identical. They teach gender codes, spelling out the relative importance of paid and unpaid work, the definitions of masculinity and femininity prevalent in the workplace (Valli, 1986; Cockburn, 1987). Vocational classrooms reproduce the class and sex segregation of the work-place, separating the males from the females and the more privileged students from the less privileged as they prepare for different kinds of jobs in different sectors of the labour market.

There are a variety of explanations in the literature for the character of vocational classrooms, some emphasizing the needs of the work-place (e.g. Lazerson and Grubb, 1974; Bowles and Gintis, 1976; Gleason and Mardle,

1980) and others emphasizing the custodial nature of schooling and the needs of teachers for order and control and for attracting students (e.g. Weiss, 1982; Cusick, 1983; Moore, 1983). This chapter seeks to answer the question of why business education takes the shape it does by focusing on the understandings and decisions of teachers. It focuses on the decisions and reasoning of business teachers because it is the teachers who in the last instance have to translate a generalized curriculum outline into a set of practices. Their accounts can be examined, just as the accounts of the students have been in previous chapters, as the product of their beliefs and predispositions, and their particular location in the school and in relation to the work-place.

I will argue that both the needs of the work-place and the need for classroom order are important to teachers, and are interpreted in ways that reproduce class and gender relations through the business education curriculum. They come together in the school I studied to produce a curriculum oriented towards specific skills training, not enquiry and criticism. Even while there are social and economic forces that might bring about change, and the curriculum shifts away from preparing secretaries for the office and enrolling only young women, towards a 'life skills' emphasis and coeducation, these changes get reinterpreted through teachers' old understandings of what it means to be employable and have an orderly class, and as a result fail to challenge the existing mode of instruction.

My argument is based on one case study of vocational teaching in one high school. This is a conservative school, where the forces for reproduction can be clearly seen and analysed. There are undoubtedly schools where reproduction is challenged more actively, and these should be studied. I do not mean to portray the impossibility of change in vocational teaching, but to analyse some of the difficulties facing those who would change. Here is a picture of stasis in the face of changing social patterns. It should inform, not discourage, attempts at reform.

The setting

The research on which this chapter is based was carried out in the autumn of 1983 in one high school, which I will call Eastside High, although this is not its real name. The school is a large comprehensive school situated in a densely populated, ethnically mixed area of Vancouver. The average income of the school catchment area is below the average for the city as a whole. So is the educational level of the adults. Five per cent of the population reported that they had a university degree; 55 per cent did not have a high school certificate. Fifty-four per cent of the population reported English as their mother tongue, 19 per cent reported Chinese, and 12 per cent reported Italian.

The eight teachers in the business department offer most of their courses at the grade 11 and 12 levels (ages 16 to 18). The courses include shorthand, general business, accounting, business communications, machine calculations and procedures, office practice, marketing and computer science. The classrooms in which the courses are taught are clustered together in one wing of the school, and the teachers have a staffroom which is rarely used by teachers outside the department.

The research was carried out by two people over a period of about four months. The research began with systematic observation of all classes. The researchers recorded what was said by the teachers and students and wrote summary field notes on each class. Some classes were observed five or six times, others were observed only twice. Course outlines were obtained, texts and materials were examined, and evaluation procedures were discussed.

An interview of about one hour's duration was taped and transcribed for each teacher. We also took notes on our informal exchanges with the teachers, on department meetings and on discussions among the teachers themselves. These notes were recorded either while the exchanges were taking place or immediately afterwards. At the end of the field work we met the teachers in several sessions to report our findings. A written report was distributed to all members of the department, so that teachers could see what was being attributed to them, and could object either to inaccuracies or to comments that they did not want reported.

Structured interviews with a random sample of 50 students in the business courses were also taped and transcribed. The researchers took notes on student conversations and on informal discussions with students in classes and in the hallways and lunchroom. A questionnaire was distributed to all the students enrolled in business courses.

The research also explored the context in which the teachers and students operated. An interview with the guidance counsellor was taped and transcribed, and observational notes were made on the counsellor's interaction with students. Official documents describing the courses, the evaluation policy and the philosophy of the department were collected. Interviews with the coordinator of business education and the career placement officer at the school board were taped and transcribed. Professional literature for business teachers was collected, and we attended and took field notes at two conferences of high school business educators.

These data collection activities produced a large filing cabinet full of evidence about the nature of the business education programme. In this chapter, I will draw primarily on observations of classrooms, teacher interviews and comments teachers made in other settings. The analysis of this material proceeded from the researchers' developing understanding of what was happening, which was checked systematically by going through the written field notes and interviews for counter-evidence, and then presenting the analysis and evidence to the teachers for feedback and suggestions.

Business education as vocational preparation

The high school has many conflicting goals, and any teacher or any course is called upon to do several things at once. Preparing students for work is only one of these goals, but it is one that is prominent in the business education area. The business department was often referred to as a 'vocational' department, and the teachers made it clear that preparation of students for office jobs was a large part of what they were about. As office jobs are held overwhelmingly by women, the business curriculum's emphasis on vocational preparation ensured that it overwhelmingly enrolled young women.

Business education has been the most consistently vocational subject taught in the public secondary school system in North America. Business courses have been included in the public school curriculum since the mid-nineteenth century, when bookkeeping and penmanship were part of what every student learned (Gidney and Lawr, 1979; Rogers and Tyack, 1982). In the early twentieth century, typewriting and shorthand were introduced into the public school shortly after they were introduced into the office, and commercial subjects were expanded and separated out from the academic mainstream to constitute a distinct vocational programme. This programme has remained surprisingly unchanged to the present day, although 'commercial' education has become 'business' education, 'bookkeeping' has become 'accounting', and 'business law' has become 'general business'.

Vocationalism pervades some business courses more fully than it does others, and the ratios of male to female students in the courses reflect the relative vocational emphasis. The courses that prepare clerical and secretarial workers (office practice, accounting, shorthand) most clearly teach specific and job-related skills and are overwhelmingly female. For example, the office practice course is supposed to 'develop skills pertinent to clerical and secretarial office procedures'. The teacher's course outline for grade 12 stated that the course would enable students to 'meet the entry requirements of selected positions'. In an interview, the teacher also emphasized vocational skills:

> I'm trying to give them employability skills as the critical thing – good skills, good mechanical skills on manipulating the typewriter and keyboard – willingness to work, never rolling your eyes, a little touch of perfectionism.

The accounting course is based on a similar premise, emphasizing the applied, office-related tasks of bookkeeping. The enrolment is overwhelmingly female, although a few young men planning to start their own businesses see it as relevant to their vocational needs. The provincial course outline says accounting 'provides basic accounting knowledge and practical applications'. The grade 12 course is a 'practical activity-based course in applied accounting reflecting current business practices'. The teacher's course description said the course was

> designed primarily to prepare students for successful entry into business employment and to provide students with the skills necessary to apply accounting principles in their personal lives.

The accounting teacher says:

Probably most students just go into a job and wind up as an accounts receivable or accounts payable or payroll clerk. So I give them something in that area – to give them practical experience at it.

When asked whether there is a relationship between what students learn and what a payroll clerk does, he replies:

Well, that would be reasonably close. We haven't got the material to duplicate a whole big job, which in the real world is repetitious. So we don't do it 26 times, maybe only do it for two weeks or one week.

He says accounting courses will help students get a job:

I have spoken to people in Manpower, and they suggest always put down the fact that you have taken accounting, even if it is not for an accounting job. It shows that you have had some business experience.

The promise of job preparation in business courses provides a reason for students, especially young women, to take the courses. Vocational preparation provides a lever for teachers to use to involve and motivate students once they are in class. One teacher, for example, told us in the staffroom:

I tell them [students] I think it's wonderful to get an A in French or Socials, but you can't go downtown and tell an employer that because they can't use it.

They all agree, in a staffroom discussion, with the teacher who argues 'I think it is wise for them to acquire these skills so they can work'. Even academic students, they say, need to get summer and part-time jobs, and would therefore benefit from the vocational preparation provided in business courses. As one teacher put it, 'Our students need to eat'.

The promise of job preparation also lays the basis for the segregation of the young women from the young men, for secretarial jobs are female jobs, both statistically and in the way they are understood by students and teachers. The students' perception of this is obvious in the following exchange:

Researcher: Why are there no males in office practice?
Female student: I think they think secretaries should be women and the guys are the bosses.

The fact of sexually segregated courses of course continues the cycle of segregation.

Researcher: How is it for guys in those courses?
Female student: I think it's really tough because they get called sissy and things like that.
Male student: At first it was pretty difficult . . . the only guy in the class. . . . I was shocked. . . . I was self-conscious about it. That's about it. Nobody bothered me about it.

The camaraderie among the young women, the gossip about clothes and food and dates during class, was one of the consequences of the gender segregation. The teacher identified with 'her girls' and talked about her own history of employment as a secretary 'made good', her family obligations and her hopes for equality for the students. She was proud of the female researchers' achievements at the university and used us as models for the students. But as she taught, she assumed a male boss and a female secretary, where the boss dictated what, when and how things were to be done, and the secretary followed orders quickly and efficiently.

This vocational promise is based on the assumption that there are specific skills that can be taught in the high school which, if mastered, will make students more productive employees who will be hired in preference to other high school graduates. Vocationalism is here being interpreted as specific skills training. The teachers' understanding of preparing young people for work means rehearsing the activities they will perform at work, reproducing the work-place in the classroom, producing the 'correspondence' Bowles and Gintis (1976) note.

The assumption that this kind of teaching will improve students' chances in the labour market must become a belief of both employers and students if it is to have effect. There are no licensing or credentialling mechanisms that enforce the taking of these courses, as there are in professional fields and in skilled blue collar ones. There is not much evidence that vocational classes provide an advantage for students in the labour market (Little, 1970; Grasso and Shea, 1979; Berryman, 1980), whether one looks at wages or unemployment rates. There is a bit more evidence for business courses when they are separated out from other forms of vocationalism (Nolfi *et al.*, 1978). But there is no evidence that one kind of course helps more than another.

Whether the labour market advantage is real or not, it seems plausible to both teachers and students. Teachers work to show students the vocational relevance of what they do. The teachers' vocational emphasis can be observed in the classroom as a quite conscious attempt to reproduce the work-place. They strive to reproduce the tasks, the social relations and the ideology of a business office. The tasks assigned in the class were the kinds of tasks students would be assigned by a boss: type a letter, transcribe a tape, draw up the books, calculate the percentages. There is little, if any, homework, essay-writing or critical analysis required. Grignon (1971) sums up this kind of classroom process as exhibiting 'technical' culture and morality, where good work resides in carrying out tasks neatly, efficiently and competently, not in explaining or understanding or analysing. He sums up the difference between academic culture and technical culture as the difference between exploring the nature of the world and learning how to perform in the world. Clearly business classes show students how to perform; they do not explore how or why these techniques have arisen or how they have been or might be managed differently.

Classrooms are organized to allow students to practise their technique. Teachers assign work tasks; students have to complete the tasks by a given date. Students wander around the classroom getting the materials they need, talking to their friends when they have a moment, and then sitting down to do their work. The classroom is set up to simulate an office. Students take turns being 'office managers', a job which includes marking other students' work, collecting and filing the work, and even clearing the garbage out of the desks ('It's an unglamorous job, but someone has to do it,' the teacher explains). The teacher is often absent from the classroom or involved in marking assignments, letting students get on with their work alone.

The business classrooms were filled with instructions about carrying out tasks correctly and carefully. In office practice:

> At the right margin you are to type your name – your first and last name can be in any order you like – then you roll the carriage back two clicks to one above the name and type the date. 'Seattle' should be on line 7 and the date on line 5.

In the accounting course:

> In this situation, the calculation goes here. The final totals go in the last column – the problem that arises here is when you don't do things consistently, the same each time.

The entire enterprise is based on the notion that there are correct procedures that students must learn. Such work is not ambiguous, subject to individual variation or conceptually difficult. Instead, it is a matter of working carefully and conscientiously at an agreed-upon procedure.

This emphasis on procedure reifies specific techniques and detaches production skills from the social and economic processes that gave rise to them and make them explicable. The division of labour between managers and clerical workers is taken for granted, as it is at work, and is not explored by students. The fact that clerical work consists of processing a series of documents that have been written by someone else and that the procedures used to do this are also derived elsewhere is not examined as a set of social relations that have been historically produced and might be otherwise. The techniques that are taught, even as they embody social conventions that have arisen in a particular mode of production, are taught as good in themselves ('be accurate', 'do what you are told', 'be consistent') and are not to be socially interrogated.

The curriculum is gender-blind in this sense. It takes for granted the gender relations of the office and does not either approve or question them. The class is all female; the boss is referred to as 'he'. It is important that a secretary embody the female virtues of supporting, smiling, dressing attractively and being generally helpful.

Social and political questions about the character of the procedures may be raised by students, but they are answered quickly and factually by teachers so that the lesson can move on to the more important basis on which students will be evaluated – their technique. For example, in an accounting class where students are learning to compute taxes, the following incident took place.

> *Teacher:* You've all got the booklets. You need one to calculate the income tax. Let's pretend a person earns $600 during a two-week period.

Look up on pages 28 and 29. The categories across the top are for the number of dependents. The first is for a single person. You then add wife, children and so on as you go across. You can't just talk about one to five dependents.

A student at this point breaks in in horror, 'You mean they take more tax if you're single? Than if you're married?'

> *Teacher:* The reason is that if you are married and have children you can't afford to pay as much as he can who is single. It doesn't take as much to live.
> *Student:* What if he wants to save money?
> *Teacher:* It's annoying when you first start to work, but that's the law – designed so you can feed your children. Now look at the next line.

The lesson continues as the teacher shows the student how to do the calculations. The teacher's lesson is planned around calculating income tax, not about the hows and whys of the income tax system and its assumptions about family relations. The lesson plan and the students' evaluation depend on being able to calculate taxes. Other issues are diversions that the serious teacher must resist.

Business teachers reproduce the work-place, not just in their reification and repetition of technique, but also in their identification with the employer's values and expectations. The courses quite explicitly assume what the teachers call 'the business point of view'.

> I try to give them an appreciation of the values and norms that exist outside in the 'real' world – so I feel that a business morality, if that is the right word – a business approach, a profit motive – those are things they should be aware of and carry with them when – when and if – they go to the work-place.

What the 'business point of view' means is learning how to be a good employee, how to value and define the world in the way that the employer does. When asked by the researcher, after a class where the 'business point of view' had been particularly evident, about the implications of such a clear value commitment in the public school classroom, one of the teachers pulled out of his filing cabinet a newspaper article quoting the premier of British Columbia as saying that the schools had been neglectful in not teaching the benefits of free enterprise. After some discussion he shrugged and said, 'It's the system we live in', but admitted, 'I guess we do indoctrinate'.

The free-enterprise ideology underlying business education can be illustrated in various ways. It appears in its crudest form when business people come into the classroom with simulation games which make 'capitalism' into a lively and entertaining exchange, while 'socialism' provides no one with any incentives to trade. It appears again in the marketing course, which is to be taught 'from a management point of view', according to the provincial course outline. Students are asked to 'sit in the chair', as the teacher put it, of the employer, and to appreciate his point of view. They do not do the same for the consumer or the employee, even though students are much more likely to have had experience in the past and to have experiences in the future as consumers and employees.

The course's ideology is called, on the course outline, 'good ol' common sense', which 'most of you already know about'. What the course is designed to do is 'reinforce and expand on' one particular form of common sense. The common sense taught in the course includes the idea that it is possible to get ahead in the business world if you show enough initiative and perseverance, and that businesses must make decisions based on efficiency and profit maximization.

Business values appear in the constant equation of doing well in school and pleasing an employer. To quote from a course outline,

> Your attendance is important to me just as it would be to an employer – you are all familiar with the bell schedule – please be on time. Again, this is important to an employer, it is important to me and should be to you, too.

Preparation for work comes to involve a general appreciation of management's point of view and the social skills involved in conforming to it.

The 'business point of view' can also be seen in what is not discussed – the point of view of labour unions, the sexual politics of the office, the rationale for organizing against the employer, gender inequality in wages, the idea that one might work to rule and not to speed up the line, the idea that technology might be used against employees, the overall idea that there might be any conflict between the interests of management and the interests of workers, or between male and female workers.

Teachers of business courses, then, derive a sense of purpose from the fact that they engage in classroom activities that clearly look like they are preparing students for work in offices. The teachers actively try to produce a congruence between school life and work life, in order to make school seem relevant and useful for their students and in order to make them 'employable'. What the teachers teach is what they think employers will have students do and believe at work, because they feel that only by teaching this can they deliver on their promise to students of making them more employable. They believe their teaching job is best performed by identifying with the employer and trying to get the students to do the same.

The emphasis on employability provides the basis for the reproduction of the social relations, the culture and the ideology of the 'businessman' in the classroom. Students are taught to identify with the employer's point of view rather than exploring their own. They learn to separate execution from conception, to value the practical and applied over the academic and abstract, and to perform concrete tasks rather than to examine how and why these ways of proceeding arose and what social relations they express. The curriculum is 'gender-blind': the fact that women's experience is different from men's is assumed, but not discussed. The gender segregation of the office is reproduced in the classroom as a fact, without comment or analysis.

Business education as classroom management

Although teachers' conscious reproduction of the work-place explains much that happens in business classrooms, there is more going on here. As all teachers do, business teachers confront the problem of how to keep 30 to 40 adolescents at a task for 50-minute periods in the confined space of the classroom. Their responses to the work-place are mediated by their immediate concerns as high school teachers. Teachers must attract and hold the attention of students in a world where students can vote with their feet. And they are more likely to attract a large clientele if they are attractive to both male and female students.

As many have noted, teachers are more often held accountable for good management than they are for what their students do or do not learn. Cusick (1983) provides an eloquent account of the public high school, showing how teachers make order in the classroom their primary goal, and consequently justify their curriculum decisions by what 'interests' students. Anyon (1981) explains class reproduction in the elementary classrooms she observes as based in teachers' assumptions about the characteristics of their students and what they 'need'.

Moore (1983) argues that the proliferation of vocational courses at further education colleges in Britain can be best understood not as a response to the needs of the occupational sectors involved, but as a response to 'the social composition of their intakes', that is, student management within the frame-work of an educational institution. As they are populated by students who are designated as non-academic, low achievers destined for low-skill jobs, vocational preparation courses simply keep the students under control and repro-duce the vertical hierarchy of the work-place through symbolic differentiation of the students in different courses. The result is that vocational students are cut off from bodies of abstract theoretical knowledge which would help them to understand their place in the world, and are taught specific skills instead.

All the business education courses are linked in some way to vocational preparation, but the stress on remediation and general interest is more obvious in some classes than in others. A course in business communication develops students' ability to write business letters, spell, punctuate and proofread. A course in business machines has students working with calculators that would be used in an office, doing maths problems that are related to business practices. Marketing has the students learn about how to market products and includes practice in a school store (considered to be enjoyable). General business covers a host of everyday issues, from renting an apartment to buying a car to getting married. In these courses the proportion of male to female students is much more equal.

Classroom management in vocational courses is in many respects like classroom management in any course. The differences arise from the assump-tion that vocational courses are for the less able, less motivated students. And the clerical courses are for young women. Although there is no official streaming in Eastside High – no levels of courses, no differentiation of diplomas, no formal designation of academic and vocational students – business education is described by students and teachers as a 'non-academic elective'. 'Non-academic' means that the business courses do not fulfil admission requirements for university. 'Elective' means that the courses are not required for high school graduation, as are English, social studies and maths.

There are three results. First, business courses are described quite openly as a 'dumping ground' for students with 'no place else to go'. Second, business courses are subject to much less scrutiny by the authorities than are academic courses. Third, teachers must ensure that their courses remain popular with students so that enrolment will continue to be high enough to justify the courses' existence. Each of these has consequences for how teachers decide what will go on in the classroom.

The structure of the school's sorting process is at the base of the belief that business students are the least competent students in the school. In the counsellor's words:

> It's a grade 12 course with no prerequisites, that any student can take. Every student must have three grade 12 courses to graduate. Therefore, the kid who's looking for a course, you know he needs three grade 12 courses, and especially if it's a kid that's your non-academic type of student, it's good, they learn some very applicable type of skills.

Moreover, students and counsellors assume it is easy to pass business courses and get a high school diploma, whatever the actual benefit of what students learn. In one teacher's words, business students 'fail their way into our courses'.

In fact, students in business courses have a wide variety of backgrounds, competencies and motives. Some are academic students who are in the courses because they want an easy credit that will allow them time to concentrate on more difficult courses. Many young women want to learn office skills so they can get jobs as secretaries. Some are students who speak English poorly, others have a difficult time with all their school work. A large number of students are looking for a course they can be assured of passing, a course that has little homework. But the great majority of students there believe they have found an 'easy' course.

The teachers react to this sorting process with some ambivalence. They frequently express frustration with the low ability and motivation of their students. At the same time, they see their particular role in the school as serving those students whom other teachers cannot or will not serve. They depend on this particular niche to ensure their courses will be well subscribed. Business teachers, therefore, adapt their curriculum to what they think will 'work' with poorly motivated, poorly prepared students. The perceived characteristics of students become important in shaping the content of business courses:

> You have to kind of watch your class and see what you've got there. And I guess pick a level at which you want to teach.

The level they pick is a low one, one that demands little except minimal cooperation from the students. No essays, no homework, little reading. Even those expectations the teacher does set can often be negotiated downwards by students. Deadlines get extended, the number of required questions goes down.[1] In one class, the teacher emphasized what was 'rock bottom' in her expectations, trying to communicate her insistence that she would not reduce them further. As the teachers explain:

> We have to keep lowering our expectations in order to let the kids get some success and in order to let them feel good about themselves.

Making onerous demands makes life less pleasant for teacher and student.

> If you start doing that you start fighting with your colleagues and hating the kids – so you just say they are nice kids and we'll give them some self-confidence. Maybe they can get out there and life will teach them.

Making demands light attracts students, avoids stigmatizing them as failures, and makes classroom management less problematic.

There is a substantial spelling, grammar and arithmetic emphasis in some of the courses. Spelling is treated as a vocationally useful skill. In the business communications course, students had to rewrite paragraphs, turning them from singular to plural, from future tense to past tense, and so on. Spelling tests were given. The machine calculations course provided practice in adding, subtracting, multiplying and calculating percentages using calculators. 'At least they improve their math by the time they get out of here,' one teacher said of the course.

What was conspicuously absent in the way of academic content was writing, reading and analysis. One teacher explained that she had once had students compose letters (rather than just copy and correct them) but that the result was of such poor quality that she did not repeat the assignment. Others explained that they could not give independent reading assignments because the students would not or could not complete them.

> When you say basic skills, that suggests that they can acquire them – I'm not sure they can.

The potential problems of managing more complex assignments with students who were not seen as capable of 'handling it' meant that they were not introduced.

What students can 'handle', then, consists of specific tasks that are easy to complete. To fail, a student must simply refuse to do the work: 'They fail themselves.' If too many students have not completed the filing exercises, the number of filing exercises required to pass goes down. If a particular exercise is too hard, it is skipped. In the staffroom there is a discussion of a student whom all agree is hopeless and 'functionally illiterate'. But one teacher says, 'I'm as guilty as anyone. She got an A for hard work'. The result of adapting to the perceived needs and abilities of students is a curriculum that demands more in the way of cooperation than it does in the way of hard work and technical or academic proficiency. One teacher describes the resulting successful curriculum as 'little modules that keep the students' interest high, lots of activity; not so academically oriented'.

The second consequence of the 'non-academic' character of business courses is that they are not closely monitored by outside authorities. It can be argued that close supervision of what is taught in schools is structurally difficult and unlikely (Lipsky, 1980; Cusick, 1983) in all subject areas. But the business area is particularly autonomous because of the lack of articulation with post-secondary education, the lack of provincial exams, and the lack of prerequisites and laddering of courses within the department. The general belief that courses should be tailored to local conditions and to students' needs pervades the field.

The autonomy of the business department is frequently pointed out by the teachers.

> One of the things I like about business education is that there is an enormous amount of freedom in content. As long as you teach the bare bones of the curriculum, you can go at it from any approach you like. So you can adapt it to what you think the kids are going to need in the real world.

> I have an autonomous feeling about it. I feel quite comfortable in making any changes to government curriculum that I can justify to myself [pause] and to the principal.

As another teacher said:

> You can justify anything in teaching in the classroom – you can justify it to the curriculum somehow.

Teachers feel not just permitted, but encouraged to define for themselves what they will do in their courses.

This relative autonomy is also noted by the guidance counsellor. The business department can 'get away with' a reasonable amount, as he put it.

> They had their own little courses set up that had no relation at all to the ministry's provincial courses – so there have been big arguments between me and the business education person about what they can and can't do. They've been allowed to get away with it.

This sense of autonomy makes understanding the teachers' views of their work important for understanding why business education takes the shape it does. Where does the freedom come from? One factor is the lack of political concern about subjects that do not articulate with the university and do not represent 'core' skills. While academic work in British Columbia high schools is increasingly facing scrutiny and standardization with the reimposition of provincial examinations, non-academic courses are still not provincially examined. Teachers still set their own requirements and do their own grading, with little supervision even at the level of the school. Moreover, business teachers are not held accountable for their students' later successes or failures, as are academic teachers in yearly reports from the university about the progress of their former students.

Second, the British Columbia guidelines were drawn up by a group of business teachers who saw flexibility as the way business courses could attract students and remain viable. As the Vancouver school board coordinator for business education put it, they were written so that one could 'drive a truck through 'em'. As business courses are electives, some schools offer a wide assortment of courses, others offer only one or two. A programme of studies that makes sense to a large department may be reduced to fewer course hours in a small department. Schools and teachers are encouraged to adapt their courses to local conditions, and thus control over the curriculum devolves to the department level.

A third consequence of business courses being non–academic electives is that business teachers feel a personal responsibility to attract students to their courses. This increases their motivation to adapt to what they think the students 'want', 'need' and are 'capable' of. As the guidance counsellor phrased the dilemma of all the elective departments:

> Everyone's looking for numbers 'cause numbers mean bodies to the department, and bodies in the department mean supplies and equipment, money, all this sort of thing.

One of the first comments the department head made to our research team was, 'Competition – that's the name of the game when you're an elective'. The teachers talk about 'selling' their courses, and about being 'in the entertainment business', believing that 'the students have to get their money's worth'. One teacher said of the grade 9 (age 14 or 15) introductory business course, 'We were actually in that course to recruit for other courses, so we geared that course to do that'.

The problem is acute because, as was noted earlier, the counsellors discourage competent students from taking business courses. The counsellor says his 'bias' is

> trying to keep as many doors open as I can so if a kid is choosing between taking the business math and Algebra 11, if there's any chance of making Algebra 11, then I'll say, 'I suggest you take the Algebra 11' – simply because it leaves that option open.

The option to go to university remains open only to the student who has taken a wide variety of academic courses.

Business courses are more likely to get maximum enrolments if both male and female students are interested in their content. To attract young men, teachers must avoid dealing only with secretarial work. This creates a push towards discussing small business, towards easy courses and towards content taken from everyone's life.

Many of the characteristics of business classes can be analysed as, and are described by the teachers as, responses to the imperatives of the school environment, and particularly to a sorting process within the school that sends students who, for whatever reasons, want an easy course to the business department. The curriculum teachers develop is premised on the low status of their students. British Columbia's ministry of education does not hold business education teachers accountable for the achievement of their students in examinations, and does encourage local flexibility. Taking this for granted, these teachers look around for ways to interest and attract students, and to provide them with some experience of success. They try to ensure that their classes are full by providing a relatively undemanding but pleasant environment for students.

The interaction of vocationalism and classroom management in a changing labour market

As we have seen, the appeal of business education is due to two factors, one vocational, the other educational. First, the programme promises to give students an edge in the labour market. Office jobs pay well for women, at least relative to other jobs that demand only high school education, and they offer more security and better working conditions. Office jobs and the proprietorship of small businesses have been attractive to a smaller but clear clientele of boys. A second promise of business education, one less proudly and unambivalently affirmed but deeply embedded, is its ability to get students who cannot handle academic courses through high school. This appeal rests on the teachers' willingness to adapt their courses so that little is demanded of students except patience. The result of these two factors has been a curriculum that emphasizes specific skills and de-emphasizes writing and reflection. It is a curriculum that reproduces the social and ideological character of the work-place in the classroom.

Today there is increasing uneasiness among business educators about the appropriateness of the curriculum they teach. At a recent meeting of Canadian business educators, for example, discussion of a presentation on changing office requirements provoked the audience into an animated debate of what was possible and desirable in business courses. The mood was pessimistic, as teachers claimed,

> Our traditional programmes don't seem to fit anymore.

> What we're doing is out of date.

> We have to rethink, or our principals will say, 'We don't need this anymore'.

Much of this uncertainty arises from changes that have taken place in the work-place. Teachers point to the way office technology is altering the nature of skills used in the office. Where typing, filing and shorthand used to be central, now word-processing, records management and micrographics are taking their place. Schools can no longer afford the machines that offices use, and business teachers are not experts in the new technology. The result is a pronounced uneasiness about the way technology is making the old curriculum obsolete.

A second change, one less specific to business education but important for it, is the rising level of unemployment, particularly among youths. Unemployment rates for young people in Canada rose from about 5 per cent in the mid-1950s to about 12 per cent in the mid-1970s to 25 per cent in 1984. Unofficial estimates of youth unemployment place it closer to 40 per cent, and in some areas the rates are still higher. The fact that there is little employment for young people leads to a good deal of questioning of programmes that are supposed to prepare them for employment.

The vocational promise of business education is being threatened by a deteriorating labour market for young clerical workers, but the educational rationale for the courses remains. In this last section, I will explore the shifting balance between vocational and educational claims, and show how a 'life skills' curriculum emerges as a solution for teachers, one that does not challenge the reproduction of gender and skills categories because it is subsumed into the old understandings of what a business course should do.

The fact that the labour market for clerical workers and for young people generally is changing is clear to the business education teachers at Eastside High. Local unemployment rates are high. Local employers no longer phone in May or June to hire graduating young women for secretarial jobs. The teachers have no confidence that their students will be able to get jobs. All of this threatens their sense of purpose and commitment.

> You try and develop them to be proficient, and you can justify all that. From a point of view. But the reality of the thing is just like what's the point if you can't get a job.

The jobs that are available for young people are in fast-food outlets and small retail stores, not in accounting, secretarial or clerical positions, or in the large businesses towards which teachers have oriented their courses. Getting the capital to set up a small business would take years of struggle for most of the students.

> You realize that most kids aren't going to do accounting when they get out – it's just a nice thing for them – it is something they can understand.

The nature of work in offices is seen to be changing in part because of the introduction of microelectronic technology, although there is little consensus about what this means. Some argue it makes the old skills unnecessary.

> Electronic typewriters – do everything automatically – centring, corrections and things like that. So I still go through and teach all these procedures – and when they get out of here they are going to realize that at a push of a button the machine will do that for you.

> We funnel people through a business education profile which is not going to be required of them anymore.

Other teachers say that the new technology demands much more from the students, and that 'their' students really cannot manage it. As one teacher put it:

> When typing covered the skills, we made sure that students could do one

good letter and get that address on an envelope, do a memo and do a simple tabular problem. Now it's necessary that they understand something about digital and analogue transmission, and all kinds of things. They have to understand a little more about electronics, physics, science – it is much more general.

Whichever position one takes, the conclusion is that business courses in the high school are less likely to give students the entry-level skills they need for 'good' office jobs. Either those skills are available to any high school graduate, or those skills are available only to very able students, but it is clear that they are not particularly available to business graduates. While typing, re-labelled 'keyboarding', becomes an increasingly universal skill taught in the early high school grades, the specialized senior-level business courses that attract and segregate young women are seen as less relevant to getting a job in the office.

If the traditional secretarial curriculum has a weaker rationale than before, what should be taught? One option is to reproduce the electronic office in the classroom, to reorganize the skills that have been taught in senior-level business courses to incorporate the new computer technology. There are many moves in this direction and much lip service is paid to it.

> We are trying to upgrade to the office of the future – on-line offices – that type of thing. Because we think that's where the kids are going to live.

> We've got to get our courses revised, to upgrade some of our skills courses, to bring in the technical advances of the last ten years.

> Somehow – I don't know how – we're going to do it.

New textbooks include descriptions of new machines. At conferences of business teachers, displays of new electronic equipment for the office are evident. New teachers who are hired for business education must be familiar with computer technology.

There are, however, a variety of problems with this approach. Many teachers believe it conflicts with the fundamental notion that business courses must be easy.

> We need techno-literate students, and I'm not sure we can do that for all our students – maybe 5 per cent – we'll put ourselves out of a job.

Or, as an Ontario business teacher put it at a conference,

> What we really need is the advanced level kids if we're going to have kids who can go out into the business world.[2]

Moreover, business software is expensive; terminals are expensive; specialized electronic office equipment is expensive. The technology is not standardized, and is quickly outmoded. At Eastside High, the advanced office practice students have access to one word-processor and one typewriter with a memory. Microcomputers are only used by business students in an accounting course, and software is in short supply.

In high schools, where a room full of electric typewriters was a luxury a few years ago, teachers do not feel they can expect rooms full of current office equipment.

> It would be nice to have a word-processing course – if it was ever affordable. Those machines are expensive.

Enterprising business teachers raise money through fund-raising activities like organizing raffles, selling donuts or providing services to the school's main office in order to buy new equipment. Teachers attempt to use work-experience placements to give their students some exposure to new technology. But raffles are time-consuming and do not generate much funding; work-placements are short, often unsatisfactory and difficult for the teacher to manage. Thus keeping up with the latest office technology seems an unlikely eventuality for high school business departments.

A second response to changes in the labour market and in the office is to reorient from teaching specific vocational skills to teaching more general and academic skills.

> The actual nature of work is changing very rapidly, and there's going to be a tremendous disruption – we don't know what these skills are going to be – so we keep talking about general skills.

This strategy arises not only from confusion, but also from the view that technology is removing the technical content of many basic-level jobs and what remains is the requirement for basic literacy, computational ability and social skills. According to the office practice teacher:

> They are still the passport. A girl has to spell better than her boss, and has to have a good memory. The employers still rely on the employee to come in and care about getting the job done on time and accurately, being able to spell, type, proofread, so you don't put something on somebody's desk that he signs that has a mistake in it.

But business teachers do not want to turn so obviously into a low-status adjunct to the English or mathematics departments. As we have seen, their emphasis is on the practical and the applied. In this context, the utility of 'academic' skills is unclear.

> If you want to work in an office, you're going to be a file clerk, what academic skills do you need other than knowing the alphabet? How many people need the math? Do you know how many times you use your math?

Dictating has been eliminated from the curriculum because secretaries do not 'need' to compose letters, and the teachers claimed the students could not see the relevance of what they were doing. The tradition of valuing practical skills over 'academic' ones, and having a distinct and vocational purpose, makes moving towards remedial academics an unpopular step for many business teachers.

A third response to the changing character of office jobs is to shift towards teaching 'life skills' instead of vocational skills. The great advantage of a life skills approach is that it maintains the vocational relevance of the traditional business education programme even as the work-place changes, and it can be readily adapted to accommodate and attract non-academic students and students of both sexes. Teaching life skills allows teachers to continue to promise their students an advantage in the labour market, for those with more life skills are more likely to be good workers. And *life* skills seem more saleable than specifically vocational skills because they apply to everyone, whatever the level of unemployment, whatever the students' vocational destination, whatever their maleness or femaleness.

The move towards life skills and away from both academic and vocational concerns has been widely noted and mostly decried in the educational literature. Recent reports on high schools in the United States (Boyer, 1983; US Commission on Excellence, 1983), studies of changes in British vocational programmes (Gleason and Mardle, 1980; Fiddy, 1983; Roberts, 1983; Watts, 1983) and some Canadian work (Grahame, 1983; Griffiths, 1983) have pointed to the increased amount of life skills teaching that goes on. Much of this work treats the life skills approach as part of a conscious state policy to keep young people docile and out of the labour market. But the appeal of a life skills curriculum must also be understood at the grass-roots level, among the teachers and students who are looking for immediate short-term solutions to the problems they face. Curriculum ideas that have political appeal but do not meet the concerns of teachers are unlikely to take root (Sarason, 1971).

The life skills approach is most apparent in the general business course at Eastside High, a course taught to both grade 11 and grade 12 students, a course described by the department head as 'a winner', of which the students said, 'it's the thing to take when you're in grade 12' and 'everyone takes GB'. Students are taught how to dress for a job interview, how to go through an interview, how to behave on the job. Business law and business terminology are taught, but in the context of students' everyday lives. Students have to go through the motions of renting an apartment, buying a used car and, the highlight of the year, getting married – complete with costumes, a reception for teachers and the principal, and confetti.

The practical framework of life skills takes for granted a particular class, gender and ethnically based version of the world, and asks students to learn about it and to adapt to it, just as vocational preparation did. Studying about credit becomes 'how to use credit wisely', studying about income tax becomes 'how to pay less income tax', studying about marriage becomes how to choose a white dress or rent a tuxedo, and studying about the labour market becomes 'how to identify the expectations of employers' and 'prepare a résumé'.

The course content continues to build in 'the business point of view' and 'an appreciation of the values and norms that exist outside in the "real" world'. One set of 'life skills' is taught. 'Life' and 'business life' are assumed to demand the same qualities. For example, the course outline states that the course will 'develop habits such as punctuality, responsibility, cooperation, diligence, initiative and honesty, which are essential in business and community life', and good behaviour in class is marked as 'personal growth and employability'.

The life skills curriculum continues to assume gender divisions without exploring them. Case studies were filled with stereotyped language, such as 'Lucy the luscious lady', 'Betty the ballerina' and the 'little old lady' who only drives her car to church on Sundays. Student groups were segregated by sex, not because the teacher suggested it, but because the students 'chose' it. The fact that the young men were at the back talking football, while the young women were at the front talking about their hair, went unremarked in class. The determination of the teachers to avoid controversy and stay with correct answers limited the classroom discussion of gender issues, forcing the discussion into private comments by students to their friends. To take the example of the classes on marriage, students were told that they had to be legally pronounced 'man and wife', and they were told that there was no legal obligation for the woman to change her name. Both of these pieces of information were given as facts. Any discussion of sexuality or of personal relations in marriage was avoided, as it could not be telescoped into the technical kind of knowledge on which the course was based. The mock marriage ceremony was carried out in class with much hilarity and western European tradition, the young men providing chairs for the brides and bridesmaids, the young women throwing their bouquets. Students' comments and laughter made it clear it was the personal and sexual relations, however, that were of most interest!

The life skills curriculum meets the needs of teachers to attract and motivate students. It is 'fun', the students told us, to plan a wedding, to learn the law related to alcohol and to try to rent an apartment. The teachers say the course 'keeps the kids happy' and is 'easy'. As it teaches a set of specific techniques with right and wrong answers, it allows a manageable classroom process and provides an easy way to generate marks.

The result is that teachers seem more content with moving the business curriculum in the direction of life skills than they do with retaining a heavy emphasis on specific and increasingly technical office skills or with emphasizing basic academic competencies. However, all three approaches can still be found in business classes with course names – 'business communications', 'general business', 'office practice' – that have changed little in 50 years. The changes occur gradually through increases in enrolments in the 'general business' course, which emphasizes life skills, and through informal adaptations of curriculum guidelines to incorporate more life skills into all courses. The processes we observed in this case study, however, suggest there will be increasing emphasis on life skills in the future.

Conclusions

This chapter has described the way the business education curriculum in one high school reproduces class and gender relations, in a variety of kinds of courses, during a time when there appears to be a general shift from 'vocational' to 'life skills' content.

The shift to life skills is a result of teachers' attempts to attract and motivate a significant segment of the high school population, under labour market conditions that are deteriorating for young high school graduates. But what looks like a change towards a more generally relevant curriculum continues a stress on mastering specific and low-level skills, within a framework that assumes gender inequality and unquestioning acceptance of the 'business point of view'. The result is a curriculum that conveys a class ideology and is blind to gender relations in all aspects of students' lives, not just in specific jobs. The skills emphasis reduces the complexity of the individual judgements with which we negotiate our way through the various settings that make up our lives to a set of agreed-upon procedures for acting, procedures which assume the employer's interest is the same as the workers'.

That the ideological character of business courses continues despite the shifting course content could be interpreted as another example of how school curriculum 'corresponds' to changes in the work-place. But such a general theoretical gloss obscures the logic of the changes at the level of the school, and does not make clear how actions by teachers are involved in creating and potentially in resisting this kind of correspondence.

The class-based assumptions and the gender blindness of the life skills curriculum are chosen and defended by the teachers. They speak of their own sense of autonomy in curriculum decisions. They provide justifications for the curriculum that are primarily based in their own concern for the employability and graduation prospects of their students. The teachers' personal political preferences and desires to defend their subject territory, significant as they are, are not directly linked to justification of the curriculum. Teachers cannot translate their personal preferences and needs into curriculum imperatives. They respond as self-conscious actors whose job is to teach a 'non-academic elective' course within an elective system in a high school in a depressed labour market. It is the ways in which they construct the needs of their students and the needs of employers that incorporate their political views into the process of curriculum determination. It is through their taken-for-granted assumptions about the nature of work and of non-academic students that the process of reproduction is ensured.

The teachers are well-intentioned, anxious that their students get jobs and become successful. It is, of course, quite unclear that the curriculum achieves the objectives they articulate. Their understanding of how best to achieve them becomes the basis for accepting or rejecting particular course contents.

A life skills curriculum, a broad curriculum introducing students to business, could potentially include issues like employment equity, sexual harassment, ergonomics and labour relations. It could explore the point of view of workers, look at the role of the public and private sectors, and examine the rights of consumers. Simon *et al.* (1991) provide an introduction to critical pedagogy in work education that would address these issues. The liberal notion of education as analysis and debate would support such a change. Some of the questions students raise, and the concerns they bring to the classroom, provide a further basis for a move in this direction.

Curricular innovations like this are periodically proposed. However, such proposals' lack of impact is remarkable. This chapter suggests some of the reasons why. It is not just a question of changing the curriculum outline or teachers' personal views of what is important and valued. A new curriculum would have to satisfy teachers' sense of what is 'needed' in a vocational course. Their account of needs is based on at least two kinds of concerns: one is what employers want; the other is what students are capable of and interested in.

The notion of what employers want would need to be reconstructed to include a more analytic, problem-solving employee. The notion of employability would need to be reconstructed to include not just what the *employer* wants, but also what the *employee* wants – a safe, equitable work-place. Ideas about what students can achieve and be interested in would similarly need to be reconstructed to include a broader range of thought and content. This might be described as raising expectations, one of the old chestnuts of educational reform. The role of the teacher is to interest students and develop their capabilities.

How can teachers' notions of employability and their expectations of students be changed? Not by preaching at them, but by showing them what is rewarded at work and what students can achieve. This would require structural changes in schools and also at work. The discussion cannot be undertaken here, but the general principle is similar to that enunciated at the end of Chapter 3. People will not be convinced that the world can change until they experience it as changed, at least in minor ways. The struggle for reform is the struggle for a sense of possibility, and the concrete experience that change *can* happen.

Notes

1. See Doyle and Carter (1984) for an illustration and discussion of this in a 'regular' class. The difference in vocational classes is that teachers assume students' abilities are much lower, so students have more room to negotiate.
2. 'Advanced level' refers to a pattern of streaming that is in place in Ontario and is somewhat different from British Columbia's system. The effects are similar, however.

6 Constructing Skill Hierarchies

The idea of skill provides a connection between the world of school and the world of work. Schools develop skills; jobs demand skills. The more skills one has, the more likely one is to get a good job. Vocational teachers in the preceding chapter justified their instruction by appealing to a common-sense notion of the skills that were needed at work. Our understanding of what 'skill' is legitimizes institutional linkages between school and work and regulates the ways young people are taught and how they come to understand their job chances and the role of their schooling.

The notion of skill is central to the way inequality is justified in the work-place. Because different jobs demand different amounts of skill, it is argued that they require different kinds of training and deserve different levels of reward. A 'skilled' job will pay a higher salary and command greater respect and autonomy for its incumbent than will an 'unskilled' job. The rationale for inequality based on skill was formulated elegantly in the functionalist version of stratification theory (Davis and Moore, 1945). It is taken up by plumbers and electricians when they defend their relatively high wages on the basis of their skill and their long apprenticeship. It is taken up by doctors and lawyers and university professors who defend their privileged positions on the basis of their complex skills and lengthy training.

As I have argued in other chapters in this book, our taken-for-granted understandings need to be critically examined. Where do they come from? How do they work to legitimate some practices and call others into question? In this chapter, I will argue that skill is not a technical property of a job that can be empirically determined by careful study, but an assessment of value that is rooted in politics: in power, in culture and in economic position.

Women have not had the power to insist that their skills be recognized and valued in the work-place. Their lack of ability to define their work as skilled is not simply a matter of cognition, but is the result of a social process that has had institutional consequences in relation to educational qualifications and opportunities for vocational training, as well as in relation to wages. That business skills are taught in the secondary school, while blue collar work is learned on the job, at community colleges and in apprenticeship programmes, is related to the ways the skills necessary for women's work – in this case clerical work – have been undervalued. To understand the organization of business education, it is necesary to look historically at how it has been understood, and to examine closely the common-sense notions of skill that continue to underlie it.

The notion of skill

The question of how we attribute a level of skill to a job is complex. How do tasks in the labour market come to be valued, to be seen by employers and employees as 'skilled'? How can we compare the value of verbal skills and physical skills, the value of social skills and technical skills? How does 'managing' as a social skill compare with dealing with customers? Our notions of labour-market skills are socially constructed and the social processes producing our designations need to be carefully examined.

In the sociological literature, Braverman's (1974) research has been an important stimulus to rethinking what counts as skilled or unskilled work. He points out that, according to census categories, work today is considerably more skilled than work a century ago. The census mirrors the assumption that life today is more complicated, because technology is more complicated, and that people have obtained more education in response to the requirements of the more complex jobs they do.

> The idea that the changing conditions of industrial and office work require an increasingly 'better trained', 'better educated' and thus 'upgraded' working population is an almost universally accepted proposition in popular and academic discourse.
>
> (Braverman, 1974, p. 424)

Braverman notes that working with machines was what originally set apart skilled factory workers from unskilled labourers in the United States' census. As an extension of this line of thinking, the census classified drivers of motorized vehicles as skilled and drivers of horse-drawn vehicles as unskilled. But Braverman comments:

> In the circumstances of an earlier day, when a largely rural population learned the arts of managing horses as part of the process of growing up, while few as yet knew how to operate motorized vehicles, it might have made sense to characterize the former as part of the common heritage and thus no skill at all, while driving, as a learned ability, would have been thought of as a 'skill'. Today, it would be more proper to regard those who are able to drive vehicles as unskilled in that respect at least, while those who can care for, harness and manage a team of horses are certainly the possessors of a marked and uncommon ability. There is certainly little reason to suppose that the ability to drive a motor vehicle is more

demanding, requires longer training or habituation time, and thus represents a higher or intrinsically more rewarding skill.

(Braverman, 1974, p. 430)

Census categories reflect common ideological assumptions and patterns of
informal learning abroad in the land: assumptions that as technology gets more
complex, jobs get more complex; that as education levels increase, the jobs
workers do become more skilled; that everyone can drive a car. What we take
to be a noteworthy skill is fundamentally shaped by what is taken for granted
in the society, what the social context is, and where and how we learn to do
something.

Having pointed out that the government's classification system does not
accurately describe skill levels, Braverman reverts to his own definition of skill,
although he has difficulty describing it in one phrase. He sees skills as
'traditionally bound up with craft mastery' and, as he indicates above, tied to
training time and the 'commonness' of skills. He assumes this definition is
shared with his readers and validated by common sense. He is uneasy with
'relativistic or contemporary notions' of skill that degrade the concept by
having it refer to those 'able to perform repetitive tasks with manual dexterity'
(p. 430). His political concern for craft workers (he was a coppersmith,
pipe-fitter and sheetmetal worker, among other things) shapes the way he
begins to think about skill himself. He points to craft skills, not to the
interpersonal and social skills involved in being a waitress or a receptionist. His
experience shapes his perceptions – understandably. None of us can avoid this.

Spenner (1983) argues that autonomy ought to be considered an aspect of
skill. Jobs that are less closely supervised should be considered more skilled
because the worker will be required to make decisions and take responsibility
for what gets done. This argument points out that one of the ways skill is socially
recognized is through the independent power and control the worker exercises.
Power relations become 'skill' differences. It allows notions of skill to become
another way of talking about power, a way that gives the power a legitimacy
it would not otherwise have.

The issue of skill is of particular concern to women, because the fact that
women workers as a group earn so much less than men has been attributed to
women's lack of skill. The assumption that the work women do demands less
in the way of achievement or skill can be found among researchers of many
different traditions. Polachek (1975, 1976) characterizes women's occupations
as 'requiring less amounts of training' and 'menial'. Women are 'still overwhelmingly slotted into specific industries and occupations characterized by
low pay, low skill requirements, low productivity and low prospects for
advancement' (Armstrong and Armstrong, 1978, p. 16). 'Women are paid less
even for the same job. They usually get less skilled jobs. They are given
proportionally less responsibility in the hierarchy, and they are the last hired
and first fired' (Castells, 1980, p. 191). Wolpe (1978, p. 294) describes women
'clustering at the lowest level of the occupational hierarchy, in terms of both
pay and skills'.

This kind of analysis accepts the notion that women's lower incomes can be accounted for by their lack of skills and it suggests that women need more skills if they are to increase their earnings relative to men's. This reasoning is implicit in much of the research that tries, in effect, to find out why women have less skill and what can be done about it. Much of the sex-difference literature has been an attempt to identify areas where women are deficient. Studies of the socialization and education of young women similarly attempt to understand the ways in which young women become deficient – learning the attitudes (passivity, fear of success) and intellectual styles (docility, dependence) that fit them for lesser areas of work (Horner, 1970; Ireson, 1978). But a more careful analysis of women's skills and of the work women do reveals that these assumptions are entirely too facile. It can be argued that, on the contrary, women's skills are superior to men's. They excel at verbal and interpersonal tasks, they get higher marks in school and they are more highly educated, on average, than men in the labour force. Such differences cannot explain why women do poorly in the labour force. They simply make the labour force statistics even less explicable.

There is also considerable evidence that the jobs women do, while they are different from the jobs men do, do not demand any less knowledge or technical expertise. Women's jobs demand as much formal schooling and are rated by the public as just as prestigious, on average, as men's jobs (Boyd, 1981). Furthermore, England *et al.* (1982) show that the jobs in which women predominate require as much 'cognitive complexity' as the jobs in which men predominate. Women use more verbal and social skills and less physical strength in their jobs than men do. But it is verbal and social skills that are related to power and higher income, and physical strength that is related to lack of power and lower incomes. Again, we find that the skills women have, far from explaining their disadvantage in the labour force, make the labour force disadvantage even harder to explain.

The problem, then, is that the skills women do have are not recognized and rewarded. With the same education and skills as a man, a woman gets paid less and gets less power and responsibility. Occupations which employ a large number of women pay less for the same skills than occupations which employ a large number of men (Oppenheimer, 1970). Occupations which employ a large number of women are less likely to provide control over the social relations of production (Wright *et al.*, 1982).

Margaret Mead (1949, p. 159) wrote:

> One aspect of this social evaluation of different types of labour is the differentiated prestige of men's activities and women's activities. Whatever men do – even if it is dressing dolls for religious ceremonies – is more prestigious than what women do and is treated as a higher achievement.

Being treated as a 'higher' achievement can easily translate in a more scientific world into being considered a 'higher' skill. Mental labour is more prestigious than manual labour; science is more prestigious than caring for children; giving directions is more prestigious than working out what they mean and following them closely. It is not clear that one is actually more difficult than another. These are cultural values – things associated with dominant values and with power are counted as higher skills.

Phillips and Taylor (1980, p. 79) have pursued this argument in relation to men and women:

> The classification of women's jobs as unskilled and men's jobs as skilled or semi-skilled frequently bears little relation to the actual amount of training or ability required for them. Skill definitions are saturated with sexual bias. The work of women is often deemed inferior simply because it is women who do it. Women workers carry into the workplace their status as subordinate individuals and this status comes to define the work they do.

Judgements about women's skills are affected profoundly by the social context, by social cues that give them meaning. A secretary may be composing letters and running the office, but because she is 'only' a secretary, the skills involved cannot be too complex. Phillips and Taylor would allow the amount of 'ability' required to differentiate legitimately among skill levels. But the same social processes mean that judgements of ability will be 'saturated with sexual bias'. Regression equations are able to show which abilities are rewarded most highly by employers today, but to build a politics on these judgements is to accept employers' existing practices as a standard for equity.

Providing an account of a worker's abilities is not a neutral descriptive process. The terms of the account are highly conditioned by the social context in which it takes place and by the social purposes to which it will be put. Labelling and valuing particular abilities involves an ongoing historical struggle between workers and employers, and between different groups of workers. Women have not fared well in these struggles. Barrett (1980, p. 166) argues that

> Women have frequently failed to establish recognition of the skills required by their work, and have consequently been in a weak bargaining position in a divided and internally competitive work force. . . . We need to know precisely how and why some groups of workers succeed in establishing definitions of their work as skilled.

Cockburn's (1983) study of workers in the printing industry provides a specific case study of how skill definitions are negotiated at work, and how class and gender shape the negotiations. She looks at the struggles compositors have waged to retain their skilled status, as technological changes have rendered their technical skills obsolete. The issue of skill, she argues, is an issue of power and control. 'There may be collective struggle over skill, but it is not about skill, it is about the value of labour power and control over production. If the weapon of skill becomes blunted, others must be sought.' Skill comes to stand for male superiority over women and for superior rights to control production and to receive economic rewards. Privileged male workers fight to maintain their skilled status and do it through collective organization even when their technical expertise no longer has a place in the work process.

Feminists must embrace this more thorough-going recognition of the social and political content of skill categories. To revalue women's skills involves seeing the ways that our knowledge and abilities have been taken for granted. It involves fighting for the revaluing of women's work, because it is important and necessary work.

Education as skill

Struggles around education and training have been central to maintaining public recognition of skilled work. Training time is often seen as a kind of proxy for the degree of complexity of a job. There is a long academic tradition that takes the length of training as a sign of skill and assumes that the time it takes to qualify for a job depends on the difficulty, complexity and breadth of understanding necessary for performing the work.

Education can, however, serve many purposes other than preparing workers for the substance of their tasks. It serves as a sign of the occupation's esoteric skills and knowledge. Long periods of training make work appear to be relatively more difficult to master and worthy of recompense for the investment students make in their studies. Moreover, the common experience of apprenticeship, of exams or of courses can enhance workers' cohesion and political power. From the medieval guilds to the rites of professional training, these experiences of socialization have been touted by the participants and analysed by academics (Becker, 1964; Brown, 1974; Rule, 1981).

The role of education in regulating access to an occupation is perhaps its most critical one. Elevated educational requirements and long training programmes reduce the number of people who are eligible to do a job and thus make the ability to do the job scarcer and more valuable. Restrictions on entry to training result in significantly high earnings for members of the occupation involved (Stoltzenberg, 1975; Sorenson and Kalleberg, 1980). Several studies of professional groups have shown how they have established their control over their areas of work by engaging in political struggles to monopolize access, to mystify and to charge high prices for the skills they have (Bledstein, 1976; Larsen, 1977; Collins, 1979). Educational credentials can also be used to segregate labour markets and to ensure higher earnings and more stable employment for a few. Craft unions have struggled to preserve apprenticeships as a sign of the skills their craft requires, and have resisted the introduction of training modules and community college programmes and the elimination of seniority clauses that regulate access to training (Thompson, 1963; Clement, 1980; Lee, 1981; Meltz, 1982). Finlay (1983) illustrates how longshoremen bargain over a training programme in an attempt to keep access to highly paid jobs restricted, even when these training programmes are not the way workers actually learn to perform their work tasks.

Even those who point to the ideological content of skill ratings (Braverman, 1974; Phillips and Taylor 1980) tend to treat time spent in training as a legitimate way to differentiate between skilled and unskilled work. Time is a useful measure for administrators, labour negotiators or social scientists trying to come up with ratings, because it can be expressed as a number and used to compare things that are actually quite unalike. Time becomes a mode of exchange of value, like money, and it creates the same problem of losing sight of what it actually represents and how it is produced. Thus time in training is turned into skill ratings, reifying skill into a unidimensional 'thing'. But Braverman for one points out that increased educational levels cannot be used as a measure of skill upgrading in the workforce.

A complete picture of the functions and functioning of education in the United States and other capitalist countries would require a thorough historical study of the manner in which the present standards came into being, and how they were related, at each step of their formation, to the social forces of the society at large. But even a sketch of the recent period suffices to show that many causes, most of them bearing no direct relationship to the educational requirements of the job structure, have been at work.

(Braverman, 1974, p. 437)

Changes in labour legislation, in the unemployment rate, in state investment in educational institutions and in employers' use of education as a screening device are some of the important things that have increased the educational levels of workers. None of these means that the skill levels of jobs have changed.

How are we to determine the amount of training 'necessary' for an 'adequate' performance of a job? Some people learn faster than others. Some employers are more demanding. Some people will already know a lot of what they need, because they have picked it up informally. The length and form that training will take is decided through political and economic struggle. Collins (1979, p. 54) comments:

The 'system' does not 'need' or 'demand' a certain kind of performance; it 'needs' what it gets, because 'it' is nothing more than a slip-shod way of talking about the way things happen to be at the time. How hard people work, and with what dexterity and cleverness, depends on how much other people can require them to do, and on how much they can dominate other people.

Lots of different kinds of training will adequately prepare people for their jobs. No single version is 'necessary'. What training programmes *do* do is control the supply of labour and certify its skill. Turner (1962, p. 184) has argued that workers are considered skilled or unskilled 'according to whether or not entry to their occupations is deliberately restricted and not in the first place according to the nature of the occupation itself'. Barrett (1980, p. 168) echoes this observation: 'Training and recruitment may be highly controlled and skill rendered inaccessible for the purposes of retaining the differentials and privilege of the labour aristocracy'.

Collins (1979) documents how some groups have successfully struggled to restrict entry through educational requirements while others have not. Doctors and engineers were able to insist on university preparation for their work; nurses, child-care workers and carpenters were not. Tool-and-die workers were able to maintain their apprenticeships on the job; clerical workers were not. Women's occupations – child-care and clerical work, for example – are much more likely to be open to people with a wide range of educational and vocational backgrounds, and therefore to be treated as unskilled occupations. Women have not had the political might to keep wages in their occupations high by restricting entry to a narrow band of suitably credentialled workers.

There is evidence that many of the skills learned at school or in formal training programmes have little direct importance on the job (Berg, 1970; Hall and Carlton, 1977). Educational attainment may act as a 'signal' or a 'screen' without imparting any necessary skills (Spence, 1973). The time training takes can vary for the same job, depending on which country workers are in, or which employer they work for. Training requirements change even when the skills involved in the work do not. For example, the training of teachers increased over the years as the demand for teachers eased and as the general educational levels of the population went up. Changes in the skills 'required' for managing a classroom have been produced by social changes extending well beyond the 'needs' of children.

To summarize, our notions of what constitutes skilled work are socially constructed through political processes that have been played out in the work-place as well as in educational institutions. Those political processes are affected by class as well as by gender, and need to be brought back into focus in order to get away from the reification of a notion of 'skill' that, if it is taken as presently constituted, serves to legitimize existing differences in income and power rather than to explain them.

The 'skilled' trades

In most employment documents and sociological texts, as well as among most workers, a 'skilled' labourer is equivalent to an artisan, a craftsperson who performs a licensed trade. The sign that a labourer is skilled rather than semi-skilled or unskilled is the existence of an apprenticeship that leads to licensing. Which trades are apprenticed, and exactly what an apprenticeship involves, varies from country to country (Reubens, 1978), but in North America apprenticeships are reserved for relatively few trades and involve periods of three to six years of on-the-job training while the trainee is employed at less than a fully trained worker's wage (Dymond, 1973).

This form of training is rarely applied to the work women do. There are only a few trades that strongly represent women – hairdressing and cooking being the main ones. In 1987, only 3 per cent of the participants registered in apprenticeship programmes in Canada were female (Statistics Canada, 1990). Briggs (1974) has pointed out that

> of the multitude of potentially apprenticeable jobs and occupations . . . those that have been recognized and approved for formal apprenticeships had with only one or two outstanding exceptions happened to fall in the traditionally male occupational category.

How does this 'happen'? The previous section of this chapter argues that we can look for the reasons in the history of political struggles over apprenticeship, rather than simply in characteristics of the work performed. Briggs herself argues that job descriptions do not show significant differences between the levels of skills required for apprenticed and much non-apprenticed and female work, even when official skill-ratings systematically under-rate the skills involved in women's work.

Apprenticeships have their origin in the practices of the medieval guilds, or 'mysteries' as they were sometimes called. The name 'mystery' emphasizes the special and complex nature of craft knowledge, and the long process of apprenticeship necessary to learn it adequately. Apprenticeships have always been subject to political struggle between labour and capital. Apprenticeships were made a universal and compulsory form of job training in England and Wales in 1563 through an Act of Parliament.

> It shall not be lawful to any person . . . to exercise any craft now used within the realm of England or Wales, except he shall have been brought up therein seven years at the least as an apprentice.
>
> (Cited in Rule, 1981, p. 95)

In fact, these regulations seem to have been mostly applied to men's work, although a few women's trades (e.g. millinery) were well-organized. Because they had to perform similar work in the home, for their families, most women learned the arts of textiles and, to a certain extent, trading (Hartman, 1979). This made it difficult to monopolize the skills, to create 'mysteries'. Women also worked in trades that were carried on as family industries with the male as head and journeyman, so that they picked up the necessary skills without being formally apprenticed (Foner, 1980).

It is unlikely that even in male trades the apprenticeship law was applied very strictly, except where the power of the craft was great enough to ensure it. However, the law acted as a symbol of the legitimate claims of the craft unions to control entry into and training for work. The repeal of the Parliamentary Act in 1814 followed a prolonged struggle between organized skilled labour and manufacturing employers seeking a free labour force (Rule, 1981).

The discussion at the time sounds remarkably similar to contemporary discussions of training requirements (Thompson, 1963, pp. 278–80; More, 1980, Chapter 3; Rule, 1981, Chapter 4). At a time when new technologies were altering jobs in the work-place and employers feared that the working classes represented a growing and serious threat, apprenticeship regulations came under attack. Much evidence was produced to show that far from teaching complex skills, apprenticeships were a way of exploiting young labourers at low wages and creating artificial shortages of workers. Adam Smith maintained that any trade, even a skilled one like watchmaking, could be learned in a matter of weeks. The craft unions fought the repeal of the law and attempted in many job-specific actions to enforce its provisions. The artisans considered that the knowledge involved their property, not to be taken from them by the state or the employer. Learning, they argued, took place on the shop floor through the precept and example of older workers. Apprenticeships also, of course, served to limit the supply of labour, to stop wages being undercut by non-union members and to enhance the status and skill of the fully apprenticed worker.

During the nineteenth century some trades were still able to consolidate their positions enough to limit, regulate and enforce apprenticeships. There is a continuing record of work stoppages and other forms of job action over apprenticeship provisions into the twentieth century (Thompson, 1963; Palmer, 1979; Kealey, 1980; More, 1980). These actions represent a continuing attempt by workers whose skills were still officially recognized to retain their power in the labour market in the face of continued reorganization of production that threatened to displace them.

> Only where working people were able to establish powerful trade societies, as in the case of male mule-spinners and the engineers, could a lengthy apprenticeship be enforced.
>
> (Lewenhak, 1977, p. 23)

Men were better organized than women to resist attacks on apprenticeships. In their struggles to maintain their skilled status, their power and their wages, the craft unions excluded women workers from training and from union membership. This was done not simply because of prejudice, but because women could be paid lower wages and used to undermine the union's position (Foner, 1980).

Women were then used by employers as strike-breakers. The fact that untrained women were used by employers to replace male workers suggests that the skill necessary for work could still be picked up more casually than through a formal apprenticeship. The apprenticeship served to control the supply of labour and to mystify the skills involved as much as it served to teach skills. The enforcement of apprenticeship regulations and the exclusion of women became tactics to preserve the power of workers who were under attack. The consequence was that women were pushed into areas of employment that did not demand an apprenticeship.

There has been much debate in the literature on apprenticeship as to whether it imparts necessary skills to workers or whether it is simply, as Lee (1981) puts it, 'a period of ritual servitude designed to reinforce exclusive unionism' (p. 58). From James Howell (1877) and the Webbs (1896) to more recent critics (Williams, 1961; Gleason and Mardle, 1980), commentators have argued that apprenticeships do not in fact teach much that is necessary for doing the job.

Others (Ryrie and Wier, 1978; More, 1980) argue that this is at least over-generalized, and that important skills are picked up through apprenticeships and are used on the job.

Whatever their training functions, it is clear that where apprenticeships exist they are an important institution in the labour market, regulating entry into some jobs. The important point is that the training has remained in a form that controls entry by demanding that trainees be hired by an employer who is willing to sponsor and subsidize their training on the assumption that the worker will be an ongoing part of the organization of production. That this form of training has been preserved, and has not been turned into either specific skill-training modules on the job, or generalized technical training in the high school or community college, is the result of continuing union pressure, an ability to import trained workers from abroad, and employers' willingness to undertake training for some workers who, they assume, will stay on the job. However, it is clear that the number of apprenticeships is still declining (Dymond, 1973; Ricketts, 1980).

Clement's (1980) study of hard-rock mining in Canada describes a contemporary example of the continuing struggle over apprenticeship. As technology has changed in mining, management has reorganized work in a way that de-skills it. Management has also replaced traditional training with a company-controlled modular training programme that teaches the particular processes necessary to operate particular machines, but provides no overall understanding of mining or the variety of technological processes involved. The union has responded by trying to introduce a 'mining-as-a-trade' programme, which would certify mining apprentices and require a three-year apprenticeship with eight weeks a year in school in addition to the time spent working in specific areas. This is an attempt by the union to counteract management's de-skilling strategy. The union has had limited success persuading the government and management to recognize the programme, although in the province of Manitoba the social democratic NDP government did so and the mining company was forced to participate.

The Canadian government is officially concerned about a shortage of 'skills', especially about the availability of people in licensed trades (Betcherman, 1980; Dodge, 1981). Government interest has drawn attention to processes of training in the trades, and has led to a new training act and a new assault on apprenticeships. Ways of increasing the supply of labour and of circumventing training requirements increase when there is a labour shortage. Research on generic skills in the trades has been funded by the Canadian Department of Employment and Immigration in an attempt to examine the transferability of skills among occupations (Smith, 1975). This has been undertaken with the explicit purpose of reorganizing training, and developing a comprehensive curriculum based in the high schools and the community colleges. Pre-apprenticeships for some trades are being introduced into the high schools. A common core programme for pre-apprenticeships in all trades is being introduced into community colleges in British Columbia. Employers complain about having to pay for training and demand more government subsidies, while they criticize the traditional apprenticeship system for being inefficient and for failing to produce enough skilled workers (Ricketts, 1980).

The result is that the use of the apprenticeship as a way of controlling the supply of labour is continuing to slip away from the unions. A more open system based in the public schools and community colleges is developing. The union's control of the content of training is also undermined. While unions have direct input into what courses will be offered in apprenticeship training, they have limited control in the public school system.

It is not clear what the result of these changes will be for women. The traditional structure of apprenticeship did not offer women much access to the trades. The demise of the apprenticeship system and the emphasis on general skills taught in educational institutions may open up recruitment and permit more women at least to compete for training places and employment. Women are more likely to be able to move into new areas of employment when these areas are expanding. On the other hand, some have argued that special initiatives for women, affirmative action programmes, and the holding of a certain quota of training 'seats' for women – all of which have recently been tried in the trades – will disappear as training is reorganized. If women do gain more access to the trades as training becomes more widely available, shorter and therefore less valued, it will continue the tradition of women moving into new areas of work as they get designated as 'unskilled'. This is a process we can see by looking at clerical work.

Clerical work

The study of clerical work is a study of how tasks with considerable technical complexity have failed to get labelled as skilled, despite some historical transitions when it looked as if this might come about. Clerical work today is quintessentially women's work. It is based in the traditional female stereotype of helpmate, where dedication to others, dependence and personal appearance are emphasized. In Canada, one-third of all employed women do clerical work. Seventy-five per cent of all clerical workers are women. Within the broad category of clerical work are more specific jobs that are even more highly segregated by sex. Secretaries and typists are female; shipping and receiving clerks are generally male (Statistics Canada, 1983a).

The average wage for clerical work is below the overall average wage for both men and women. Clerical workers have little access to power and authority. Career ladders are short. Training requirements are few.

Clerical work, particularly in the specific areas that are overwhelmingly female, requires a specific technical skill – typing – that is not taught on the job, and must be learned by a worker before job entry. Clerical work, particularly female clerical work, also demands considerable language skill. Clerical workers deal with the written word. The necessity for language skills is pointed to in the complaints of employers about the spelling and grammar of their female clerical employees (Hall and Carlton, 1977). Often numeracy skills are also demanded, as well as familiarity with calculators and, increasingly, computer keyboards.

Skill estimates of clerical work in the *Canadian Classification and Dictionary of Occupations* (CCDO) are based on training time, and are low. A clerk-typist is rated as having a general educational requirement (GED) of three, signifying applying 'common-sense understanding', making arithmetical calculations and copying language. The specific vocational preparation (SVP) rating is three, which indicates the job can be learned in between thirty days and three months.

There is no official licensing or credentialling process that qualifies someone to work at clerical or secretarial tasks. Training for clerical work is available widely in the public high schools, at community colleges and in private training 'colleges'. It must be acquired by an employee at her own expense before entrance to the job. The location of training in public high schools is very important in making it universally accessible at an early stage in the educational process. Even many young women who do not anticipate clerical jobs take typing 'in case' they will need it. The preceding chapters have shown how important the existence of clerical training is for young women's planning of their lives and for their experience of school.

The result is a large pool of labour so identified with women that the assumption that all women can type becomes prevalent. Clerical skills become part of every woman's skills, along with the ability to manage her personal appearance, support the men around her and handle interpersonal relations. The training does not appear scarce, long and arduous, but easy, taken for granted (as long as you are female) and thus no skill at all. At the same time, men do not have these skills and are therefore disqualified from a wide range of clerical jobs.

How did the close supervision of clerical workers and the wide-open organization of training come to be combined with the necessity for specific technical skills and considerable language proficiency? Clerical work has changed from the nineteenth century, when it was a male bourgeois occupation where complex skills were learned on the job and combined with substantial responsibility, to a female proletarian occupation in the twentieth century, where skills are learned off the job and are not combined with authority and responsibility. A complete account of this cannot be given in a few pages here. What I will do, however, is argue that the skills necessary for the work did not determine the organization of work and training. Instead, struggles over work and training have shaped our notions of skill.

Davies (1983, p. 5) claims that 'The typical clerk in the early 19th century office was an aspiring businessman, apprenticed to the petite bourgeoisie or capital class'. Master craftsmen such as bookkeepers controlled the office, and apprentices learned their craft on the job, advancing through promotions to positions of greater responsibility. None of these workers were women.

Although many nineteenth-century employers and clerks saw little value in formal business training in the public schools (Atherton, 1952), approving experience as the best teacher, some did find uses for public education.

Lockwood (1958, p. 20) quotes the following requirements for a clerk in London in 1878:

> A little instruction in Latin, and probably a very little in Greek, a little in Geography, a little in Science, a little in arithmetic and bookkeeping, a little in French, with such a sprinkling of English reading as may enable a lad to distinguish Milton from Shakespeare are considered enough.

These requirements reflect the secondary school curriculum of the time. The combination of 'academic' (Latin, Greek and Shakespeare) and 'vocational' (bookkeeping) courses was taken for granted. Bookkeeping was an accepted part of the public school curriculum at the elementary and secondary levels. Penmanship was another clerical skill taught in the public schools, considered in fact a core skill equivalent in importance to arithmetic and writing. The acceptance of clerical training in the schools is illustrated by Dewey's use of bookkeeping as an example of the old, dry academic approach in 1900:

> The joint stock company was invented, compound partnership disappeared, but the problems relating to it stayed in the arithmetics for two hundred years. They were kept after they had ceased to have practical utility, for the sake of mental discipline – they were 'such hard problems you know'.
>
> (Dewey, 1956, p. 77)

The class position of clerks was marginally bourgeois. Incomes for clerical work were higher than for blue collar work (Coombs, 1978; Lowe, 1982). Relations between employers and clerks were to be based on trust and considerable autonomy for the clerk. 'The only way to be sure that a bookkeeper or clerk had tallied a column of numbers accurately was for the employer to repeat the task himself', Davies (1983, p. 21) points out. Trust was developed through a personal relationship in a small office, an apprenticeship system offering possibilities for promotion and responsibility, and the recruitment of workers from bourgeois backgrounds.

In the late nineteenth century, office work expanded rapidly. As it expanded, jobs were differentiated, supervision was increased, working conditions and rewards deteriorated, and significant parts of the work were feminized. In Canada, clerical work more than doubled from 2 per cent of the workforce in 1891 to 5 per cent in 1901, and by 1911 had almost doubled again to 9 per cent. The percentage of clerical workers who were women rose from 14 per cent in 1891 to 22 per cent in 1901, and to 33 per cent in 1911 (Lowe, 1980).

Around the turn of the century, the typewriter introduced a new technical skill into the office. It was not immediately clear who would learn it, and how its relationship to the rest of the jobs in the office would be worked out. An advertisement from Shaw's Business College in Toronto in 1902 maintained the image of stenography as appropriate for men, and as a stepping-stone into management positions.

> To young men we wish to place special stress upon the excellent opportunities presented to them in the work of a stenographer. It is not

only a congenial and profitable occupation in itself, but the intimate acquaintance with the business which they must necessarily acquire is very often the means of securing rapid promotion to positions of greater responsibility and trust.

Typing, said the College, 'may well be considered a necessary qualification of every aspirant, for a position in the commercial field' (Shaw, 1902). Such advertising was harking back to an earlier day, however, trying to resurrect patterns that were rapidly becoming obsolete. The feminization of stenography proceeded quickly. In 1891, 65 per cent of typists and stenographers were women. By 1901, this reached 80 per cent, by 1911 it was 85 per cent, and by 1931 it was 95 per cent (Marks, 1984).

Even when stenographic skills became identified with a distinct group of female office workers, their relative 'skill' status was not immediately clear. Lowe comments on the potentially advantageous position of stenographers:

> Mechanization afforded considerable socioeconomic status and craft like work to a select group of female clerks. Early stenographers closely approximated the ideal of craft work, as evident in the range of their skills and their greater mastery and control over the work process.
>
> (Lowe, 1980, p. 377)

Stenographers earned relatively high wages to begin with, substantially more than teachers and industrial workers (Coombs, 1978; Lowe, 1982; Marks, 1984). It was pointed out in an advertisement aimed at women from Hamilton Commercial College in 1885 that stenographic positions 'require less arduous work and are better paid, than teaching in public schools' (Marks, 1984, p. 45). In 1892, Brockville Business College pointed to examples of teachers who had taken their courses and become stenographers at wage rates double what they earned as teachers (Marks, 1984).

As we know, however, typists and secretaries were restricted to dead-end jobs and their wages fell relative to other workers. Gender itself was an important factor in this process. Women were cheaper to employ than men, they were educated and they were increasingly available for wage labour. Women were considered less suitable for management than men and less suitable for training because of their gender and their primary location in the family. The use of gender in hiring policies and guidelines for promotion and training within the office was often explicit. When the number of women in clerical positions in the Canadian federal civil service grew at the turn of the century, the civil service commission became alarmed at the potential deterioration in the number of training positions for men. They introduced regulations limiting women to the third (lowest) category of clerical positions, whatever their examination results qualified them for (Archibald, 1970). Even within the third division, women were restricted to 'suitable' jobs that did not involve travel, handling large registers or carrying 'files and books up and down ladders' (Lowe, 1980, p. 375). Thus gender, not skill, was built into the very shape of the clerical hierarchy as it emerged. Women's skills were explicitly discounted because women had them. There is evidence that despite the official regulation of women to low-level, less 'skilled' positions, women continued to perform duties that went well beyond their job descriptions. Marks (1984, p. 83, Table 3) calculates that between 1895 and 1911 one-third of the women employed as stenographers and typists in the Ontario government were performing executive or supervisory work either in combination with their clerical tasks or alone.

Besides gender, there is the issue of class. Why did clerical workers not organize to maintain wages and power? Although there are a few instances of increasingly hard-up bank clerks trying to form collective associations with the help of American unions (Coombs, 1978; Lowe, 1987), they had little success. The bourgeois tradition of clerical work for male workers was an important factor. This class status built in individual identification with the employer and the continuing hope for upward mobility, rather than working-class identification. For women, clerical work remained a relatively well-paid job through the First World War, and it attracted middle-class women with a tradition of gentility to uphold (Aron, 1981).

The lack of collective organization of clerical workers meant they were unable to restrict entry and exert much influence on the form of training that emerged. This training was controlled by the needs of employers and the entrepreneurship of the owners of private business colleges.

Clerical training outside the work-place expanded dramatically in the last half of the nineteenth century. Private business school entrepreneurs promised success through business training, drawing on the new-found belief that one should and could translate one's personal abilities and character into a career (Bledstein, 1976). The increase in the kinds of jobs in the office, the fact that specific skills certainly helped workers perform their jobs better, and the relatively open competition for office employment made business training attractive. This training was quite unregulated until the turn of the century, and anyone who could pay fees could find a place at a business school. Unlike the carefully controlled examination system in place in the public schools, private business schools offered credentials for all, a fact that quickly devalued the training they provided. Although in 1896 the Canadian Business Education Association was founded to combat abuses, it was too late to reverse the pattern of offering business training of variable quality, to all who wanted it and could pay.

Public school training also expanded rapidly. At the turn of the century, the course of studies at the public high school was differentiated so that commercial education became a separate, lower-status programme, a programme teaching typing and stenography, directly related to preparing young women for office jobs. The clear streaming of courses in the high school came at a time when educators were arguing for the incorporation of vocational education courses into the high school curriculum. In fact, of course, vocational content in the form of bookkeeping and penmanship had long been in the high school. The origin of many other subjects was also vocational – Latin for the clergy being the clearest example. What was novel was the progressive reformers' arguments that an 'academic' curriculum was elitist and that schooling had to be adapted to the needs of working-class children. They also argued that vocational courses would make pupils more productive and well-paid workers, and would mesh schooling with the economy to make it more efficient (Lazerson and Grubb, 1974).

The debate between employers and labour over vocationalism in the high school curriculum tended to ignore commercial education and focus primarily on skilled blue collar work; there was some agreement that home economics should be the equivalent for young women. Employers saw vocational education in technical and industrial areas as a potential means of breaking workers' control over skills training. Bowles and Gintis (1976, p. 193) quote the United States National Association of Manufacturers as saying, 'It is plain to see that trade schools properly protected from the domination and withering blight of organized labour are the one and only remedy for the present intolerable conditions'. Rogers and Tyack (1982, p. 282) describe the response of business as a 'noisy, ambitious campaign to insert training for jobs into schools'. While there is more evidence of business apathy in Canada than in the United States (Stamp, 1971), business seems to have supported the introduction of vocationalism into Canadian schools (Dunn, 1979).

Labour was split on the wisdom of more vocational schooling, wanting to use it to increase access to advancement, but fearing management's motives. Some Canadian working-class testimony to the Royal Commission on Technical Education in 1913 opposed more technical education in schools on the grounds that it would lead to a congested labour market and would teach skills imperfectly (Schechter, 1977). However, the Trades and Labour Congress declared itself in complete sympathy with the Commission's recommendations to increase funding for technical education. They wanted recognition of the value of their knowledge.

Although home economics was part of the new vocational curriculum package, its politics were somewhat different. Lobbying for home economics did not come from business and labour, but from reformist women's groups who wanted women's work recognized and provided with a scientific base. While some feminists argued that women should be included in the industrial education courses instead of being segregated into home economics (Powers, 1984), by and large the introduction of home economics provided an agreed-upon way to introduce vocational classes for young women while keeping them out of industrial education.

The fact that business education was rarely mentioned during these often heated debates is at first puzzling, as the proliferation of business schools indicated the appropriateness of school-based training for these jobs. Reasons for the silence can be found in the class and gender character of business education. There was not much opposition to what had become the accepted and growing practice of offering business courses in the schools. The business curriculum was already enshrined as a 'middle-class' version of vocational schooling, so the rhetoric about adapting schools to working-class students seemed irrelevant. The discussion between labour and capital over the merits of business education did not take place because clerical workers were not organized, and did not have any control of training to begin with.

While the introduction of industrial education, home economics and business education as separate programmes in the public schools took place in the early twentieth century, this 'victory', as it was called, obscures the fact that there were important differences in the meaning of vocational training in the three programme areas. Most apprenticeships continued outside the school, and school-based industrial training was not producing students qualified for skilled industrial jobs. Home economics was largely directed towards young women's work in the home. Only in business education did the training for specific jobs come to be lodged in public schooling, as the rhetoric of vocational education suggested and as employers had demanded.

The politics of skill in classrooms today

Today, clerical work remains an area where skills are not recognized, where women experience the disjuncture between what they do and what others see. Clerical workers in a contemporary Canadian study of office training articulated their sense of being undervalued in a variety of ways:

> I don't think a lot of people realize that a lot of work done in offices isn't done by the boss. . . . Most of it is done by the staff and everyone doesn't look at it that way.

> A man [manager] was hired at one time who had no experience, and he got twice as much wages as I did. You know, I had to train him. And it really got under my skin.

> Well, if the boss is a poor writer and he says 'fix everything' you know you've got to fix his punctuation and grammar and everything. If you don't know yourself then you are sending out sloppy letters, so it's poor.

The work, the knowledge, the language skills that these women have are clear to them and provide the motivation for them to engage in further education. But their frustration is that their skills are not visible to others, and are not rewarded by high wages or respect in the office. They may have better language skills than the boss and more knowledge of how the office runs, but theirs remain dead-end, low-pay, 'low-skill' jobs.

The reorganization of clerical work with the introduction of computer technology reopens the question about the 'skill' of clerical workers. As the cost and complexity of office machinery increase, jobs are reorganized and their 'skill' characteristics and training requirements are up for discussion again. As 'information systems' replace typing and filing documents, some argue that the access of clerical workers to training, promotion opportunities and independent responsibility can and must increase. They argue that the new technology is a complex one, demanding a level of sophisticated understanding that was not necessary with typewriters. For one community college instructor describing her understanding of what is necessary in training competent secretaries, the computer adds one more skill to an already full programme:

> We try to emphasize that this isn't the end of the road, that they are going into a career, a secretarial career. That they specialize. Either they go the legal secretarial route or any of those areas they might see as a speciality. Then they've got to look at the professional aspect of it too. There's organizations and there's further education. Education for skill development, because they don't get a great deal of bookkeeping or accounting at this level. . . . Of course now they're also looking at the computer aspect.

'The computer aspect' conjures up visions of advanced mathematics and science courses, as well as a level of abstract reasoning that was not previously required. Again, teachers describe their views of skill change:

> I think word-processing is a fairly conceptual thing. It takes a bright kid. You can't take the average kid I see in a classroom today and say they're capable of composing on a word-processor.

> There seems to be . . . a greater demand for a person we used to call the 'Girl Friday', only this person needs to be able to work with a micro-computer, needs to be able to do word-processing, spreadsheets, database analysis and computerized accounting.

Some students also respond to the excitement and additional insight they get from learning about technology:

> It opens the door – that's a bad analogy, but it opens the door just enough to see what the possibilities are out there. Like in the computer and word-processing . . . just what it is capable of – wow! It's amazing. We are just using software, and we are just using word-processors, but you can just see it – you know, envision the whole Greater Vancouver, that massive conglomerate, down there, all put on a little disk. It's fantastic! Legal – you can see all of a sudden the whole Canadian . . . the law system . . . the Forces . . . the good parts and the bad. You can see a little bit on how it works, how it is set up. It gives you sort of food for thought. Things that you may have accepted before and got mad about because you never understood. Well, at least that's what I mean – opening a bit of light and gives you some understanding. . . .

> It goes more in depth into the type of filing, storage and everything like that . . . in the word-processors and data-processors. We are learning more about the insides, more about what they can do. It seems like we are learning a lot about data storage. I just handed in a report yesterday on databases – that kind of thing.

In response to these kinds of views, longer, more specialized programmes are started with the idea of 'upgrading' the work and the workers, attracting skilled people and increasing pay levels. Technology seems to some to offer a moment wherein training requirements can increase, and the consequent recognition of skill will lead to better pay and more responsibility for workers. On the other hand, some argue that technology will further reduce the skill levels associated with secretarial and clerical work. As spelling checkers are built into word-processing programs, the language requirements for doing a good job as a secretary decrease. As documents can be given a standard format at the press of a button, the need to learn about and aesthetically judge letter formats disappears. As word-processing pools are set up like factory production units to keep the expensive machinery busy at all times, the diversity of tasks and flexibility of judgement required in a more traditional clerical job are eliminated. A teacher describes what she sees happening to clerical jobs:

> It's work for drones. They don't want highly educated people who are ambitious and have a wide variety of skills. And they don't pay very much.

A student describes the training:

> Well, it's very simple. Because we're taking secretarial level, of course. You don't have to be brilliant, right? It's laid out and it's a certain procedure that you learn. You take it step by step. Which one you would use and that.

Courses that channel clerical students into a de-skilled and technical version of clerical work proliferate. In British Columbia schools, for example, 'data processing' is the technological component of the business education curriculum. The stated objectives of the course include that 'students will learn to process data with (a) edged notched cards, (b) embossed plates, (c) carbon paper'. They will 'prepare source documents for input' using a variety of techniques and they will learn to 'use a variety of input media and devices' (British Columbia Department of Education, 1981). They are learning to feed the machine, but they are not officially expected (considered able) to understand how computers work. Understanding the technology is reserved for academic students in mathematics departments who take 'computer science' instead. If this version of clerical work becomes the predominant one, the knowledge and skills that clerical workers have, and their access to advancement, to power and decent salaries, will be reduced.

So the political struggles over the nature of clerical work, its requirements, its skills and its training continue. The argument is carried on partly in disputes about what kind of training is necessary for clerical workers in the 'information office'. How much do they need to know about computers? Do they need more sophisticated language skills or less language skill? Do they need to know about the organization of offices or just about how to perform specialized tasks? Should training be carried out more directly in the work-place? Should it also be carried out more directly in relation to the power and organization of the work? What is a fair wage? Should clerical workers unionize? Should they consider themselves 'professionals'? Will jobs be organized to provide variety and flexibility or to have workers perform narrow and specialized functions? It seems unlikely that any simple answer can be given to these questions.

Increasing differentiation of clerical jobs highlights the importance of the politics in particular work-places and educational institutions.

Conclusion

This discussion of women and skill has argued that skill ratings of jobs, which seem neutral and descriptive, actually construct an understanding of the value of work, and do so in a way which has devalued the work women do. Definitions of how skilled a job is need to be seen not as neutral descriptors of the nature of the work, but as socially constructed labels that serve to explain and justify the work's relative economic advantage or disadvantage. These labels and these definitions are constructed out of political struggles that are constantly waged in the work-place and in educational institutions. Workers and employers try to give their own skill-definitions a social basis in the organization of training programmes and requirements, and in the organization of supervision and autonomy.

Women have fared relatively poorly in these struggles because of their lack of economic and political power. They have not been able to insist on the value of their work by making it a scarce commodity or by organizing collectively to gain control of job entry or of the production process. Clerical work, while it involves a considerable degree of literacy and significant technical skill, is not seen as 'skilled' work. It is not seen as difficult to learn. Knowing about the work is not seen to justify a worker's right to decide on how the work should be done; knowing the job well does not qualify a worker for high wages and promotion into managerial responsibilities. This definition of the work has come about through specific historical transformations in which both the class position and the gender position of clerical workers were critical. The transformations continue to occur, and with increasing awareness of the problem, working-class women can organize to insist on their own value.

7 Directions for Policy and Research

Like much literature in the sociology of education, this book has explored the process of social reproduction – here, as it occurs in the passage of young people from school to work. My work was shaped by a desire to emphasize human agency in the context of structural analysis, and to understand gender as integral to social structure. It was not intended to be a disinterested piece of research, but to further critical feminist scholarship and to illuminate practice. In this final chapter, I will review what has been argued, and explore the implications for policy and pedagogy.

The research starts with the accounts young people give of their movement from school to work. It takes these accounts seriously, assuming that the young people interviewed are thoughtful and purposeful, and learning from what they say about their experiences. But the text also looks at their accounts critically, trying to understand where the young people's words and concepts come from, and how the institutions and culture in which they live shape their accounts and affect their actions as they move through school towards the work-place.

How do working-class youths end up in working-class jobs? Willis's (1977) question is central, and has been explored here in a context different from the Birmingham inner city where he did his study. The Canadian youths in this book are neither as class-conscious nor as resistant to mainstream culture as the 'lads' in *Learning to Labour*. But they 'choose' vocational courses, and as soon as they graduate they leave school for working-class jobs with a feeling of release. They leave school in a variety of ways, and with some feeling of failure, but with a sense that they are making the best of their lives, in a world they describe as stacked against them in many ways. Their approach is individualistic, and the taken-for-granted nature of school, of gender relations and of job opportunities is the background against which they operate.

Moreover, why do young working-class women end up accepting responsibility for domestic labour and choosing to enter a lower-paying, female sector of the labour market? This question is not asked by Willis. The young women in this study act thoughtfully and responsibly to achieve what they can within a world they did not create, and they end up recreating the world they are not happy with. They see what men are like; they see what jobs pay and how one gets trained for them; they see the lack of child-care options. Within the world as they experience and know it, they do their best. The young men take their gender privilege equally for granted. The result is the reproduction of gender divisions, not because they are desired, but because these young people don't believe the world can be otherwise.

My analysis starts with the accounts of young people, but it ends with historical and institutional enquiry into some of those patterns at school and work that the young see as so intractable.[1] What was striking to me in what the young people said, was what they took for granted: that men couldn't bring up children; that school was boring; that clerical jobs required a simple skill that could be picked up in a few courses in high school; that students who had rehearsed routine technical tasks would be more employable. These assumptions grew from their experience of the world, which they interpreted and understood from within their culture and ideology. These assumptions became central to the actions and understandings that led to the reproduction of existing inequalities. They made young women feel powerless and limited their sense of what was possible. They provided reasons for valuing low-paying jobs. For the teachers, they justified a form of vocational teaching that stopped enquiry.

Willis described confidently the ways in which his lads 'penetrated', in other words, understood correctly, the social order, and the ways in which they did not. I am more sceptical that any single account, or group of accounts, can reveal the truth. I have come to think of the role of the social scientist as one of engaging in conversation, providing alternative accounts for people to consider. Social science becomes critical pedagogy, not confined to the school. Human cognition is a human practice, rooted in social conventions and full of personal, cultural and political blind spots. Postmodern theorists have pointed convincingly to the partiality of any account, including any academic account. Language can conceal and obfuscate, texts can be seen to 'universalize the particular and the idiosyncratic, privilege the ethnocentric, conflate truth with those prejudices that advantage the knower' (Hawkesworth, 1990, pp. 145–6). The postmodern critique makes a convincing theoretical case for appropriate humility, and should make anyone sceptical about dogmatic claims of truth. Feminist theory has, since its arrival on the academic scene, engaged in a similar critical inspection of objective and universal claims to truth. Feminist theorists must not fall into the trap of seeing their own work as the one reasonable and warranted truth.

I see the work of the social scientist, rather, as interpretive, as offering alternative ways of seeing the world. With Hawkesworth (1990), I see these not just as alternative fictions, however, but as accounts that come closer to adequacy because they are well grounded in empirical enquiry, in the collective thinking represented by the academic literature and in the political debate of the feminist movement. I see my work as an attempt at critical feminist interpretation, rethinking the world in a way that serves equality, rethinking it also on the basis of systematic enquiry.

A critical feminist epistemology must avoid both the foundationalist tendency to reduce the multiplicity of reasons to a monolithic 'Reason' and the postmodernist tendency to reject all reasons *tout court*. Keenly aware of the complexity of all knowledge claims, it must defend the adoption of a minimalist standard of rationality that requires that belief be apportioned to evidence and that no assertion be immune from critical assessment. . . . In providing sophisticated and detailed analyses of concrete situations, feminists can dispel distortions and mystifications that abound in malestream thought.

(Hawkesworth, 1990, p. 147)

Social science can suggest a rethinking of the taken-for-granted by providing accounts of how existing social practices came to take the form they do, and thus how they might be different. Human action produces social life. Existing institutions and practices are not the outcome of natural laws or biological imperatives, but of human conflict and struggle. Showing how the struggle works involves historical analysis and institutional analysis, not just the exhortation of individuals. Any particular research project can take on only a small part of this analysis, consider only a few of the concepts that seem to matter in a particular context. But the research can come up with accounts that challenge the taken-for-granted, the hegemonic versions of social relations that form such an essential part of social reproduction, for human constructions can be reconstructed.

Historical and institutional analysis goes beyond the experience of the people who produce the accounts which provide the starting point. But the analysis should connect with these accounts, by referring to some of the central concepts used in them and throwing back a more problematic version of the world (Smith, 1990). In this way, social science can have some impact on the world it studies – for example, on schools and teachers and employers – while it remains in a dialogue with people.

The metaphor of a conversation with the social scientist suggests a world of equal power relationships, where listening to others is possible, and choices are based on consent and evidence. This is not the world as we know it, even while it serves as an ideal version of what social science might contribute, and as a model for which to strive. Actually, the social scientist has relatively much power in some settings – I think particularly of the young women asking for advice, and little in others – educational policy in Canada has been largely uninterested in social science. Those with interests to defend are often understandably uninterested in the intellectual validity of the concepts they use. Social scientists must be seen to be trustworthy, a question not just of their evidence, but also of their political purposes and ideals (Donmeyer, 1985).

This is because the social location of social scientists informs and constrains their interpretations. The state of the academic field at any point in time, the university's allocation of work and rewards and, most importantly, one's own biography and political commitments shape one's scholarship. While pushing against the taken-for-granted and trying to turn every concept upside down to see if it works better that way is one of the attractions of academic work, it is not possible to think outside some ordinary knowledge that becomes clear only in retrospect (Lindblom and Cohen, 1979). The process of research is a process of narrowing things down so that they become manageable. This means developing a consistent set of questions to guide the narrowing. Feminist scholarship pursues questions that matter to women, questions about why their power to shape their own lives has been diminished and how it might be increased. These purposes frame both what is researched and how it is researched and reported. The changing concerns of feminism and the changing state of academic discourse are reflected in scholarship.

The exclusion of some areas of enquiry from this text speaks of the way I narrowed my own research questions. The exclusions are patterned by my concerns at the time, by the ease of carrying out research in the area and by the culture of academic enquiry in which I am steeped. Issues of sexuality and of cultural and racial reproduction are the most obvious omissions. Today each receives more attention than it did ten years ago, although the lack of research on ethnic and racial issues in relation to class and gender is still astounding.

'Politics' and 'struggle' are words I use to describe the action that has been taken and might be taken to change things. While it is becoming increasingly clear in the literature on educational reform that educational questions are questions of morality and purpose, rather than technical questions about means, it is more common to speak of these dilemmas as ethical than as political (Gilligan *et al.*, 1990; Goodlad *et al.*, 1990). However, the political language captures better for me the unequal power relations that characterize action, and the collective nature of the action necessary for change. Seeing the provision of concepts and understandings as political also engages the analyst in the struggle, for however we frame our accounts, they have consequences for the relations of power among people.

The relationship between changing concepts and changing power relations is a dynamic and complex one, as I have indicated in several chapters. Concepts about how the world actually works are located in one's experience of the world. Simply explaining that things can be different will not change the mind of a young woman whose experience convinces her that they cannot be. She would be unwise to jettison her own experience of the world in favour of what she is told by an expert, whether social scientist, teacher or guidance counsellor. But experience is not apprehended directly. It is apprehended through a set of concepts and understandings, an ideology, that makes sense of it. Changing these concepts can change the meaning of 'experience'. So social science and critical, social pedagogy can contribute to change.

A change in concepts occurs most easily when one's own life provides experiences that can be seen as evidence for change. The belief that men cannot bring up children is challenged most directly when a young woman has a father who is competent and loving with children. The belief that women won't be hired into blue collar jobs is challenged when an employer actually hires a dozen young women for such positions. Structures do change, new options do open up. Life is not static; power is not a thing but a relation that is constantly negotiated. Critical social science and critical pedagogy are grounded in awareness of the material world, but offer an appreciation of its flux and changing meaning for all of us.

More concretely, the implications of the analysis in this book for research and policy can be taken up in relation to three foci: young people, the school and the work-place. Each is a vast area for study and policy-making, but general directions for change consistent with this analysis can be suggested for each.

Adolescents and their careers

One reason why young people are of such concern to us is that they are poised between childhood and the adult world, still young enough for us to treat them as malleable and interested in learning from adults, but old enough for their choices and aspirations to be consequential, for themselves and for society. In them we see both the results of early socialization and the anticipation – or anticipatory socialization, as some academics would put it – of adult labour markets and family patterns. They are a focus for change, the new generation, and a repository of early learning from the old generation, especially from their parents. As a result, they are a focus for our hopes and fears about the future as well as an intriguing subject for the analyst who is wondering how best to understand what they do and say.

Young women are a group that stir strong emotions for a feminist of the 1970s like myself. They are also analytically important because of what they may teach us about change and persistence in patterns of gender inequality. Will they continue traditional patterns or will they demand equality? Are they continuing to make traditional choices and think traditional thoughts, or has the resurgence of the women's movement had an impact on the way they approach adulthood? Those of us who have struggled for change wait eagerly to see if the new generation will take up the torch, or whether they will let feminism fade – and if so, why.

A Canadian government study of adolescent girls called *What Will Tomorrow Bring?* (Canadian Advisory Committee on the Status of Women, 1985) is an example of the kind of study that frequently bears witness to this interest in female adolescence and points to some of the difficulties in producing a useful analysis of the questions involved. The concern behind this study was 'that adolescent girls are not adequately being prepared, or preparing themselves for a changing world'. In other words, the concern was that young people be as committed to a new feminist version of the world as the feminist researchers who carried out the study. Unfortunately, the young women were not. They often wanted a husband and children and a house surrounded by a white picket fence. Their visions of the future did not include poverty, single parenting or going into non-traditional jobs. These visions were, as researchers put it, 'romanticized, traditional and stereotypic'. The study concludes that young women need more counselling, more education and more realism.

In this study (and I use it only as an example of policy-oriented research by a women's branch of government committed to social change for women), there is an equation of 'realism' with adopting new and more equal conceptions of the role of women. But what is realistic may not be what is progressive. In many cases, I would argue, traditional choices appear the most 'realistic' to the young women involved. The persistence of traditional choices among young women can be accounted for precisely by their realism, by their attempts to come to grips with the world as they know it. It is not that young women live in a romantic fog of misperception. The problem rather is that the world they experience and come to know is thoroughly sexist, offers them few opportunities and is generally stacked against them.

How do analysts, as outsiders, know what is 'realistic' for someone else? A young woman's reality must be carefully explored in dialogue with her, not glibly assumed to be the same as a college-educated woman researcher's. Talking with young women allows us to understand the world from their points of view, and to challenge our own. It is this that is exciting, not just measuring what we find against our own standard, for then others will always be found wanting. Research should be less interested in telling young women what is wrong with their views and choices – there are enough critics out there already – than in understanding how they arrive at their choices. My assumption is that feminist researchers should listen carefully, with awareness of the particular context involved and empathy for the speaker. To have women's voices heard, not silenced, is central to feminist theory and practice. To listen to, write about and validate what young women tell us is an important role for an academic feminist. After all, young women will generally know more about themselves and the world they live in than we outsiders do. If they did not, it would not be interesting to talk to them.

This sometimes appears to be a conservative stance – it listens sympathetically even to very right-wing views, it is not as quick to be critical of existing patterns and choices as others might be – but for me it is part of feminism to listen carefully to other women (and to people generally) and to assume they know what they are talking about. As Giddens (1979, p. 5) puts it in discussing structuration, 'every social actor knows a great deal about the conditions of reproduction of the society of which he or she is a member'. This stance does not preclude criticism and change. Rather, I think it leads to more informed criticism and to changes that are fundamental instead of cosmetic. It locates the problem not in 'the victim', but in the social arrangements that take away from people the power to achieve their goals. It leads to arguments addressed to those in powerful positions, those who hire, teach, counsel or shape government policy, rather than arguments addressed to individual young women.

For what is striking is how even young women with a desire for change think little change is realistically possible without unacceptable levels of self-sacrifice, risk-taking or unhappiness. To quote Hoggart (1960, p. 322) again, these young women 'remove the main elements in the situation to the realm of natural laws, the given and the raw, the almost implacable material from which a living has to be carved'. Knowing the forces arrayed against them, they do not dare to ask for more, to say no, to struggle for themselves.

Intervention to interrupt the reproduction of class and gender inequality in the high school could involve responses directed at the young people themselves, or directed at the setting within which they act. The first response offers many options. One of the more promising involves strengthening young women's resistance, by providing models of courage and support for their risk-taking. As Gilligan *et al.* (1990) put it, young women need the security to find their own voice, to ask disruptive questions out loud. A pedagogy that gives voice to women's concerns and validates them is clearly important.

For young men, the implications for pedagogy are less clear. Given the extreme sexism of some of the young men, the problem becomes interrupting their assumption of privilege, having them understand their power and their misogyny, rather than giving them a voice. Holding up to them young women's accounts can help make their assumption of power visible, and induce guilt in some. Supporting some of the more egalitarian young men in their sense of fair play begins to change the social milieu in which they all have to act. But it is not at all clear that a critical awareness can be induced without social sanctions for the overt expression of misogyny. Weiss (1990) has argued that in a deindustrializing America, white working-class males are so threatened by their loss of a traditional masculinity along with a loss of job opportunities that the new right is very attractive to them. Public displays of abuse and violence against women have been receiving more media attention in Canada since the murder of 14 women engineering students by a man out to shoot 'the feminists' in Montreal in 1989. What combination of increased hostility by men and increased public anger by women this represents is not clear. While the solution to young men's assumption of power over women lies partly in education, it also lies in structural change and clearer sanctions.

The second response means turning to institutional change, to the context in which young people act, in order to provide a critique of the 'natural laws, the given and the raw', and demonstrate that change can take place. Young women do not have primary responsibility for this kind of change, although their changed responses would change the context in which young men have to act. Being confronted with young women who demand equal relationships or no relationships will produce a changed set of rewards and sanctions for male behaviour. But it is the school, the work-place, the state that primarily organize the settings within which young people act. The possibilities and directions for change in school and in the labour market are the ones to which I now turn.

The school: rethinking vocational education

What is taught in school matters. Teachers provide an account of how the world works and they qualify and certify students for the job market. The organization and stratification of knowledge in the school, the specific inclusions and exclusions of knowledge, tend to be taken for granted by those in the school, but must be understood as historically, ideologically and politically based choices. What is the possibility of changing the stratification of knowledge in secondary schools? What is the possibility, especially in vocational classrooms, of a critical pedagogy that holds up existing patterns of gender and class inequality for examination?

Vocational education has often been criticized for reproducing the divisions of the labour force, and reducing knowledge to specific skills and techniques. This book adds to such criticism. The vocational objectives of schooling get bad press among educators. Education should be for the love of learning, the joy of discovery, the development of the mind. Stressing the economic value of education seems sordid and narrow, even if it is increasingly necessary, for 'other people's children' (Grubb and Lazerson, 1982). Most liberal educators prefer to ignore or deny the economic uses of schooling, arguing that education is not about getting students jobs or increasing their economic competitiveness, but rather about their social and intellectual growth.

This suggests that the best solution would be simply to abolish vocational education in favour of a liberal education for all. Adler (1982), Bloom (1987) and Hirsch (1987) argue along these lines. It is possible to find labour-union spokespersons who agree. But the struggle to incorporate what we now call vocational subjects into the curriculum at the turn of the century was strongly supported by segments of the labour movement who saw the existing curriculum as elitist, based in the lives of the middle classes. They wanted the curriculum broadened to incorporate the knowledge of working people, to insist that this knowledge was worthy and worth teaching. 'Really useful knowledge' for all classes surely should be taught in schools.

The struggle to include vocational subjects was won just after the turn of the century, and has been seen by some historians as a disaster.

> The triumph of vocationalism marked the victory of the market revolution in education and the defeat of Whig and radical republican conceptions of society and education premised on visions of a 'classless society and common schooling'. . . . [It] made possible the transformation of public education into an adjunct of the labor process and the labor market. . . . [It] stratified educational credentials in a wholly new way and strengthened the connection between schooling and the system of stratification.
>
> (Hogan, 1985, p. 193)

Or, as Katznelson and Weir (1985, p. 151) put it,

> The conflicts over vocational education proved to be the last site where a class-based battle was fought over whether the ideal of the common school would be replaced by a highly stratified and differentiated system of public education.

When vocational subjects were included, they were included as an addendum to the existing curriculum. They were to be studied only by the lower streams of students, segregated and separated from the academic curriculum, where such studies still remain.

Today, we should rethink the distinction between liberal and vocational education in order to enrich both. The arguments for including vocational knowledge in the curriculum were good ones. They drew on both the dignity and value of labour and a progressive pedagogy that integrated activity with thought, the practical with the theoretical. The problem was the clear distinction that was drawn between the vocational and the academic, once vocationalism was institutionalized.

Vocationalism should mean education for work in its broadest and most humanistic sense. The distinction between vocational and liberal studies is based on dichotomies that are philosophically inadequate and socially pernicious. The attempt to divorce academic education from any practical concerns is just as destructive to academic education as the divorce of practical education from academic concerns has been. It separates knowledge from experience, theory from practice, and thought from action. But experience informs knowledge, theory informs practice, thought informs action and action informs thought. A curriculum that recognizes this and incorporates both intelligence and execution, mind and body, is what we want for all our young people (see also Silver and Brennan, 1988; Spours and Young, 1988). Challenging this division inscribed in knowledge offers the possibility of structurally interrupting the reproduction in the school of the class and gender distinctions that permeate the work-place.

Work makes intellectual as well as personal and technical demands upon workers. Different kinds of work make different kinds of demands, but recognizing the skill and knowledge all people bring to their work is part of challenging class and gender divisions at work. The integration of conception and execution must be translated into educational programmes as well as into social and technical relations in the work-place. To re-frame education for work in a way that recognizes this is not to invent some new concept of vocationalism. The liberal arts were once closely tied to education for the church and for the professions, and their practical focus did not devalue them.

The origins of the vocational–liberal education distinction can be found in the class system of the Greeks. Aristotle prescribed a liberal education for the citizens, and a vocational education for the slaves, foreigners and women. For the Greeks, the search for truth was the highest ideal. Knowing for the sake of knowing, uncontaminated by practice, was the sign of the free man. A citizen

> must not lead the life of mechanics and tradesmen, for such a life is ignoble and inimical to virtue and the performance of civic duties. . . . To young children should be imparted only such kinds of knowledge as will be useful to them without vulgarizing them . . . wherefore we call those arts vulgar which tend to deform the body, and likewise all paid employments, for they absorb and degrade the mind.
>
> (Cited in Charlton, 1986, p. 2)

Dewey is perhaps our most venerable critic of the way these dualisms are constructed, and the pernicious implications they have for education. His educational prescriptions of 1916 go against the idea that activity and thought are quite different activities, calling for an education that incorporates action and relevance into all areas of the curriculum. He wrote that 'only superstition makes us believe the two are necessarily hostile so that a subject is illiberal because it is useful, and cultural because it is useless' (Dewey, 1966, p. 258). He argued that all education is education for a calling, if calling is interpreted broadly enough, and that good education is education that integrates the concerns of real life and the activities of the child into the experience of learning. His view was taken up by supporters of vocational education and continues, sometimes, to lend to vocational education a rhetoric of progressive pedagogy.

Dewey also pointed out that the distinction between academic and vocational education had its root in social inequality. He added that, 'While the distinction is often thought to be instrinsic and absolute, it is really historical and social' (p. 260). Aristotle's distinction was based in a social order that distinguished free men from everyone else. Aristotle argued that different kinds of education were necessary to keep social distinctions clear: 'If they [free men] habitually practice them [manual activities] there will cease to be a distinction between master and slave' (Dewey, 1966, p. 260). Dewey's commitment to democracy led him to argue for a curriculum where intellectual and manual work were combined, where all would work and all would share in thinking and doing.

> We are in a position honestly to criticize the division of life into separate functions and of society into separate classes only so far as we are free from responsibility for perpetuating the educational practices which train the many for pursuits involving mere skill in production, and the few for a knowledge that is an ornament and a cultural embellishment. Ability to transcend the Greek philosophy of life and education is not secured by a mere shifting about of the theoretical symbols. . . . Important as these theoretical and emotional changes are, their importance consists in their being turned to account in the development of a truly democratic society, a society in which all share in useful service and all enjoy a worthy leisure.
>
> (Dewey, 1966, p. 256)

What we refer to as liberal education was, in the sixteenth century, vocational preparation for the literate male minority who were destined to govern. Classical languages and bookish learning were preparation for religious vocations. The sons of the aristocracy were prepared to rule through exposure to classical languages and those *studia humanitatis* that would inculcate gentility. In the last half of the nineteenth century the examinations that were increasingly required for entry to the army and the civil service in Britain were based on the classical curriculum, ensuring that 'the classical curriculum became more "useful" while still presenting the strong advantage for the would-be gentleman of being decidedly not "utilitarian" ' (Reid and Filby, 1982, p. 25).

Raymond Williams (1961, p. 142) writes:

The old humanists muddled the issue by claiming a fundamental distinction between their traditional learning and that of the new disciplines, notably, science and technical education. . . . As educational history shows, the classical linguistic disciplines were primarily vocational, but these particular vocations had acquired a separate traditional dignity, which was refused to vocations now of equal human relevance.

What was considered the modern and practical curriculum in the nineteenth century consisted of English, science and mathematics, subjects which were increasingly important for making a living in commerce and industry. Such knowledge was taken up by the new professional classes, and became the mark of the professional, as opposed to the 'mechanick'. As influential groups like navigators and physicians began to base their expertise in theoretical knowledge, acquired through bookish education, liberal education came to include the sciences. What was useful in preparing middle-class men for work became the accepted academic curriculum.

A feminist critique of the curriculum can be argued along the same lines. The gender distinction exists in Aristotle, right alongside the class distinctions. Dewey points out that for Aristotle 'women are classed with slaves and craftsmen as factors among the animate instrumentalities of production and reproduction of the means for a free or rational life' (Dewey, 1966, p. 253) and that 'slaves, artisans and women are employed in furnishing the means of subsistence in order that others, those adequately equipped with intelligence, may live the life of leisurely concern with things intrinsically worthwhile' (p. 253). As women's role was to serve men, their education was to remain practical in its orientation, firmly separated from men's and lower in status.

In the 'domestic labour debate' feminists argued with Marxists that domestic labour should be seen as productive labour, that Marxist theories of labour, with typical masculine shortsightedness, excluded women's work in the home, when it was critical to production.

The distinction between women's knowledge and men's knowledge has been just as deeply ingrained in the curriculum as the distinction between vocational and liberal knowledge. Women's knowledge has been vocational, designed for the practicalities of being a woman, designed for the private sphere. The rest of the curriculum has been designed to educate men for the public sphere. At the same time that the labour movement was arguing for the inclusion of vocational subjects in the curriculum, the women's movement was arguing for including domestic science. The movement pointed out that the existing curriculum was a curriculum for men, and that women's work in the home was valuable, skilled and worthy of a place in the public school curriculum. The success of the reformers in including domestic science in the curriculum was seen as a victory by many. But the implementation of this victory meant the segregation and devaluing of women's special knowledge in home economics courses, not the general recognition of the value of this knowledge.

What is necessary is a reincorporation of education for the private sphere into our conception of education for everyone. Jane Roland Martin's work points in this direction. She has argued that both the content and the structure of schooling have been designed to prepare young people for a male world. The school has been justified as preparation for the public, productive sphere, for work and for citizenship. In the public sphere, men have played dominant roles, and women have been excluded, by custom, tradition or law. The very idea of the humanities was tied to civic life and leadership in the public arena. Liberal education was based on the needs of the cultivated gentleman.

Schooling has ignored the private sphere. Learning for family and personal life has been relegated to the family. As a result, Martin argues, the ideal of the educated person has been based on the male stereotype – objective, analytic, rational and interested in ideas and things, but not nurturing, empathic, intuitive or supportive. Education has emphasized the development and application of reason and objective judgement; it has separated the mind from the body, thought from action and reason from emotion.

But even Jean-Jacques Rousseau, who outlined such a curriculum for his hero Emile, realized it was not adequate for a society. Rousseau assigned to Sophie, Emile's sister, the womanly arts of caring, bringing up children and soothing the fevered brow of the public man. To educate the whole person, and to ensure the survival of our society, Martin argues, we must not ignore those tasks and qualities that have been assigned to women and to the private sphere; rather, we must integrate them into the mainstream, into the public school system. We must build nurturing capacities and an ethics of caring into the curriculum for all our students, and not depend on women to learn it privately and do it for us all.

Martin does not think, as most women reformers did at the turn of the century, that this means incorporating home economics into the curriculum, even for male as well as female students. As Martin (1985, p. 198) emphasizes,

> If education links nurturing capacities and the 3Cs [of caring, concern and connection] only to subjects such as home economics that arise out of the reproductive processes, we will lose sight of the general moral, social and political significance of these traits. So long as rationality and autonomous judgment are linked exclusively with the productive processes of society, the reproductive ones will continue to be devalued. . . .
> When the productive/reproductive dichotomy and its accompanying hierarchy of values is rejected, teaching methods, learning activities, classroom atmospheres, teacher–pupil relationships, school structures and attitudes towards education may all be affected.

What is striking is the similarity between her arguments about overcoming the productive–reproductive dichotomy and Dewey's arguments about overcoming the mental–manual dichotomy. Both dichotomies serve to reproduce in the school the hierarchies and divisions that occur outside the school. Both work within taken-for-granted dichotomies in the culture and the experience of young people in the society. Neither is a necessary distinction, and the hierarchy of value attached to the distinction is not necessary either.

Interrupting reproduction through the school involves interrupting these structural continuities between school and work.

The teachers I interviewed would define the ideal of sexual equality in the school as gender blindness. Gender differences should not matter. Young women should be treated just like young men, within the existing structure of the school. Both sexes should strive for the highest levels of achievement. They should take Algebra 11 if they can possibly manage it, for it leads to higher-status education at the university and ultimately a better pay-off at work. They should have access to home economics as well as carpentry and choose freely. They should get the same treatment in class, the same privileges and the same penalties for failing to do their best.

Gender blindness means silence on gender issues. It accepts the existing structure of the school and its subjects as a given, excluding discussion of the 'private' issues of gender. While individual teachers might choose to incorporate a wider range of topics and value positions into their class, without a significant shift in the definition of what counts as school knowledge we cannot expect to see changes in what most teachers do in the classroom. Until vocational teachers see that ethics and literacy and understanding are issues related to work and issues that can involve a class of adolescents, their version of vocationalism as 'employability' will continue to narrow every initiative that is taken to broaden the curriculum. Until they see that thinking critically about gender relations, sexuality and culture is part of 'life skills', and part of what the school has a responsibility to teach, the private will continue to be silenced, not examined, in the school.

Linking school to work

The young people discussed in this book believe that to stay in school is to improve one's chances in the job market. The teachers and the guidance counsellors also tell them that skills developed in school will translate into improved economic success. Functionalist theory and human capital theory are based on exactly this premise. But the assumption of a critical sociology of education, as articulated persuasively by Bowles and Gintis (1976), is that the 'IQ ideology' is a means of legitimating inequality rather than an accurate representation of how people find jobs or get rewarded for their work.

In Chapter 6, I argued against any notion that the link between school and work is a transfer of skill for money. People are not rewarded at work with a salary and responsibility level equivalent to the skills and understandings they bring to their work. Instead, I argue, what people are paid reflects their power in the work-place. Some groups of workers have been able to achieve higher wages than others, through a variety of means using resources of different levels and kinds. Some of these resources are ideological. Some workers have convinced others their jobs are difficult, or they have appealed to sexism or to racism. Some of these resources depend on collective organization or strategic access to power. Some workers have restricted access to their jobs through guilds and professional licensing, or have organized strikes, or have had direct access to those who set the wage scales. Some of the differences in wages have a long historical tradition; some are newly arrived at as new types of work appear. These and similar processes have determined wage structures.

The conclusion is that only if skill is translated into power in the work-place does it result in higher wages. Because of its ideological currency in indus-trialized societies, skill is a resource that can be used in the struggle for higher wages. But women have not been very successful at this. The jobs of women systematically pay less than those of men for the levels of skill they demand, using the most conventional definitions of skill. Years of education and training is perhaps the simplest and most conventional indicator of skill. Women in the labour force have more education than men in the labour force, even though women are paid much less (Boyd, 1981; Gaskell, 1982; Picot, 1983). If women were paid for their education as much as men are paid for their education, women would be much better off.

When more complex measures of skill are used to compare men's and women's occupations, we continue to find that women are paid less than men for the same skills. Women earn less than men when their jobs have equivalent requirements for education, experience, skill and working conditions (Oppen-heimer, 1970; England *et al.*, 1988). Several studies have found that the percentage of females in an occupation depresses wages even after measures of skill-demands, as described in the (American) *Dictionary of Occupational Titles*, are controlled (England and McLaughlin, 1979; Treiman and Hartman, 1981; England and Norris, 1985). England *et al.* (1982) conclude, based on these ratings, that 'females actually have an advantageous occupational skill distribu-tion on balance' (p. 163), meaning that the skills women are more likely to have (social and literacy skills, by and large) are skills that in the labour force as a whole tend to be rewarded with higher wages than the skills men have (physical strength, in particular). This advantage is offset by the combination of extreme occupational segregation and the depressing effect on wages of the concentration of women in an occupation.

The women's movement has recognized the fact that women are not paid as much as men for the same skills, as these skills are usually defined, and that skill is an ideological resource for women. This argument for higher wages has been well used recently in struggles for pay equity legislation. In many parts of the USA, and in several provinces in Canada, pay equity schemes have been argued for and won (Acker, 1981; Cuneo, 1990). Pay equity legislation demands that employers replace market mechanisms for setting wages with a job assessment scheme that evaluates every job for its skill, effort, responsibility and working conditions. The legislation has been resisted by employers at the level of the legislature, and at the level of implementation. Even with all this resistance, it has resulted in wage increases for women workers that range from slight to substantial.

Much of the ideological power of pay equity lies in its promise of a process that substitutes objectivity for politics, technical expertise for power relations. A pay equity committee judges the worth of a job by assigning points on an agreed-upon scale. Numbers seem objective and neutral. The scale is based on criteria that are shared within the committee, can be communicated to the sceptical and, if need be, argued about in court. Where collective bargaining, the market and employers' decisions have demonstrably disadvantaged women, a technical process that insists on 'unbiased' assessments of the characteristics of jobs and therefore of their worth seems enormously promising.

The question is whether buying into an ideology of skill is beneficial in the long run. Is the promise real or illusory? Can employers, or management consultants, or even teams of workers and managers, come up with assessments that are not biased? Can assessments of jobs be made objectively, without a political point of view implicit in the analysis? The simple answer is no. Any rating scale, any determination of job value, is based on judgements which can be politically contested. The job evaluation process involved in pay equity looks like a technical process, but it is a political one.

This kind of argument is not a new one for feminist analysis. Revealing the hidden ideological underpinnings of 'objective assessments' has been grist for the feminist academic mill. Feminist scholarship has continually pointed to the ways in which taken-for-granted, neutral and objective judgements are actually partial, if not completely wrong and misguided. Feminist analysis has shown that what has been taken as objectivity and political neutrality has too often been simply what powerful males think and say. 'Subjectivity' and 'politicization' enter in when someone with less power raises questions. This general lesson applies to the determination of pay equity.

My argument, in short, is that there is no one correct, objective version of how much skill is involved in doing a job. In making statements about and evaluations of skill, we stand in our historical time and place, in our culture. We stand in traditions of thought that have been thoroughly dominated by men and by the bourgeoisie. And we come face to face with basic questions of value, of power, of women's place in the world. What less powerful workers do has been construed as lacking in skill. When people overlook women's skills, devalue them, give them low ratings, it is not a technical glitch, but a reflection of the status and power women have not had in the world.

Women have not had the power to insist upon the recognition and value of their skills in the work-place. Their lack of ability to define their work as skilled is not simply something that has occurred in people's heads, but is a social process that has had institutional consequences in relation to educational qualifications and opportunities for vocational training, as well as in relation to wages. The ways this works are various. Women's skills have often been considered part of their femaleness, and therefore not to be counted. Being polite and helpful and 'attractive' in particular ways are learned, but considered personality, not skill. Many of the things that women do at work tend to be taken for granted in this way, and not seen as skills.

When skills are recognized, evaluating their relative complexity and worth is equally complicated. Are technical skills more valuable or more complex than social skills? What are the relative importances of the ability to manage social interaction, the ability to put up with routine tasks, the ability to analyse problems? Do supply and demand determine the value of a skill, even if they do not determine the value of a job? Is it a question of how well the enterprise could function without a particular skill? Can we measure the use value and the exchange value of a skill? Different things will count in different circumstances. Different people will count different things.

The question of learning time as a measure of skill is also much more ambiguous than it appears. A job that takes longer to learn appears to be more skilled. But whose learning time and what circumstances should we take into account? The length of time someone is required to attend a training programme to get a credential is likely to differ from the amount of time it actually takes a person to learn the job.

The process of evaluating skills is a highly political, contextual and ideological one. 'Skill' is a category that gives status and importance to work in common parlance and in wage negotiations. Skill categories are ideological categories, used to justify and challenge existing hierarchies at work. Indeed, some would argue that skill designations are nothing more than power relations expressed in the form of skill. The more important, highly paid, powerful work must by definition be more 'skilled'. We treat mental work as more skilled than manual work, reflecting the power managers have over manual workers. Characteristics of powerful positions – autonomy, supervision of less powerful workers, making judgements for others – are what we count as higher-order skills. Our ideas about skill are continually constructed and reconstructed in the politics of the work-place. Attaching numbers to skill does not change this fundamental fact.

The pretence that skill can be objectively determined will be used to justify gender inequalities that remain after pay equity committees have ruled on how jobs are unequally skilled. As England and Norris (1985, p. 638) put it,

> Regression analysis can tell us the relative returns to the job characteristics of heavy lifting and finger dexterity. Employers may pay a premium for heavy lifting rather than painstaking finger dexterity precisely because heavy lifting is done by men and finger dexterity is more often required in women's jobs. But a method that puts variables tapping finger dexterity and lifting into a regression to tap whether they are part of the policy of wage setting will not count pay differences between predominantly male lifting jobs and female jobs requiring finger dexterity as discriminatory. That is, the coefficient on sex composition will be determined net of the effects of these differences.

If a skill is valued because it has been associated with men's work, and if we are not critical of these traditional judgements, gender inequity will be built into wage rates more securely than ever.

Of course the argument gets applied to all wage differentials, not just the differences between male and female wages. The entire hierarchy of wages can be justified and 'rationalized' through a pay equity policy that ties wages to objective judgements of value. This is sometimes the appeal of pay equity for employers who would like to reduce the relative wages of skilled blue collar workers.

The process of defining and valuing the skills necessary for a job is a complex one that is based on someone's point of view. It has rarely taken the point of view of women workers. The devaluation of women and their work has shaped the assessment of women's skills, and affected the kind of training women receive for their work. Training programmes symbolize skill and restrict job entry. Women workers have not been able to insist on long and regulated training programmes. They have not been able to insist that on-the-job training be provided.

Pay equity is a means for women to achieve increased wages. I would not argue against its use. But it should be used with a recognition, not a conceal-ment, of the politics of skill attribution. Politics, power and struggle remain, as pay equity policies are used to reshuffle wages in the work-place. Pay equity legislation should be used to raise consciousness about women's skills and training at work. It should be used to show more workers that their skills are important, and that they can legitimately make demands based on them.

How pay equity is implemented, and how it is discussed by unions and employers and lawyers and all of us is what becomes critical. The legislative requirement for pay equity committees means that the question of what skills are required at work must be confronted and discussed by management and workers. If the discussions simply leads everyone to discuss where on a taken-for-granted scale of value their own job fits, the politics of pay equity will consolidate in the work-place a version of skill that was arrived at with little input from women. If the scales themselves are discussed and re-evaluated, there is an opportunity for a fundamental revaluing of work, and particularly of women's work.

There seems to be preliminary evidence that pay equity discussions in the work-place can either entrench the legitimacy of existing versions of skill or raise questions about existing structures. Women do sometimes discover, as they discuss the skills involved in their work, that they have skills they had never thought about, and they force their fellow workers and their employers to recognize it too. But without support for this, the process can confirm for women their place at the bottom, and legitimate ways of valuing that obscure women's skills. It depends on how the process is seen and how it is im-plemented.

The relation between education and work is not a mechanical one, much though legislative initiatives like pay equity and other job evaluation schemes may be pushing in this direction. There were historical periods when attending school had little impact on success at work. Young men dropped out of school early to work, while young women more often stayed in the protective environment of the school. As schooling developed stronger links with work, ideologies justifying work-place arrangements through schooling also de-veloped. What will happen in the future depends on who stands to benefit from what kinds of actual and perceived linkages. At the moment, women will benefit from stronger linkages, because women have schooling and skills, but not wage parity with men.

No single kind of linkage seems essentially more progressive than another.

In different times and places, different kinds of linkages will contribute to more equality. What needs to be kept in mind is the fluctuation, the myriad possible patterns that have been and might be tried. Only with a sense of the alternatives can political choices about what to argue for be made.

From here

There is no one right answer to questions about how to improve the chances for young people, how to create a school curriculum that is equitable and stimulating, how to improve women's status at work and challenge class inequities. What schools and social science *can* do is reframe some of the issues, and provide new ways to think about them and new ways to investigate them. The particular answers must be arrived at by those who have to live with the arrangements devised. The answers change with the people, the time, and the institutional and cultural context.

The young people whose lives and opportunities are discussed here exist in a Canadian city that has its own history and social organization; the schools they attend are particular; the labour market they were entering has changed since this research was done. The experiences of these young people cannot be generalized to the experiences of other young people in different times and places.

At the same time, the organization of class and gender categories and their relation to the school and to work are not peculiar to this setting. The unequal locations of women and men in relation to school and work, and the inequity between those who do manual labour for low wages and those who do mental labour for higher wages, exist across schools and labour markets. The processes that maintain the inequities can be seen and confronted generally.

The vision of school and work proposed here would open the school to a broader set of curriculum issues and to a more critical discussion of them. It would not link the school to work by developing specific job-skills in the classroom or by espousing an ideology that differences in wages must be justified by differences in schooling. It would, however, see vocational concerns as school concerns, and recognize the importance of work done in the home as well as in the office and factory. Schooling would develop its links with all spheres of life, and teachers would strive to provide a sense of possibility for all students.

Note

1. See Dorothy Smith (1990) for an argument expanding this approach as feminist method.

References

Acker, S. (1981). No woman's land: British sociology of education, 1960–1979. *Sociological Review*, **29** (1), 77–104.

Adler, M.J. (1982). *The Paidea Proposal: an Educational Manifesto*. New York: Macmillan.

Almquist, E.M. and Angrist, S.S. (1975). *Careers and Contingencies*. Port Washington, NY: Dunnellen.

Anyon, J. (1981). Social class and school knowledge. *Curriculum Inquiry*, **11** (1), 3–42.

Anyon, J. (1983). Intersections of gender and class: accommodation and resistance by working class and affluent females to contradictory sex role ideologies. In S. Walker and L. Barton (eds), *Gender, Class and Education*, pp. 19–38. Lewes: Falmer Press.

Apple, M. (1982). *Cultural and Economic Reproduction in Education*. London: Routledge and Kegan Paul.

Archibald, K. (1970). *Sex and the Public Service*. Ottawa: Queen's Printer.

Armstrong, P. and Armstrong, H. (1978). *The Double Ghetto: Canadian Women and Their Segregated Work*. Toronto: McClelland and Stewart.

Arnot, M. (1981). *Class, Gender and Education*. Milton Keynes: Open University Educational Enterprises.

Aron, C. (1981). To barter their souls for gold: female clerks in federal government offices, 1862–1890. *Journal of American History*, **67** (4), 835–53.

Atherton, L.E. (1952). Mercantile education in the ante bellum south. *Mississippi Valley Historical Review*, **39**, 623–40.

Barrett, M. (1980). *Women's Oppression Today: Problems in Marxist Feminist Analysis*. London: Verso.

Bazalgetti, J. (1978). *School Life and Work Life: a Study of Transition in the Inner City*. London: Hutchinson.

Becker, H. (1964). *Human Capital Theory*. New York: Columbia University Press.

Behn, W., Carnoy, M., Carter, M., Crain, J. and Levin, P.H. (1976). School is bad: work is worse. In M. Carnoy and H. Levin (eds), *The Limits of Educational Reform*, pp. 219–44. New York: David McKay Company.

Benbow, C.P. and Stanley, J.C. (1980). Sex differences in mathematical ability: fact or artifact? *Science*, **210**, 1262–4.

Benbow, C.P. and Stanley, J.C. (1982). Consequences in high school and college of sex differences in mathematical reasoning ability: a longitudinal perspective. *American Educational Research Journal*, **19** (4), 598–622.

Benbow, C.P. and Stanley, J.C. (1983). Differential course taking hypothesis revisited. *American Educational Research Journal*, **20** (4), 469–573.

Berg, I. (1970). *Education and Jobs: the Great Training Robbery*. New York: Praeger.

Bernard, J. (1981). *The Female World*. Chicago: Aldine.

Bernstein, B. (1975). *Class, Codes and Control: Volume 3. Towards a Theory of Educational Transmission*. London: Routledge and Kegan Paul.

Berryman, S.E. (1980). *Vocational Education and the Work Establishment of Youth: Equity and Effectiveness Issues*. Santa Monica, CA: Rand Corporation.

Betcherman, G. (1980). *Human Resources Survey*. Ottawa: Economic Council of Canada.

Bielby, D. (1978). Career sex-atypicality and career involvement of college education women. *Sociology of Education*, **51** (1), 7–28.

Blackburn, R.M. and Mann, M. (1979). *The Working Class in the Labour Market*. London: Macmillan.

Blau, P. and Duncan, O. (1967). *The American Occupational Structure*. New York: John Wiley & Sons.

Bledstein, B.J. (1976). *The Culture of Professionalism*. New York: Norton.

Bloom, A. (1987). *The Closing of the American Mind*. New York: Simon and Schuster.

Boudon, R. (1973). *Education, Opportunity and Social Inequality*. New York: John Wiley & Sons.

Bourdieu, P. and Passerson, J.-C. (1979). *The Inheritors*. (Trans. Richard Nice.) Chicago: University of Chicago Press.

Bowles, S. and Gintis, H. (1974). IQ in the United States class structure. In A. Gartner, C. Greer and F. Reissman (eds), *The New Assault on Equality: IQ and Social Stratification*, pp. 109–51. New York: Harper & Row.

Bowles, S. and Gintis, H. (1976). *Schooling in Capitalist America: Educational Reform and the Contradictions of Economic Life*. New York: Basic Books.

Boyd, M. (1981). Sex differences in the Canadian occupational attainment process. *Canadian Review of Sociology and Anthropology*, **19** (1), 1–28.

Boyer, E. (1983). *High School: a Report on Secondary Education in America*. New York: Harper & Row.

Braverman, H. (1974). *Labor and Monopoly Capitalism*. New York: Monthly Review Press.

Briggs, N. (1974). *Women in Apprenticeship: Why Not?* (Manpower Research Monograph no. 33). Washington, DC: Department of Labor.

British Columbia Department of Education (1981). *Curriculum Guidelines*. Victoria, BC: Government Printer.

Brown, P. (1987). *Schooling Ordinary Kids*. London: Tavistock.

Brown, R. (1974). The attitude to work, expectations and social perspectives of shipbuilding apprentices. In T. Leggat (ed.), *Sociological Theory and Survey Research*, pp. 109–51. London: Sage Publications.

Burawoy, M. (1979). *Manufacturing Consent: Changes in the Labor Process under Monopoly Capitalism*. Chicago: University of Chicago Press.

Burstein, M. (1975). *Canadian Work Values*. Ottawa: Department of Manpower and Immigration.

Canadian Advisory Committee on the Status of Women (1985). *What Will Tomorrow Bring? A Study of the Aspirations of Adolescent Women*. Ottawa: Government Printer.

Canadian Council on Social Development (1977). *Youth and Employment: the Need for Integrated Policies*. Ottawa: Canadian Council on Social Development.

Castells, M. (1980). *The Economic Crisis and American Society*. Princeton, NJ: Princeton University Press.

Centre for Contemporary Cultural Studies (1981). *Unpopular Education*. London: Hutchinson.

Centre for Educational Research and Innovation (1983). *Education and Work: the Views of the Young*. Paris: OECD.

Charlton, K. (1986). The liberal–vocational debate in early modern England. In J. Burstyn (ed.), *Preparation for Life? The Paradox of Education in the Late Twentieth Century*, pp. 1–18. Philadelphia, PA: Falmer Press.

Cicourel, A. and Kitsuse, J. (1963). *The Educational Decision Makers*. New York: Bobbs-Merrill.

Clark, B. (1960). The cooling out function in higher education. *American Journal of Sociology*, **45**, 569–76.

Clement, W. (1980). *Hard Rock Mining*. Toronto: McClelland & Stewart.

Cockburn, C. (1983). *Brothers: Male Dominance and Technological Change*. London: Pluto Press.

Cockburn, C. (1987). *Two Track Training: Sex Inequalities and the YTS*. Houndrills, Basingstoke: Macmillan Education Ltd.

Collins, K. (ed.) (1977). *Youth and Employment: a Sourcebook*. Ottawa: Canadian Council on Social Development.

Collins, R. (1979). *The Credential Society*. New York: Academic Press.

Coombs, D.C. (1978). *The Emergence of a White Collar Labour Force in Toronto, 1895–1911*. Unpublished doctoral dissertation, York University, Toronto.

Corrigan, P. (1979). *Schooling the Smash Street Kids*. London: Macmillan Press.

Coser, R.L. and Rokoff, G. (1971). Women in the occupational world: social disruption and conflict. *Social Problems*, **18** (4), 535–54.

Cuneo, C. (1990). *Pay Equity: the Labour Feminist Challenge*. Toronto: Oxford University Press.

Cusick, P. (1983). *The Egalitarian Ideal and the American High School*. New York: Longman.

David, M. (1980). *The State, the Family and Education*. London: Routledge.

Davies, M. (1983). *Women's Place Is at the Typewriter: Office Work and Office Workers*. Philadelphia, PA: Temple University Press.

Davis, K. and Moore, W.E. (1945). Some principles of stratification. *American Sociological Review*, **10** (2), 242–9.

Davis, S. and Haller, E. (1981). Tracking ability and SES: further evidence on the revisionist–meritocratic debate. *American Journal of Education*, **89**, 283–304.

Davison, P.E. and Anderson, H.D. (1937). *Occupational Mobility in an American Community*, Stanford, CA: Stanford University Press.

Delamont, S. (ed.) (1984). *Readings in Interaction in the Classroom*. London: Methuen.

Dewey, J. (1915). *The School and Society*. Chicago: University of Chicago Press.

Dewey, J. (1956). *The School and Society*, revised edition. Chicago: University of Chicago Press.

Dewey, J. (1966). *Democracy and Education*. New York: The Free Press. (Originally published in 1916.)

Dodge, D. (1981). *Labour Market Developments in the 1980's*. Ottawa: Employment and Immigration Canada.

Donmeyer, R. (1985). The rescue from relativism: two failed attempts and an alternative strategy. *Educational Researcher*, **14** (10), 13–20.

Doyle, W. and Carter, K. (1984). Academic tasks in classrooms. *Curriculum Inquiry*, **14** (2), 129–49.

Dreeben, R. (1968). *On What is Learned in School*. Reading, MA: Addison Wesley.

Dunn, T. (1979). Teaching the meaning of work: vocational education in British Columbia, 1900–1921. In D.C. Jones, N. Sheehan and R.M. Stamp (eds), *Shaping the Schools of the Canadian West*, pp. 236–56. Calgary, Alberta: Detselig Enterprises.

Dymond, W.R. (1973). *Training for Ontario's Future: Report of the Task Force on Industrial Training*. Toronto: Ministry of Colleges and Universities, Manpower Branch.

Economic Council of Canada (1965). *Towards Sustained and Balanced Economic Growth: Second Annual Review*. Ottawa: Queen's Printer.

Edwards, R. (1979). *Contested Terrain: the Transformation of the Workplace in the Twentieth Century*. New York: Basic Books.

England, P., Chassic, M. and McConnock, L. (1982). Skill demands and earnings in female and male occupations. *Sociology and Social Research*, **66**, 147–68.

England, P., Farkas, G., Kilbourne, B. and Dau, T. (1988). Explaining sex segregation and wages: findings from a model with fixed effects. *American Sociological Review*, **53** (4), 544–58.

England, P. and McLaughlin, S.D. (1979). Sex segregation of jobs and male–female income differences. In R. Alvarez, K. Lutterman and Associates (eds), *Discrimination in Organizations*, pp. 189–213. San Francisco: Jossey-Bass.

England, P. and Norris, S. (1985). Comparable worth: a new doctrine of sex discrimination. *Social Science Quarterly*, **66**, 627–43.

Farrar, E., De Sanctis, J. and Cowden, P. (1980). *The Walls Within: Work Experience and School Reform*. Cambridge, MA: Huron Institute.

Fiddy, R. (1983). *In Place of Work: Policy and Provision for the Young Unemployed*. Lewes: Falmer Press.

Finlay, W. (1983). One occupation, two labor markets. *American Sociological Review*, **48**, 306–15.

Finn, G. and Miles, A. (1982). *Feminism in Canada*. Montreal: Black Rose.

Foner, P. (1980). *Women and the American Labor Movement*. New York: The Free Press.

Freeman, R.B. and Wise, D.A. (1979). *Youth Unemployment: Summary Report*. Cambridge: National Bureau of Economic Research.

Furnham, A. (1985). Youth unemployment: a review of the literature. *Journal of Adolescence*, **8**, 109–24.

Garet, M.S. and Delaney, B. (1988). Students, courses and stratification. *Sociology of Education*, **61** (2), 61–77.

Gaskell, J. (1973). *The Influence of the Feminine Role on the Aspirations of High School Girls*. Unpublished doctoral dissertation, Harvard University.

Gaskell, J. (1977). Sex role ideology and the aspirations of high school girls. *Interchange*, **8** (3), 43–53.

Gaskell, J. (1982). Education and job opportunities for women: patterns of enrolment and economic returns. In N. Hersom and D. Smith (eds), *Women and the Canadian Labour Force*, pp. 257–306. Ottawa: Minister of Supply and Services.

Gerson, K. (1985). *Hard Choices: How Women Decide about Work, Career, and Motherhood*. Berkeley: University of California Press.

Gibbins, R., Ponting, J.R. and Symons, G. (1978). Attitudes and ideology: correlates of liberal attitudes towards the role of women. *Journal of Comparative Family Studies*, **9** (1), 19–40.

Giddens, A. (1979). *Central Problems in Social Theory*. London: Macmillan.

Gidney, R.D. and Lawr, D.A. (1979). Egerton Ryerson and the origins of the Ontario secondary school. *Canadian Historical Review,* **9** (4), 442–65.

Gilligan, C. (1982). *In a Different Voice.* Cambridge, MA: Harvard University Press.

Gilligan, C., Lyons, N. and Hammer T. (1990). *Making Connections: The Relational Worlds of Adolescent Girls at Emma Willard School.* Cambridge, MA: Harvard University Press.

Gleason, D. and Mardle, G. (1980). *Further Education or Training?* London: Routledge and Kegan Paul.

Goldthorpe, J.H., Lockewood, D., Bechhofer, F. and Platt, J. (1969). *The Affluent Worker in the Class Structure.* Cambridge: Cambridge University Press.

Goodlad, J., Soder, R. and Sirotnik, K. (eds) (1990). *The Moral Dimensions of Teaching.* San Francisco: Jossey-Bass.

Grahame, P. (1983). *Life Skills, Autonomy and 'Really Useful Knowledge'.* Paper presented at the annual meeting of the Canadian Society for the Study of Education, Vancouver, British Columbia, June.

Grasso, J. and Shea, J. (1979). *Vocational Education and Training: Impact on Youth.* Berkeley, CA: Carnegie Council on Policy Studies in Higher Education.

Griffin, C. (1985). *Typical Girls? Young Women from School to the Job Market.* London: Routledge and Kegan Paul.

Griffiths, A. (1983). *Skilling for Life/Living for Skill: the Social Construction of Life Skills in Ontario Schools.* Unpublished (mimeographed) paper, Ontario Institute for Studies in Education, Department of History and Philosophy.

Grignon, C. (1971). *L'ordre des choses.* Paris: Editions de Minuit.

Grubb, N. and Lazerson, M. (1982). *Broken Promises: How Americans Fail Their Children.* New York: Basic Books.

Hall, O. and Carlton, R. (1977). *Basic Skills at School and Work.* Toronto: Ontario Economic Council.

Hall, S. and Jefferson, T. (1977). *Resistance Through Rituals: Youth Subcultures in Post-War Britain.* London: Hutchinson.

Halsey, A.H., Heath, A.F. and Ridge, J.M. (1980). *Origins and Destination: Family, Class, and Education in Modern Britain.* New York: Oxford University Press.

Hartman, H. (1979). Capitalism, patriarchy and job-segregation by sex. In Z.R. Eisenstein (ed.), *Capitalist Patriarchy and the Case for Socialist Feminism,* pp. 206–47. New York: Monthly Review Press.

Hawkesworth, M.E. (1990). *Beyond Oppression: Feminist Theory and Political Strategy.* New York: Continuum.

Heyns, B. (1974). Selection and stratification in schools. *American Journal of Sociology,* **79**, 1434–51.

Hirsch, E.D. (1987). *Cultural Literacy: What Every American Needs to Know.* Boston: Houghton Mifflin.

Hogan, D. (1985). *Class and Reform: School and Society in Chicago, 1880–1930.* Philadelphia: University of Pennsylvania Press.

Hoggart, R. (1960). *The Uses of Literacy.* Harmondsworth: Penguin.

hooks, b. (1984). *Feminist Theory: from Margin to Center.* Boston: South End Press.

Horan, P. (1978). Is status attainment research atheoretical? *American Sociological Review,* **43**, 534–40.

Horner, M.S. (1970). Femininity and successful achievement: a basic inconsistency. In J. Bardwick (ed.), *Feminine Personality and Conflict,* pp. 45–74. Belmont, CA: Brooks Cole.

Howell, J. (1877). Trade unions and apprenticeship. *Contemporary Review,* **30**, 833–57.

Ireson, C. (1978). Girls' socialization for work. In G. Stromberg and S. Harkness (eds), *Women Working*, pp. 176–200. Palo Alto, CA: Mayfield Press.

Janeway, E. (1980). *Powers of the Weak*. New York: Knopf.

Jencks, C., Bartlett, S., Corcoran, M., Crouse, J., Eaglesfield, D., Jackson, G., McClelland, K., Mueser, P., Olneck, M., Schwartz, J., Ward, S. and Williams, J. (1979). *Who Gets Ahead: the Determinants of Economic Success in America*. New York: Basic Books.

Jencks, C., Smith, M., Acland, H., Bane, M.J., Cohen, D., Gintis, H., Heyns, B. and Michelson, S. (1972). *Inequality*. New York: Basic Books.

Jenkins, R. (1983). *Lads, Citizens and Ordinary Kids*. London: Routledge and Kegan Paul.

Katz, M. (1968). *The Irony of Early School Reform: Educational Innovation in Mid-Nineteenth Century Massachusetts*. Cambridge, MA: Harvard University Press.

Katznelson, I. and Wier, M. (1985). *Schooling for All: Race, Class and the Decline of the Democratic Ideal*. New York: Basic Books.

Kealey, G. (1980). *Toronto Industrial Workers Respond to Industrial Capitalism, 1867–92*. Toronto: University of Toronto Press.

Kerckhoff, A. (1990). *Getting Started: Transition to Adulthood in Great Britain*. Oxford: Westview Press.

Kuhn, A. (1978). Structures of patriarchy and capital in the family. In A. Kuhn and A.M. Wolpe (eds), *Feminism and Materialism*, pp. 42–67. Boston: Routledge.

Labour Canada (1977). *Women in the Labour Force: Facts and Figures*. Ottawa: Women's Bureau.

Larsen, M.S. (1977). *The Rise of Professionalism*. Berkeley: University of California Press.

Lather, P. (1986). Research as praxis. *Harvard Educational Review*, **56** (3), 257–77.

Laws, J.L. (1976). Work aspirations of women: false leads and new starts. *Signs*, **1**, 33–50.

Lazerson, M. (1971). *Origins of the Urban School Public Education in Massachusetts, 1870–1915*. Cambridge, MA: Harvard University Press.

Lazerson, M. and Grubb, N. (1974). *American Education and Vocationalism*. New York: Teachers College Press.

Lee, D.J. (1981). Skill, craft and class: a theoretical critique and a critical case. *Sociology*, **15**, 56–78.

Lees, S. (1986). *Losing Out: Sexuality and Adolescent Girls*. London: Hutchinson.

Lein, L. *et al.* (1977). *Working Family Project Final Report: Work and Family Life*. Wellesley, MA: Wellesley College Research Center for Research on Women.

Levy, B. (1972). Do schools sell girls short? *Today's Education: Journal of the National Education Association*, **61**, 27–9.

Lewenhak, S. (1977). *Women and Trade Unions*. London: Ernest Benn.

Lindblom, C. and Cohen, D. (1979). *Usable Knowledge: Social Science and Social Problem Solving*. New Haven, CT: Yale University Press.

Lipsky, M. (1980). *Street Level Bureaucracy*. New York: Russell Sage.

Little, J.K. (1970). *Review and Synthesis of Research on the Placement and Follow-Up of Vocational Education Students*, ERIC Research Series no. 49, VT 010 175. Columbus, OH: Center for Vocational and Technical Education.

Lockwood, D. (1958). *Blackcoated Worker*. London: George Allen and Unwin.

Lorde, A. (1984). *Sister Outsider*. Trumansburg, NY: Crossing Press.

Lowe, G. (1980). Women, work and the office. *Canadian Journal of Sociology*, **5** (4), 361–81.

Lowe, G. (1982). Class, job and gender in the Canadian office. *Le Travailleur*, **10**, 11–37.

Lowe, G. (1987). *Women in the Administrative Revolution.* Toronto: University of Toronto Press.

Maccoby, E. and Jacklin, C. (1974). *The Psychology of Sex Differences.* Stanford, CA: Stanford University Press.

McRobbie, A. (1978). Working class girls and the culture of femininity. In *Women Take Issue,* pp. 96–108. Birmingham, University of Birmingham, Centre for Contemporary Cultural Studies, Women's Studies Group.

Mangum, G. and Walsh, J. (1978). *Employment and Training Programs for Youth: What Works Best for Whom?* Washington, DC: US Department of Labor.

Marks, L. (1984). *New Opportunities Within a Separate Sphere: a Preliminary Exploration of Certain Neglected Questions Relating to Female Clerical Work, Focussing on Stenography in Canada, 1890–1930.* Unpublished MA thesis, Department of History, York University, Toronto.

Martell, G. (1974). *The Politics of the Canadian Public School.* Toronto: James Lewis & Samuel.

Martin, J.R. (1985). *Reclaiming a Conversation: the Ideal of the Educated Woman.* New Haven, CT: Yale University Press.

Mead, M. (1949). *Male and Female.* New York: Dell.

Meece, J.L., Eccles, J., Kackala, C.B., Goff, S.B. and Futterman, R. (1982). Sex differences in math achievement: toward a model of academic choice. *Psychological Bulletin,* **91**, 324–48.

Meisner, M. (1975). No exit for wives: sexual division of labour and the cumulation of household demands. *Canadian Review of Sociology and Anthropology,* **12**, 424–39.

Meisner, M. (1981). *The Domestic Economy: Now You See It, Now You Don't.* Paper prepared for Social Sciences and Humanities Research Council of Canada conference on women in the labour force, Vancouver, Canada, January.

Meltz, N. (1982). *Economic Analysis of Labour Shortages: the Case for Tool and Die Makers in Ontario,* Occasional Paper no. 15. Toronto: Ontario Economic Council.

Menzies, H. (1981). *Women and the Chip.* Montreal: Institute for Research on Public Policy.

Minh-ha, T. (1989). *Woman, Native, Other: Writing Postcoloniality and Feminism.* Bloomington: Indiana University Press.

Moore, R. (1983). Further education, pedagogy and production. In D. Gleeson (ed.), *Youth Training and the Search for Work,* pp. 14–31. London: Routledge and Kegan Paul.

More, C. (1980). *Skill and the English Working Class.* London: Croom Helm.

Nelson, R.W. and Nock, D. (1978). *Reading, Writing and Riches: Education and the Socioeconomic Order in North America.* Kitchener, Ontario: Between the Lines Press.

Nolfi, G.N. *et al.* (1978). *Experiences of Recent High School Graduates.* Lexington, MA: Lexington Books/D.C. Heath & Company.

Oakes, J. (1982). Classroom social relationships: Exploring the Bowles and Gintis hypothesis. *Sociology of Education,* **55**, 197–212.

Oakes, J. (1985). *Keeping Track: How Schools Structure Inequality.* New Haven: Yale University Press.

Oakley, A. (1974). *The Sociology of Housework.* New York: Pantheon Books.

Olsen, T. (1978). *Silences.* New York: Delacorte.

Oppenheimer, V. (1970). *The Female Labor Force in the U.S.* Berkeley, CA: Institute of International Studies.

Organization for Economic Cooperation and Development (1977). *Entry of Young People into Working Life.* Paris: OECD.

Ornstein, M.D. (1976). *Entry Into the American Labor Force*. New York: Academic Press.

Osterman, P. (1980). *Getting Started: the Youth Labor Market*. Cambridge, MA: MIT Press.

O'Toole, J. (1973). *Work in America*. Cambridge, MA: MIT Press.

Page, R. and Valli, L. (1990). Curriculum differentiation. *Interpretive Studies in US Secondary Schools*. Albany: State University of New York Press.

Palmer, B. (1979). *A Culture in Conflict: Skilled Workers and Industrial Capitalism in Hamilton, Ontario, 1860–1914*. Montreal: McGill University/Queen's University Press.

Panel on Youth of the President's Science Advisory Committee (1974). *Youth: Transition to Adulthood*. Chicago: University of Chicago Press.

Parsons, T. (1959). The school class as a social system: Some of its functions in American Society. *Harvard Educational Review*, **29** (4), 297–318.

Persell, C. (1977). *Education and Inequality*. New York: The Free Press.

Phillips, A. and Taylor, B. (1980). Sex and skill: Notes towards a feminist economics. *Feminist Review*, **XXX**, 79–88.

Picot, W.G. (1983). *University Graduates and Jobs: Changes During the 1970s*. Ottawa: Minister of Supply and Services.

Polachek, S. (1975). Discontinuous labor force participation and its effect on earnings. In C. Lloyd (ed.), *Sex Discrimination and the Division of Labor*. New York: Columbia University Press.

Polachek, S. (1976). Occupational segregation: an alternative hypothesis. *Journal of Contemporary Business*, **5**, 1–12.

Porter, J. (1965). *The Vertical Mosaic*. Toronto: University of Toronto Press.

Porter, J., Porter, M. and Blishen, B. (1982). *Stations and Callings: Making It Through the School System*. Toronto: Methuen.

Powers, J. (1984). *Feminist Politics, Pressure Groups, and Personalities: Trade Training Versus Home Economics in Smith-Hughes*. Paper presented at the annual meeting of the American Educational Research Association, New Orleans.

Prendergast, S. and Prent, A. (1980). What will I do? Teenage girls and the construction of motherhood. *Sociological Review*, **28** (3), 517–32.

Reid, W. and Filby, J. (1982). *The Sixth: an Essay in Education and Democracy*. Lewes: Falmer Press.

Reubens, B. (1978). *Review of Foreign Experience in Youth Employment and Public Policy*. Englewood Cliffs, NJ: Prentice-Hall.

Ricketts, M. (1980). *A Time for Action: a Survey of Critical Trade Skills in the Lower Mainland*. Vancouver, BC: Vancouver Board of Trade.

Rinehart, J.W. (1978). Contradictions of work-related attitudes and behaviour: an interpretation. *Canadian Review of Sociology and Anthropology*, **15**, 1–15.

Roberts, K. (1983). *School Leavers and Their Prospects: Youth and the Labour Market in the 1980's*. Bury St Edmunds: Open University Press.

Rogers, D. and Tyack, D. (1982). Work, youth and schooling: mapping critical research areas. In H. Kantor and D. Tyack (eds), *Work, Youth and Schooling*, pp. 269–94. Stanford, CA: Stanford University Press.

Rosenbaum, J. (1976). *Making Inequality: the Hidden Curriculum of High School Tracking*. New York: John Wiley & Sons.

Rowbotham, S. (1973). *Women's Consciousness, Man's World*. Harmondsworth: Penguin.

Rubin, L.B. (1976). *Worlds of Pain: Life in the Working Class Family*. New York: Basic Books.

Rubin, L.B. (1979). *Women of a Certain Age: the Midlife Search for Self.* New York: Harper & Row.

Rule, J. (1981). *The Experience of Labour in the 18th Century.* London: Croom Helm.

Ryrie, A.C. and Wier, A.D. (1978). *Getting a Trade.* London: Hodder & Stoughton.

Sarason, S. (1971). *The Culture of the School and the Problem of Change.* Boston: Allyn and Bacon.

Schechter, S. (1977). Capitalism, class and educational reform. In L. Panich (ed.), *The Canadian State,* pp. 373–416. Toronto, University of Toronto Press.

Sennett, R. and Cobb, J. (1972). *The Hidden Injuries of Class.* New York: Knopf.

Sewell, W. and Shah, V.P. (1968). Parents' education and children's educational aspirations and achievements. *American Sociological Review,* **33** (2), 191–209.

Sharp, R. and Green, A. (1975). *Education and Social Control: a Study in Progressive Primary Education.* London: Routledge and Kegan Paul.

Sharpe, S. (1976). *'Just Like a Girl': How Girls Learn to Be Women.* Harmondsworth: Penguin.

Shaw, W.H. (1902). *The Story of a Business School.* Toronto: Shaw College.

Silver, H. and Brennan, J. (1988). *A Liberal Vocationalism.* New York: Methuen.

Simon, R., Dippo, D. and Schenke, A. (1991). *Learning Work: a Critical Pedagogy of Work Education.* New York: Bergin and Garvey.

Smith, A.D.W. (1975). *Generic Skills Research and Development.* Prince Albert, Saskatchewan: Manpower and Immigration, Training Research and Development Station.

Smith, D. (1977). *Feminism and Marxism.* Vancouver, BC: New Star Books.

Smith, D. (1990). *The Conceptual Practices of Power: a Feminist Sociology of Knowledge.* Toronto: University of Toronto Press.

Sokoloff, N. (1980). *Between Money and Love.* New York: Praeger.

Sorenson, A. and Kalleberg, A. (1980). An outline of a theory of the matching of persons to jobs. In I. Berg (ed.), *Sociological Perspectives on the Labor Market,* pp. 49–74. New York: Academic Press.

Spady, W. (1970). Educational mobility and access: growth and paradoxes. *American Journal of Society,* **73,** 273–86.

Spence, M. (1973). Job market signalling. *Quarterly Journal of Economics,* **87,** 355–74.

Spenner, K. (1983). Deciphering Prometheus: temporal change in the skill level of work. *American Sociological Review,* **48** (6), 824–37.

Spours, K. and Young, M.F.D. (1988). *Beyond Vocationalism: a New Perspective on the Relationship Between Work and Education,* Working Paper no. 4. University of London, Institute of Education, Centre for Vocational Studies.

Spring, J. (1972). *Education and the Rise of the Corporate State.* Boston: Beacon Press.

Stamp, R. (1971). Technical education, the national policy and federal–provincial relations in Canadian education 1899–1919. *Canadian Historical Review,* **52** (4), 404–23.

Stanworth, M. (1983). *Gender and Schooling: a Study of Sexual Divisions in the Classroom.* London: Hutchinson.

Statistics Canada (1980). *Women in the Labour Force: 1978–1979.* Ottawa: Ministry of Labour.

Statistics Canada (1983a). *Women and the Labour Force Part 1: Participation.* Ottawa: Ministry of Supply and Services.

Statistics Canada (1983b). *Women and the Labour Force Part 2: Earnings.* Ottawa: Ministry of Supply and Services.

Statistics Canada (1990). *Women in Canada: A Statistical Report.* Second Edition. Ottawa: Ministry of Supply and Services.

Stoltzenberg, R.M. (1975). Occupations, labor markets and the process of wage attainment. *American Sociological Review*, **40**, 645–65.

Tanguy, L. (1985). Academic studies and technical education: new dimensions of an old struggle in the division of knowledge. *Sociology of Education*, **58** (1), 20–33.

Thomas, R. and Wetherall, D. (1974). *Looking Forward to Work*. London: HMSO.

Thompson, E.P. (1963). *The Making of the English Working Class*. Harmondsworth: Pelican Books.

Thurow, L. (1975). *Generating Inequality*. New York: Basic Books.

Tolson, A. (1977). *The Limits of Masculinity*. London: Tavistock.

Treiman, D.J. and Hartman, H. (1981). *Women, Work and Wages: Equal Pay for Jobs of Equal Value*. Washington, DC: National Academy Press.

Turner, H.A. (1962). *Trade Union Growth, Structure and Policy*. London: Allen and Unwin.

US Commission on Excellence in Education. (1983). *A Nation at Risk*. Washington, DC: Government Printing Office.

Valli, L. (1986). *Becoming Clerical Workers*. Boston: Routledge and Kegan Paul.

Vanfossen, B., Jones, J.D. and Spade, J.Z. (1987). *Curriculum Tracking: Correlates and Consequences*. Paper presented at the annual meeting of the American Educational Research Association.

Venek, J. (1974). Time spent in housework. *Scientific American*, **231**, 116–20.

Venek, J. (1980). Household work, wage work and sexual equality. In S.F. Berk (ed.), *Women and Household Labor*, pp. 275–91. Beverly Hills, CA: Sage.

Wallace, C. (1987). *For Richer, For Poorer: Growing Up in and out of Work*. London: Tavistock.

Watts, A.G. (1980). *Work Experience Programmes: the Views of British Youth*. Paris: OECD.

Watts, A.G. (1983). *Education, Unemployment and the Future of Work*. Milton Keynes: Open University Press.

Webb, S. and Webb, B. (1896). *The History of Trade Unionism*. London: Longmans, Green and Company.

Weiss, J. (1982). The advent of education for clerical work in the high school: a reconsideration of the historiography of vocationalism. *Teachers College Record*, **83** (4), 613–36.

Weiss, L. (1990). *Working Class Without Work: High School Students in a Deindustrializing Economy*. New York: Routledge, Chapman and Hall.

Whitty, G. (1985). *Sociology and School Knowledge: Curriculum and Theory, Research and Politics*. London: Methuen.

Williams, R. (1961). *The Long Revolution*. London: Chatto & Windus.

Willis, P. (1977). *Learning to Labour*. Farnborough: Saxon House.

Willis, P. (1981). Cultural production is different from cultural reproduction is different from social reproduction is different from reproduction. *Interchange*, **12** (2–3), 48–67.

Wolpe, A. (1974). The official ideology of education for girls. In J. Ahier and M. Flude (eds), *Educability, Schools and Ideology*, pp. 138–59. London: Croom Helm.

Wolpe, A. (1978). Education and the sexual division of labour. In A. Kuhn and A. Wolpe (eds), *Feminism and Materialism*, pp. 290–328. London: Routledge.

Wotherspoon, T. (1987). *The Political Economy of Canadian Education*. Toronto: Methuen.

Wright, E.O., Costello, C., Hachen, D. and Sprague, J. (1982). The American class structure. *American Sociological Review*, **47** (6), 709–26.

Yankelovitch, D. (1974). *The New Morality: a Profile of American Youth in the 1970's*. New York: McGraw Hill.

Name Index

Subject Index